'For a long time, Wilfred Bion's thinking was considered eccentric, even foreign or paradoxical, in comparison with that of classic psychoanalysis, or it has been used in a sloganistic manner by extracting the most original concepts and turning them into catchwords that are incredibly distant from his initial communicative intentions. Rugi manages to bring him back into the scene by clarifying the origins, which concern Bionian's complete production in its entirety, and relating it in a consistent and careful manner to that of Freud's. The result is a book that is both an excavating and an opening, highly useful and indispensable "Memory for the Future."'

Lorena Preta *an ordinary member of the SPI and the IPA, head of the international research group Geographies of Psychoanalysis and former director of the magazine Psiche and of Spoleto Scienza*

'Rugi approaches the concepts of Time and the Unconscious through his own process of dreaming Bion's thinking. He aims to make it accessible not only to specialists, but also to a wider audience. He invites us to find out about the internal coherence in the unexpected continuity between the earliest insights into groups, and the latest thoughts on factual transformations. This exploration does not always remain static, but turns on itself; expanding, specifying and delineating from different points. Rugi's description of Bion clinical material provokes a process of identification and the passion of discovery.'

Antònia Grimalt, *M.D., a training and supervising analyst for the Spanish Society (SEP-IPA), editor of Bion, Intuition and the expansion of psychoanalytic theory and Bion and Intuition in the clinical setting, by Routledge*

'A timely and valuable text as through two fundamental themes of psychoanalysis, time and the unconscious, it clarifies the Freudian roots of Wilfred R. Bion's thinking, and highlights the profound differences and the richness of a new paradigm that is still evolving.'

Sarantis Thanopulos, *ordinary member of the SPI with training functions, and the current President of the SPI*

Time and the Unconscious

Bion's *unfashionable* thought is a challenge for our times in which anaesthesia and mass thinking prevail. The themes this book addresses are time and the unconscious.

In the present/past, the here and now reveals its relationship with the unredeemable time, which conditions our behaviour and is at the root of a state of hallucinosis in the form of a short-sighted view that is distorted by deep-seated wounds. This book also highlights the resonances with contemporary epistemology and physics that underlie the new paradigm of psychoanalytic field theory. The topic of the unconscious raises questions about its origin and the difference between the Bionian and the Freudian unconscious. In Bion we see an evolutionary, process character emerge, with a double movement of repetition and expansion within a single system in unstable equilibrium, for which there is no conscious feeling that does not also carry with it the shadow of the unconscious.

Drawing on psychoanalytic and philosophical concepts this book is essential reading for psychoanalysts, psychotherapists, philosophers and anyone who wishes to understand more fully what it means to be human.

Goriano Rugi, M.D., psychiatrist, psychotherapist, is a member and training analyst of the Italian Institute of Group Psychoanalysis (IIPG). He teaches at the IIPG School of Specialisation in Milan and at the European Research Institute of Psychoanalytic Psychotherapy in Padua. He is a trainer and supervisor at various institutions. He lives and works in Verona. His best-known works are *Transformations of Pain* (2015), *Diagnosis and Mental Disorders* (2018) and *Time and the Unconscious* (2023), Milan, FrancoAngeli.

Psychoanalytic Field Theory Book Series

The *Psychoanalytic Field Theory Book Series* was initiated in 2015 as a new subseries of the *Psychoanalytic Inquiry Book Series*. The series publishes books on subjects relevant to the continuing development of psychoanalytic field theory. The emphasis of this series is on contemporary work that includes a vision of the future for psychoanalytic field theory.

Since the middle of the twentieth century, forms of psychoanalytic field theory emerged in different geographic parts of the world with different objectives, heuristic principles, and clinical techniques. Taken together they form a family of psychoanalytic perspectives that employs a concept of a bi-personal psychoanalytic field. The *Psychoanalytic Field Theory Book Series* seeks to represent this pluralism in its publications. Books on field theory in all its diverse forms are of interest in this series. Both theoretical works and discussions of clinical technique will be published in this series.

The series editors are especially interested in selecting manuscripts which actively promote the understanding and further expansion of psychoanalytic field theory. Part of the mission of the series is to foster communication amongst psychoanalysts working in different models, in different languages, and in different parts of the world. A full list of titles in this series is available at: https://www.routledge.com/Psychoanalytic-Field-Theory-Book-Series/book-series/FIELDTHEORY

Time and the Unconscious

Daring and Creativity in Wilfred R. Bion

Goriano Rugi
Foreword by Giuseppe Civitarese

R Routledge
Taylor & Francis Group

LONDON AND NEW YORK

First published in English 2025
by Routledge
4 Park Square, Milton Park, Abingdon, Oxon OX14 4RN

and by Routledge
605 Third Avenue, New York, NY 10158

Routledge is an imprint of the Taylor & Francis Group, an informa business

Published in Italian 2023 by FrancoAngeli *(Tempo e Inconscio)*

British Library Cataloguing-in-Publication Data
A catalogue record for this book is available from the British Library

Library of Congress Cataloging-in-Publication Data
Names: Rugi, Goriano, author.
Title: Time and the unconscious: daring and creativity in
Wilfred R. Bion / Goriano Rugi; foreword by Giuseppe Civitarese.
Other titles: Tempo e inconscio. English
Description: Abingdon, Oxon; New York, NY: Routledge, 2024. |
Series: Psychoanalytic field theory series | Includes bibliographical
references and index.
Identifiers: LCCN 2024008142 (print) | LCCN 2024008143 (ebook) |
ISBN 9781032655215 (hardback) | ISBN 9781032658346 (paperback) |
ISBN 9781032658346 (ebook)
Subjects: LCSH: Bion, Wilfred R. (Wilfred Ruprecht), 1897–1979. |
Psychoanalysis.
Classification: LCC BF109.B54 R8413 2024 (print) |
LCC BF109.B54 (ebook) | DDC 150.19/5—dc23/eng/20240226
LC record available at https://lccn.loc.gov/2024008142
LC ebook record available at https://lccn.loc.gov/2024008143

ISBN: 978-1-032-65521-5 (hbk)
ISBN: 978-1-032-65834-6 (pbk)
ISBN: 978-1-032-65523-9 (ebk)

DOI: 10.4324/9781032655239

Typeset in Times New Roman
by codeMantra

Contents

Foreword

Giuseppe Civitarese

New Ontologies for Psychoanalysis

It is high time that Goriano Rugi's contributions to the interpretation and development of Bion's thought were better known, both in Italy and abroad. Rugi writes about Bion with a clear and fluent style, with competence, with courage and with the characteristic absence of any hint of vanity or authorial pomposity. Those who know him will spontaneously identify in these stylistic notes so many characteristic features of his personality. He is a Tuscan and that is good enough. He can be simple, direct and reserved, but always with a glimmer of loving irony in his gaze and a minimal but healthy distance from things in a way that would be less immediate and "obvious" to others.

In *Time and the Unconscious*, the challenge is no small one because of the subjects tackled (nothing less "time", and then the "unconscious", which can be said to be no less enigmatic even though it has been widely explored by generations of psychoanalysts). The approach is not academic. Convinced that Bion must be understood as a whole, holistically, Rugi approaches the concepts of time and the unconscious in a broad way. For the journey, one must equip oneself well and choose one's travelling companions wisely – Nietzsche, Serres, Han, Bateson, Rilke, Dostoevsky, Eliot, Borges, Wittgenstein, Merleau-Ponty, Heidegger, etc. The journey is definitely an intertextual one.

Right from the subtitle, we are first confronted with Nietzsche. The reference to *Unfashionable Observations* is explained, and it is clear what *outdatedness* consists of: going against the grain, daring to disturb the universe of what is already known and canonised. Furthermore, after placing Bion as the champion of "becoming real" under the banner of Nietzsche, Rugi differentiates the two authors, creating another paradox! Therefore he places the purpose of everyone's life in "becoming what one is", that is, in being able to broaden the boundaries of the soul as much as possible, and thus to make actual the potentialities that often remain only virtual.

Finally, and we are only at the beginning, Rugi unites the two authors, and himself with them, in the bond of a profoundly ethical principle, and one that, in my opinion, should be the pole star of any treatment of psychic pain. It is when he quotes Bion on the subject of the envy of growth-enhancing objects as the origin of the impulse to inhibit. Now the "impulse to inhibit" is not very different from the concept expressed in the fragmentary memoirs in which Nietzsche writes that he considers those who aim to shame others to be bad.

Speaking of quotations, we know how difficult it is to paraphrase Bion, because style is as essential to the expression of thought as content. We also know how the habit of quoting him can sometimes become excessive and represent a kind of negative use of Bion, not to think but to avoid the pain inherent in thinking (remember? Tolerating the pain of absence). And indeed, one of Rugi's beautiful insights is where he questions the beauty of theories and, with Maturana and Varela, the aesthetic seduction they exert, but immediately afterwards giving us a complex conception of the aesthetic: the opposite of what one might vacuously mean by ornamental or "aestheticising".

No: the very birth of the subject is aesthetic, since it occurs through waves or vibrations in the form of sensations, and where the challenge is to move from disorder to order. And just as aesthetic (holistic) is the birth and development of the models and theories of psychoanalysis, from Freud to Klein, from Ferenczi to Fairbairn, but also Winnicott, Meltzer, Abraham and Torok, Grotstein, Tustin, Resnik, etc. all authors with whom Rugi demonstrates his familiarity and ability to integrate in a rigorous but inclusive thought.[1]

In this book, you will find the quotations often surprising because they are not among those now used as "advertising" and degraded to commonplace, but instead weave harmoniously into the conversation to which Rugi invites the reader. This means that "in a long and arduous apprenticeship" Rugi has made Bion's ("difficult") thought his own. He has "re-dreamed" it, and is now able to speak not from a position of mere knowledge, but is able to share the experience he has gained from a long habit of working close to psychic pain and from studying Bion and other authors of psychoanalysis.

Here is an example of what Rugi's sharp eye can spot at a glance and delight the reader with: Kleinian theories "bear a great resemblance to sin:

everybody is against them, but everybody practises them in secret". In addition, the game of interpreting the generative ambiguity of the phrase would be dizzying, since Bion is talking about his ex-analyst's theories and thus about his "sins" and the intimacy of their relationship.

In the following example, however, Rugi, with his usual perspicacity, reveals a deep affinity between Bion and Han, the philosopher who makes "smoothness" the hallmark of our society: "Even any roughness of our system that might facilitate the lodgement of the germ of another idea is smoothed and polished" (Bion, 1977b, p. 46). And here the discourse expands to society and the political relevance of war. One of the points in which I most agree with Rugi is when he mentions the pitfalls of new technologies and the need to rethink the very notion of our humanity. His reflection resonates not only with the Freud of the malaise of civilisation and the founder of modern critical theory, but also with the fundamental contribution we owe on this question to the great speculative thought of the last century and until now, at least from Husserl to Agamben.

These authors are among those who have developed new ontologies (Nancy: *A Thought on Existence*) that emphasise the radically social nature of the subject, for example: Heidegger's fundamental ontology, Merleau-Ponty's ontology of the "flesh" or Nancy's ontology of we/being together/being with. However, if it is true that "there is no difference between the ethical and the ontological", as the latter author makes clear in an iconic way, then it is also ethical to rethink care and the essence of therapeutic action as an art of emotional bonding and expansion of "we". This Rugi asserts in his own way, recalling the interpretive key of Borges' short story "The Writing of God": that there is nothing in language that does not imply the whole universe. This is how we could read Freud's mysterious remark that "Psyche is extended; knows nothing about it".

It is true that there is no growth without pain, but not all pain is necessary. Not, for example, is the "iatrogenic" pain inflicted by guilt-ridden or subtly ideological interpretations which in reading what would be evil in the other, end up establishing relations of domination (Kernberg).

Rugi's style is enveloping and almost seductive. For those who are fond of psychoanalysis, of Bion, of the problem represented by the nature of the human being, this book is an opportunity to lose oneself in a conversation that is at once calm and adventurous, fruitful and pleasant. Every step of the way, the reader feels grateful for the beauty of the places they explore or glimpse at, but also for the guidance that accompanies them. Faced with some difficult turns (Bion uses a difficult language and his is a difficult thought), Rugi almost always manages to suggest the right attitude to face them and to convey a sense of security (the Wordsworthian "recollection in tranquillity" comes to mind).

Bion's difficulty is a recurring theme. I think that Freud is by no means always "easy", and neither is Winnicott, as the adoption of an everyday language, but soon bent to his theoretical and expressive needs, might suggest. However, it is true that Bion poses particular problems because of his idiosyncratic use of logical or mathematical formalisms, etc. Rugi wonders whether to take the *easy* route of presenting an isolated Bion, closed off in his world of interrelated concepts, or the *difficult* route of not artificially severing the deep and living roots that connect him to other classical and contemporary authors. Why is this the "difficult" way? Because it requires a good skill as a translator from one conceptual universe to another, while knowing that each concept cannot be translated without remnants, because it lives in its own specific network of similarities.

Once the strategy has been chosen, it remains to identify the tactics. Here, the tactic is to face the battle by trying to make clear the positions occupied in Bion's theory: the concepts of time and temporality, on the one hand, and those of the unconscious, on the other. We can immediately see a certain boldness in this, since time is by definition the mystery (St Augustine: the closer you look at it, the less you understand it, Rugi would say that the thing is "frightening"). But it is understandable when we think of the scandal that has now spread to all quarters of psychoanalysis of the Bionian precept that invites us to listen without memory (as if to say without time). From the Alpes to the Manzanares, the heart-rending cries of desolate vestals of reality resound: "But reality matters!"

Of course, it matters, but psychoanalysis has never been about material or historical reality. The reality that matters to us is the psychic reality, of the dream, of the internal world, and not that hastily causal and de-responsibilising way of thinking which explains and thus trivialises the present with the traumas of the past – which is even worse. Traumas with respect to which the analyst should withhold an analytic listening (of the unconscious meaning of the conversation) and limit themselves to "bear witness", a term by which we mean a nefarious sentimentality, that is "iatrogenic" (and incomprehension of another scandalous Bion's precept: to listen without desire).

What these non-critical critics struggle to grasp, and which they have transformed into a criticism of slogans and harps of thought with respect to both the intrinsic paradoxicality inherent in being (like *Dasein*) and to the models that try not to evade confrontation, is that the subject is always also intersubject (a "we"), and therefore the presumed pure memory of the trauma. Even wanting to forget that psychoanalysis is born when it frees itself from the thought of this concreteness and discovers the phantasm ("I no longer believe in my *neurotica*"), from another point of view it is the story that the subject incessantly makes of themselves, but intertwined with others, to come to exist in every thousandth of a second. This, therefore, can very well be listened to as an account of the state of vitality in the here and now both as individual threads of being and as the points where these threads knot in "we". But if it is a story that coincides with existing and with existing mutually, it means that it is not made up only of words, but of a body (not only that of words) and of actions. More correctly we should say of, trying once again to say the unspeakable of the dialectical fibre of being: of intercorporeity.

The attention to the present, already a Kleinian inheritance, is for Bion a real shibboleth, because in no other author is it so extreme. Third surprising quotation and possible criticism to be addressed to the critics of "dream-like memory" is: "If [the analyst] witnesses certain facts he is under an obligation to state his evidence; equally, he must not report what he does not see. Otherwise he is guilty of fraud". The expression "guilty of fraud", which he throws like a stone at all those who obviously do not follow his own strict principles, is one that is not to be forgotten. Bion is always demanding, sometimes even intransigent, but, as Rugi points out, he also displays "an extraordinary capacity for irony, even about his own theories".

In fact, one could collect a florilegium of quotations in which, from time to time, he takes a swipe at the analyst-propagandist or advertiser, or the one who does not know how to use intuition, or the one who arrogantly looks down on patients and colleagues, etc. We deduce that in Bion there is a constant ethical questioning ("an immense need for ethical and professional rigour") and that treatment only makes sense if it is ethical – not in the banal sense of observing the rules of morality, but in the profound sense of respecting the other.

And here Rugi very aptly underlines the importance in Bion's thought of a concept that I think is still waiting to be fully developed, that of the "protomental system" and the inaccessible state of the psyche or personality.

Why has it not been developed? Because it would require familiarity with ontologies that radically heal the insidious split between mind/body, matter/life, flesh/spirit.

As I write these notes, I realise that I have only reached page 25, that I have only gone through the preface and introduction! In the little space I have left, how am I going to finish my preface so that my preface is a short introduction that invites the reader to read, and not a second and inappropriate Introduction? If I recount this little personal drama, it is to give an idea of the richness of the book, of how it invites a slow and meditative conversation and not the hasty rush of a superficial and "polished" reading. The only solution is to limit ourselves to a few summary hints and then leave the pleasure of discovery to the reader. Rugi approaches the theme of time in Bion primarily from the problem posed by memories of the non-declarative type, stratifications of meaning embodied in the body, inaccessible states of the psyche; then he questions in depth the very structure of lived temporality and its relation to linear and measurable time. Here he encounters some of the most formidable questions of all. For example, is there a time before the emergence of the subject?

I would venture to answer that with a "no" as we know it as lived temporality and "objective" time, in the absence of the subject and its *necessary* connection with the "seeing itself seen" (Valery, Magrelli) in which self-reflexivity consists, it would be problematic to answer in the affirmative. Indeed, a time that distances itself from the subject seems inconceivable, almost a contradiction in terms. But immediately the idea arises that, in the abstract, there must be something that we would perhaps call by another name, perhaps "difference".

But how to conceive the relationship between pure difference, to be clear what we hypothesise that led to the proto-sensitivity (or "visibility" for Merleau-Ponty) of the "folds" in matter (Deleuze) and the very human anguish of frozen time? It is anguish that makes little Marcel clearly choose, to snatch a goodnight kiss from his mother – when she finally climbs the stairs to go into his room – to endure what he imagines as the martyrdom of the most certain ousting of the family nest. The guilt appears to him enormous and irredeemable, but the fever of "objectness" that burns him is too much, as well as that which makes Phaedra delirious in Racine's Hippolytus, or in the famous ode of Sappho taken as an example of the sublime by Longinus.

Turning instead to the subject of the "unconscious", I fully agree with Rugi that it is the subject of a strange theoretical obscurantism. Analysts are afraid to realise how shaky the ground is on which they stand, namely, their theory of the unconscious. Thinking of the theory of the unconscious as a plurality of theories is the site of a real removal of "burning" content. Perhaps this gives us a sense of the clumsy attempts to cling to conceptions of history and trauma that take us back to when Freud still believed in his neurotics – essentially to before Freud.

So there is a sense of quiet freedom in these pages. Each major author innovates on the main concepts that inevitably revolve around our view of the unconscious processes of the mind and changes that view: period. The first topic is different from the second, and this is different from the way Freud suggests the function of dreaming and thus of the unconscious in *Beyond the Pleasure Principle,* and it is also different from the Kleinian idea of the theatre of the mind and the Bionian notion of the unconscious as a psychoanalytic function of the personality and as infinite. Rugi quotes some respectable authors who grasp at straws to say otherwise, and one wonders, for example, what somersaults they would do to justify "Saint Winnicott's" rejection of Freudian metapsychology.

So where does Rugi land in his analysis of the concept of the unconscious? To Merleau-Ponty's ingenious formula: "perception is unconscious"; and then, knowing that in *The Visible and the Invisible,* the same author sought to purify his own thought of the idealistic residues that might still cling to the centrality still attributed to the eye of the perceiving subject. We would rather say, with an even more outrageous but comprehensive notion, that *the unconscious is the flesh* (Vanzago). The idea, I repeat, is the counterintuitive but brilliant one of the subject seen within the framework of a field ontology: of the subject as group and proto-mental system.

Incidentally, whether the unconscious is timeless, as Freud says, is debatable. Temporality is inherent in meaning. Every sentence has an obvious temporal development and could not have been otherwise. But what does "timeless" mean? Perhaps that we live in different worlds in our dreams, as if they were all present and not divided into past and present? But isn't that how we live even when we are awake, if it is true that we dream both day and night? In fact, as Rugi writes well following Bion, we are all our past *now*, in the present. We return to the point that we cannot rely on a net dichotomy of primary process/secondary process. This is Bion's scathing critique of Freud in the 1962 essay "A Theory of Thinking".

Rugi has aptly titled a small chapter "What is at stake in the concept of the unconscious". The refinement of our conception of the unconscious processes of the mind, rather than the fetishisation of Freud's "dark and malevolent", is now central to the future of psychoanalysis: at stake is the possibility of its true ethical re-foundation, or de-arrogation or de-ideologisation. I no longer look at the other or myself with suspicion – inevitably judging him or her, even as I bask in my own sentimental permissiveness – and instead trust both as capable of shaping emotional experience and thus of arriving at existence. I mention only that the last section deals with the subject of intuition, which is as elusive as it is enigmatic, but which finds its perfect place in the context of the book's discourse. One need only think of the special relationship that intuition has with the lightning-fast temporality of the ideo-affective synthesis with which we usually identify it.

In conclusion, even looking at the international scene, I don't think there are many authors who would prove to be worthy of Rugi's book. That is, that they would be able to render in a serious, calm, cultured, reflective, literally "understanding" way, an author with a thousand facets and so still "outdated" – even when he is accepted but only to be immediately misconstrued. The capacity for dialogue that Rugi demonstrates with respect to other strands of psychoanalysis, and in particular to the classical sphere, as well as with numerous authors of literature and philosophy, as we know among the most important sources of inspiration for Bion, but also with the neurosciences, it's highly admirable. Whatever the level of knowledge of the reader, his way of conceiving Bion and psychoanalysis will come out changed, full of questions, ready to turn over the pages and re-read at least the many points underlined or highlighted in order to be able to find them again easily.

There are many memorable passages: the Proustian time thirsting for bodies to be transformed into unrecognisable puppets; the meditation on the sense of pain, today often spectacularised and degraded; the Falstaff character, more real than a real person who actually exists; the many points where we convincingly see a Bion moving more and more towards a vision of individual therapy that is first relational and then specifically group or towards a transpersonal field; images of the infinite spatiality of psychotic panic; the shift from an epistemological to an ontological vision – not only in Ogden's sense but also as an anticipation of a new ontology, no longer atomistic or dualistic – of the subject. The idea that thinking in terms of events rather than substances helps us to penetrate more deeply into the nature of things; the clarification and closure, once and for all, of the misunderstanding of Bion as a philosopher or "mystic", and so on.

On this last point, no one could put it better than Rugi: "But all these ideas, like stray thoughts, enter into his elaboration of the concept of time only after he has already encountered the time-wasting patient and many other clinical experiences of the destruction and creation of time and space in the analysis room. The result is something completely new, different, in which clinical experience, and therefore empirical work, always remains the true foundation, the true source, to which he always returns". This is another way of speaking of Bion's "strange empiricism" and of recalling the beauty of psychoanalysis as a discipline whose uniqueness lives in the Freudian *junktim*, the exciting and indissoluble mixture of theory and empirical research, of passion for meaning and closeness to psychic pain.

(Moena, January 2023)

Note

1 On the connection between the birth of the psyche and aesthetics, also in relation to art, see Civitarese 2017; Civitarese 2020.

Preface
Why Bion and why now?

Why present the thought of Wilfred R. Bion, and why now? And above all, how can we present it in an accessible way not only to specialists, but also to a wider audience? An audience that still has the desire to understand and think about itself in relation to the context, times and reality in which it lives. The proposal to present Bion as an out-of-date thought may appear to be a philosophical whim, even inappropriate, but Bion's relationships with philosophy are perhaps more complex and profound than he would have liked. Bion made philosophy his fundamental basic attitude; that disturbing questioning that demands the persistence of the question within every query. Hence the impossibility of developing a thought in a complete, concluded, linear way, because thinking is made of paradoxes, which pulsate at the heart of thought itself and make it impossible to proceed linearly. These are the *philosophical paradoxes*, which one cannot fail to encounter when thinking and trying to understand life.

One of the quotes that Bion loved most was "La réponse est le malheur de la question", a famous phrase by Blanchot that he learned from Green. Bion never gives direct answers, which saturate the question, or rather the asking. His intent is always to open up to thought, to be a stimulus to thinking. Bion's thought is therefore "out-of-date" because it is uncomfortable, even irritating, in times in which mass thought and anaesthesia prevail; in times when it is usual practice, supported by dominant science, to reduce emotional and relational problems to simple cognitive learning operations. Being "out-of-date", going against the dominant mentality, is perhaps the destiny of every creative person, of every innovator, and Bion certainly has been this from the beginning. The "out-of-date", starting from Nietzsche, is moreover the true soul of true thought, at least the philosophical one which, as Deleuze (1968) indicates, is always unfashionable, that is against this time and in favour of a time to come. Bion, however, did not just go against the grain, he had a stubborn, absolute determination in trying to achieve his objectives, which were nothing else than to verify and sometimes formalise his extraordinary intuitions. In this sense, Bion truly embodies that empiricist soul, of which Deleuze speaks, as an inexhaustible and fantastic creation of ever-new concepts that emerge in the encounter of the here and now; concepts that are never the same, starting from an ever-moving horizon, which repeats and differentiates them. An empiricism, therefore, is rooted in the infinite and always different repetition of the clinical encounter, without ever being an empirical particularity, nor an abstract universal, but an encounter, with a hic et nunc, which in its continuous shifting and disguising itself, always tends to create the new. For this reason, Bion's tension towards mysticism and formalisation reveals what Deleuze calls a *Cogito* for a dissolved Ego.

In doing this, Bion often finds himself overturning common thought, codified theories, but mostly he leaves aside those that now seem to him to be worn-out coins. He did this with almost all psychoanalytic theories, those of Freud on the unconscious and dreams, those of Melanie Klein, and finally with those of Bion himself, showing in *A Memoir of the Future* an extraordinary ability to distance himself even from his own ideas, or at least by the rigidity of one's own jargon. In *The Italian Seminars,* Bion (1977a, p. 110) observes that "when we secrete an idea, or when we produce a theory it seems that at the same time we emit calcareous material, we become calcified, the idea becomes calcified".[1] For this reason, theories are not so important as thinking itself, which for Bion means being able to process thoughts, taking on the responsibility of thinking, staying in touch with one's emotional experiences, and therefore being able to be more true, authentic and even more real.

The idea that guided the group that welcomed Bion in Italy in July 1977, starting with Francesco Corrao, was that one cannot be a Bionian, but only oneself, because this is his fundamental teaching; becoming oneself and accepting all the risks. This is the profound meaning of Parthenope Bion's work "Why we cannot call ourselves Bionians" (1987). Therefore, the risk of becoming oneself may also be that of realising that some Bionian ideas have gradually taken on less correspondence in clinical practice. Moving away from the teacher is not a real risk, but moving away from oneself is. That is losing contact with one's own deep, inaccessible, but always active parts, or not listening to one's own wild thoughts, which however ridiculous, stupid or fantastic they may be, is giving up: one must have the courage to welcome such thoughts. These strange thoughts are in the air, somewhere, looking for a thinker – who could be one of us.

Bion invites us to respect these 'strange' thoughts; to which we must give temporary accommodation and clothe them with words suitable for public expression. The creative process is thus painful, and passes through the courage to express one's errant thoughts, whatever they may be, even in fear of the reception they will receive. Bion (1970, p. 129) writes "What is required is not the decrease of inhibition but a decrease of the impulse to inhibit; the impulse to inhibit is fundamentally envy of the growth-stimulating objects". Rather than Kleinian envy, as a constitutional element, Bion, however, addresses fears and blockages that prevent the individual from getting in touch with himself, because if hopes are deceitful, fears can be lies.[2] Indeed, fear as a lie implies a lack of faith, first of all in the truth and so in our ability to accept it. In order to express a wild thought, therefore, there must be someone who is ready to accept it, but this someone must, first of all, be ourselves: "There is always one person who can hear what you think – and that is you" (Bion, 1977a, p. 143). And yet for Bion the process of subjectification is complex, uncertain, non-linear, and does not occur in solitude, but only in relational relationship. Becoming oneself, should not be understood as a narcissistic distancing of the individual from the group, but as a parallel and concomitant process of differentiation of the individual in the group, which implies the growth of both. In this sense, Bion's thought is unfashionable in a very different way from that of Nietzsche. The philosopher works by aphorisms, criticising current morality, from scattered, sometimes irreconcilable thoughts, and showing the opposite horns of paradoxes. Bion inhabits the paradox by wearing the uncomfortable garb of the "tragic man" who seeks to realise his own Self, despite the adversities of life, the tragic lack of physical and mental strength, and of course death.

The tragic, Natoli (1986) reminds us, does not lie in suffering, but rather in the way in which in suffering one is instituted. In fact, the tragic is imposed precisely in the very claim to exist. Pain and the claim to exist are the same thing. This is why man is tragic in his nature, and Greek tragedy represents the theatre of the soul – the inevitable clash between its dark and irreconcilable forces. Like Nietzsche, Bion too looks at becoming, but not at the becoming of the "Over-man", nor at the becoming of the spirit through the Hegelian synthesis. Growth for Bion is always painful and contradictory, but without glory and presents stumbling blocks, yet consists of passion for the truth, enthusiasm and even beauty. This is why Grotstein (2007) states that the true kōan that remains at the bottom of Bion's work is that each person becomes what he or she accepts to suffer.

Bion's thinking is, therefore, difficult, and his idea of thinking requires courage, the ability to tolerate the frustration of not understanding, the patience to pause in the chaos, to tolerate pain, paradox, complexity, to keep alive the ability to observe without thinking, to apply the practice of doubt and to learn from experience, and from one's mistakes. Can we honestly say that our age recognises itself in this way of thinking? That it feels comfortable in this disposition to think in the way of Bion?

Contemporaneity seems to be characterised by a dramatic crisis of thinking, or rather of the ability to think, to experience emotions and the very experience of reality. The simplest, most immediate ways are sought in drugs or surgical solutions, while growth models and desire itself are increasingly delegated to media algorithms and artificial intelligence. The capacity to think, the last real defence against barbarism and a specific sign of our exceptional place in the cosmos, no longer seems to enjoy the esteem that many thinkers had accorded it, and in any case, it does not enjoy good health. Man is no longer just a fragile reed, but a reed that thinks, as Blaise Pascal wrote that all our dignity as human beings was collocated in the ability to think. Is this still the case?

In fact, our post-modern age is rapidly moving towards a world we do not know, the "infosphere", where technologies interact with other technologies, making humans increasingly marginal and less involved in the processes (Floridi, 2014). Humanity is rapidly moving from Newtonian space, animated by objects and people, to the "infosphere", where the virtual is part of the real and the real is part of the virtual, implying a radical transformation of the environment in which we live. In the face of these changes, we urgently need to ask ourselves how the new media and new technologies are changing the texture of reality, our society and our behaviour. Indeed, it is becoming increasingly clear that these changes require a rethinking of the very concept of human being. The spectre of the post-human, long hovering between art and science, now wanders into the spaces of the everyday, increasingly virtual, leaving the subject disoriented and confused. The post-human shift arises from the convergence of post-humanism, as a critique of the humanist ideal of man as universal representative, and post-anthropocentrism, which questions the claimed superiority of human being and recognises the need to abandon species-specific hierarchy and affirms biological egalitarianism. Placing human being in a broader context, in a vision that is no longer hierarchical, that takes into account the idea of the environment and our negative impact on it, is indeed the real challenge of a present that is always late in thinking about a possible future. The current generation, defined as the "Anthropocene generation", is now aware of the lasting and dramatic disasters that man has caused and is causing on the planet, but it does not seem capable of responding with a thought that is also a shared future project.

As I write, the war in Ukraine rages on, and no one can say how it will end, a tragedy that is difficult to talk about. It seems like a return to the past, a war from another time, but it is not. It is a war of *our time*, in which we see the return of the ghosts of land ownership, of raw materials, even of the fear of hunger and cold. And in a world that has lost faith in dialogue, where fear dominates, and the ideas of freedom, self-determination and democracy are seriously threatened, as they are being crushed by imperialisms of all kinds. This is mass thinking and at the same time proof that thinking is dangerous, because totalitarianisms do not tolerate thinking that presupposes freedom and respect for the other. That is all totalitarianisms: there are no good or bad totalitarianisms. It is enough to read the conversation between the communist teacher Mostovskoj, imprisoned in a Nazi camp, and Liss, the camp commander – in one of the most beautiful dialogues in literature that Vasily Grossman (1980) has given us in *Life and Fate* – to understand that Nazism and communism, or rather "dictatorship of the proletariat", as Lenin preferred, are actually the two faces of the same problem.

Ours is an age of catastrophic change and our world is going through a dramatic crisis. Past and future are colliding like tectonic plates. On the one hand, we are witnessing the proliferation of highly advanced theories and currents of thought; on the other, we are experiencing ancestral struggles. How do we reconcile the real and the virtual, the closed and the open, repetition and singularity, method and creativity, invariance and emergence, in a world in which we struggle to recognise ourselves and the other?

If we do not want the various post-human theories to become a flight into a distopic future, with its absurd excesses like Cancel Culture, we must find the strength to observe reality, to recognise that we live in paradox, and that our achievements always have a dark edge, i.e.,a shadow line. Post-human theories rightly criticise the conception of the world and of human beings as dualistic entities, structured according to the principles of the dialectical opposition of inside/outside, and move towards a neo-materialist conception of subjects and processes of relations within networks of relations. In these theories, the human/non-human, nature/culture relationship becomes a *continuum*, and yet they seem to underestimate the risks connected to uncontrolled biogenetic development, to robotics, to artificial intelligence, which minimise and endanger the distance of post-human culture from much less noble projects, such as the so-called transhumanist project, a *human enhancement* compressed into a robotic and dehumanising determinism, What about the recent idea of breeding human embryos in incubators, without any input or contact with the parents? What is post-human, transhuman, inhuman? What remains of the *human quality* based on memory, affection and relationships? We may think that in these incubators the foetus enjoys infinite serenity, a perfect environmental quality, but to reduce environmental (and relational) quality to quantitative biomedical and nutritional parameters managed by artificial intelligence is in fact to breed meat robots. Thinking about the quality of human relationships is, therefore, a priority. Every psychoanalyst knows that totalitarianism is not only outside us, it also lurks inside us, making us less free, and inhibiting our creativity and that of others around us. The outside and the inside are not so separate, there is no outside that does not carry the shadow of the inside, and vice versa. Is relationship, or rather the quality of human relationship, destined to become one of the great narratives in its twilight? In a world where 2 out of 10 children at age 1 and 6 out of 10 at age 2 now habitually use touchscreen devices such as tablets or smartphones, where parents are beginning to be replaced by electronic tools for storytelling, playing, interacting, how much does relationship matter? And above all, how much are we still able to relate empathically, to provide tenderness, patience, a sense of presence and the ability to pay attention?

When Bion and Winnicott placed the quality of the relationship at the centre of the development of the mind and of pathology, downplaying the importance of the constitutional aspect, they in fact made a real revolution in the pathogenesis and therapy of mental disorders. Beginning with Bion and Winnicott, authors of all such trends, they show an unusual agreement in attributing to the family the function of modulator of psychic pain, which remains a central task in the development of the child and his ability to learn to tolerate contact with the inner and outer world, to transform primitive emotions and to develop symbolisation processes. Parental figures thus retain a central role as mediators of suffering and the traumatic nature of reality, as in all forms of learning, and the deficiencies or distortions of these functions remain at the root of much psychopathology. Indeed, recent studies in this field tend to trace the origins of even today's technological addictions to various forms of emotional neglect in the early years of life. Oedipus, in his various declinations, thus seems to hold a firm position as the organiser of the child's mental development.

Nevertheless, shrewd philosophers such as Michel Serres (2015) dismiss as a strange and petty limitation the tendency of psychologists of all orientations to construct personal identity through parental relationships. For Serres, identity is constructed not only in relation to the human environment but also in relation to all other beings, animals and plants, even the rocks and water that surround us. And Serres is right. A stone, however, remains a stone and can also be used to hit you; we can only grasp the beauty of a stone if someone has taught us to love it. Any knowledge that has to do with human life always and only passes through an affection that helps us to understand its meaning and its beauty. Serres is also a fervent advocate of the virtual, saying that after the "hard" age of artefacts, we have entered a "soft" age. He heralds the dawn of a new world, that is an age in which we are free to live virtually in which everyone can connect with whomever they want, and finally think for ourselves without anyone telling us who we are, because the Net makes us all *co-acting, cogitating,* actors in an era of mass democracy where everyone can be at the top, but in fact where there is no top anymore. For Serres, the virtual is our virtue. It is open to all metamorphoses and thus to the new ways of thinking. In the ideal network, now real, for Serres each individual can come into contact with one or more others, regardless of distance and alienation. In his hymn to the technological god, however, Serres seems to forget the price that man must pay for this lightness associated with the sweet age. Curiously, it is the neuroscientists who remind us that every time we entrust a human function to a machine, we are taking something out of our lives and our brains. Entrusting memory, the ability to orient, to organise, to calculate, to avoid the complexity and harshness of the real, to live in the virtual, depending on preferences, to think with responses programmed by algorithms, and a thousand other issues related to control and programmed conditioning, do not seem to be highly conducive to growth and creativity. In short, these wonderful tools that we have in our hands and pockets (at least for the moment) and that tend to replace our brains, make our lives easier, but beyond a certain level they make us regress destructively, and according to many, we have already crossed that line. Today, research tells us that the smartphone has become a transitional object, i.e.,a bodily extension and sometimes a prosthesis, on which we are increasingly dependent and, above all, that our cognitive capacities have been declining rapidly for years.

Alongside philosophers like Serres, who are very "fashionable" in their thinking, there are others who seem to be sounding the alarm about everything we can call fashionable. Among them is Byung-Chul Han, a South Korean philosopher of German culture who is very involved in social debate. In his lucid and rigorous analyses of the contemporary world, Han (2020) points out that ours is a society without pain, reduced to permanent anaesthesia, incapable of recognising truth and facts, and detached from reality. Mass anaesthesia and mass thinking, but also closure to the other, because the wound that hurts is a primordial opening to the other. Han's analyses are sharp, bordering on provocative, in fact. Even at the cost of irritation, the South Korean philosopher seems willing to undermine our certainties, to reveal the restlessness behind the anaesthesia and torpor that plague our consciences. In his complex path, Han comes to identify "smoothness" as the hallmark of our time. Smoothness neither hurts nor resists. This is the art of Jeff Koons, with his reflective sculptures, a mirror-like smoothness in which the viewer is reflected, asking only for a "wow". In this way, beauty is polished, stripped of all its jolts and wounds. Aestheticisation shows itself in the mode of anaestheticisation (Byung-Chul, 2015).

Han does not quote Bion. His vast culture fishes in the sphere of philosophy and aesthetics. However, a profound affinity emerges between the ideas of the philosopher Han and those of the psychoanalyst Bion. Both do not fail to connect growth and thinking to experience, and to the relationship with truth and reality, and both place pain in a central position. For Byung-Chul (2020) – pain is a midwife of the New, of the completely Other: – the negativity that interrupts the Same. And in the face of pain, the mind imagines Beauty, which is the complementary colour of pain. Bion does not glorify pain, but he knows that the fight against pain is only done through the experience of pain, and therefore an analytic therapy can only be painful; and this is the price everyone must pay to stay in touch with their emotional truth. The greatest pain is to avoid the pain itself, because it reduces anaesthesia. Man's ability to tolerate pain, then makes a difference and some patients confuse feeling pain with suffering it, but those who cannot tolerate pain are not even capable of suffering pleasure. Pain is, in consequence, necessary, at least to the extent that it represents the price of our ability to feel and experience emotions. In this sense, there is no growth, no creativity and no beauty that does not arise from pain: Beauty is nothing but dire at its beginning. It is the idea with which Rainer Maria Rilke (1923), in the *Duino Elegies*, forever linked pain and beauty. And there are many who think that beauty will save us, recalling Dostoevsky in *The Idiot*, where Prince Myshkin says that beauty will save the world. Dostoevsky, however, wondered what beauty and said that it is difficult to evaluate beauty, and that he was not prepared, because beauty is an enigma.

Negativity, depth and roughness thus mark the relationship with beauty, which remains a mystery. In Dostoyevsky, as in Han and Bion. It is interesting to note that in *A Memoir of the Future*, Bion (1977b, p. 46), actually anticipates Han's idea of smoothness: "Even any roughness of our system that might facilitate the lodgement of the germ of another idea is smoothed and polished". For Bion (ibid., p.48), the night, dreaming and even delirium and hallucination are roughness in relation to daylight: imperfections in which "an idea might lodge and flourish before it can be stamped out and 'cured'". The similarities between Han's thought and Bion's are, therefore, striking. Both join the long list of unfashionable thinkers that began long before Nietzsche.

The problem, however, is not to unite Bion with counter-current voices, of which there is no shortage, nor to carry on a close comparison between the two thinkers. Bion is not a philosopher and it would be a mistake to think of proposing the mental attitude of a psychoanalytic setting as a vision of the world. More interesting would be to understand whether Bion's theory of the development of thinking can actually tell us something about where the current technological evolution risks leading. In other words, is Bion's theory of thinking a theory limited to psychoanalytic practice or is it a general theory of the development of the ability to think? Bion (1961) himself poses this question at the very beginning of *A Theory of Thinking*, pointing out the similarity of his theory to philosophical theories. Naturally, like any psychoanalytic theory, his theory of thinking has practical aims and needs to be empirically verified. Bion, therefore, points to the space of analysis, the analytic work, as the natural place for his theory. This does not detract from the fact that the patient-analyst relationship is placed in analogy with the mother-child relationship and is thus immediately proposed as a more general theory of the development of the capacity to think. In fact, Bion's theory of thinking requires the patience to tolerate the pain of absence, thinking is *tolerated pain*. And this implies the importance of the quality of the relationship in analytic work, and of course in the mother-child relationship. Perhaps the boundary between the philosophical and psychoanalytic theory of thought is thinner than Bion himself was prepared to admit, and analytic work is, in reality, a laboratory in which a natural process that accompanies us from birth is repeated, i.e.,the incessant work of developing our capacity to think, to expand our mental space, even to construct our unconscious. In fact, for Bion, the unconscious is developed as a function of the personality, and starts from the primary relationship, which, distinguishes itself as the psychoanalytic function of the mind, and is realised as the capacity *to perceive* reality, according to an integrated functioning, by bringing together the different points of view; conscious/unconscious, and which leads to the capacity to make sense of experience. Thinking is, therefore, a process of continuous becoming, and every thought, the thought, grows old and eventually becomes a brake on thinking itself. It is the idea that becomes "-calcified-". Thoughts are thus reduced to formulas, to slogans. They undergo a viral mutation. A virological reproduction that turns them into commonplaces, and condemns them to endless repetition in a vacuum of meaning. It is this slide into routine that devitalises true thought and creates pockets of habit, of non-thought, that prevent any change. So all of Bion's work is about developing the human capacity to think. And thinking means being able to feel free to become ourselves, to regain contact with our split parts – not alive/not dead – but enormously active, and to reduce the impulse that inhibits our potential. It is in this perspective that Bion's thinking is "unfashionable", and perhaps for that very reason extraordinarily *daring* and *creative*.

Notes

1 The page indications refer to Bion's original works reported in References.
2 Bion quotes a verse from Arthur Hugh Clough, an English poet of the 1800s.

Introduction

Why does one choose a theory?

Bion's thought is complex, requires a long and arduous apprenticeship and does not lend itself to easy reduction to this or that theme. It is as if it must be understood as a whole or it must be abandoned. That is why more than a few specialists prefer to ignore it. Why, then, is Bion's theory chosen by an increasing number of psychoanalysts and psychotherapists, and why are his citations in international indexes constantly increasing?

We must, therefore, ask ourselves why one model or theory is chosen and not another. Maturana and Varela (1980) have no doubts. It is the "aesthetic seduction" that favours the choice of a frame of reference based on the desires and functions to be fulfilled in the cultural and material world in which we live. The choice is thus made on *aesthetic grounds*. More recently, McAllister (1998) hypothesises a recursive relationship between aesthetic and empirical choices, with the possibility that if an empirical theory works, it may lead to a change in the aesthetic criteria themselves. Perhaps then it is also necessary to understand that Bionian theory works and, above all, *how* it works; to grasp its close connections with the clinic, with life and with the wider process of knowledge development. Understanding the more general empirical and heuristic aspects of a theory could, therefore, help us to better appreciate beauty itself.

In his tireless search for the structures and forms of life, Gregory Bateson (1979) had come to favour aesthetics and the idea of a fundamental unifying beauty. The traces of the living are the symmetries, the spirals, the proportions, the organisation, the connections, the structures that connect. From this perspective, for Bateson, the "aesthetic" is what is sensitive to the structure that connects, and beauty is the fundamental unifying force: the only one that can oppose the authority and dominance

DOI: 10.4324/9781032655239-1

of quantitative science. What beauty is, however, remains a mystery. Friedrich Cramer (1988) observes that beauty emerges only at the frontiers of chaos, along a dangerous path, tense between two precipices: that of the dissolution of all order on the one hand, and that of becoming rigid in symmetry and order, on the other.

This position seems to be closely related to Bion's theory. Bion is convinced that science does not have the adequate tools to objectively study human life, and often cites Heisenberg's Uncertainty Principle as the basis of an intrinsic limitation of knowledge. But this did not stop him from looking for order and invariants precisely where chaos is greatest, that is in human relationships, starting with groups. This is Bion's strange empiricism, which in the infinite multiplicity and variability of the clinical encounter maintains a constant tension towards formalism and even mathematism, and at the same time the need to return constantly to the sources of creativity, to the chaos of the dissolved Ego and to the uncertainties of relationship. In this aspect, we intuit and recognise beauty in its theory, because, as Cramer (1988) suggests, *beauty is created in the union of chaos with islands of order.* For this reason, beauty is never separated from a sense of vertigo and the restlessness of the uncanny. Bion's thought is always in a precarious balance between order and disorder. He tries to insert formal elements right where the chaos is greatest and to find invariants in the continuous flow of events. For this reason, his theory cannot be linear, but involves a series of models that work now in synergy, now in antagonism, now in an oscillating way, in an attempt to grasp the complex passages of vital processes, always poised between organisation and anti-organisation, abstraction and concretisation, factuality and counterfactuality.

The gestalt of Bion's theory: internal coherence, complexity, fractal structure

What then are the characteristics that identify the gestalt of Bion's theory, an overview of it, so that it can be recognised in its qualities as an aesthetic, and therefore transformative object?

I propose three elements: *internal coherence, complexity, fractal structure.*

These three elements cannot be thought of separately, because they are interrelated and together they make Bion's theory a single body; a set of models that refer to each other, intimately linked and functionally coordinated.

This aspect implies a first epistemological or methodological problem, that of its possible deconstruction, that is, whether Bionian theory can be taken "in pieces" or whether it should be taken "in toto". My hypothesis is that its particular structure makes its partial use and even partial knowledge unlikely. This is why it is rarely seriously refuted, but rather ignored, and the various quotations used by authors who are not familiar with it as a whole often have the devastating effect of advertisements.

As far as **internal coherence** is concerned, there is a surprising continuity between the earliest insights into groups and the latest thoughts on factual transformations. Bion's theory is endowed with an internal coherence that runs through it from beginning to end. This does not mean that it always remains the same, but that it returns to itself, expanding, specifying itself, delineating itself from different points, constantly stressing its limits, and often the reader's, but maintaining an underlying coherence. In this way, it is characterised as a dual-group model, in which the differences between individual and group analysis tend to blur, and which today flows into the so-called *Bion Field Theory*. Certain initial assumptions of *group experience*, such as the proto-mental system, are never fully replaced by the later beta-element model. The proto-mental system is bracketed, remaining silent, only to reappear in *A Memoir of the Future,* as an imaginative conjecture and narrative formulation of an inner group life in which the primitive parts of the personality carry out their thinking through the body:

> I cannot make anything clear to Psyche unless I borrow a bellyache or headache or respiratory distress from somitic vocabulary for any of these post-natal-structures. I believe in mind and personality as there is no evidence whatever for anything but Body.
>
> (Bion, 1979, p. 20)

Bion, therefore, suggests that the embryonic stages may have their own distinct representation in the structure of the self and that therefore the life of the mind involves a kind of inner dialogue which may be concordant or discordant. Meltzer (1986), admits to being troubled by the proto-mental system hypothesis, which implies the evocation of a primitive, tribal life deep within the mind, a life that may emerge as group behaviour or express itself through bodily processes. This hypothesis leads Meltzer to suggest a clash of systems, a kind of political conflict between the parts that are more attuned to the basic emotional level and the rational, less authentic parts.

The terms of this conflict revolve around the fear of exclusion from the group and the prize of a place in the power system.

Internal coherence and continuity, albeit in an increasingly complex context, have been widely acknowledged by various authors. Mauro Fornaro (1990) proposes a unified reading of Bion's theory within a biopsychosocial paradigm that links the proto-mental system to the concept of projective identification, as an exchange within a common trans-individual space and of the indistinction between mind and body. Eugenio Gaddini (1981), for example, stresses the continuity between the group in itself and the internal groupality of each individual, the functioning of which, close to that of the body, remains one of the most fundamental discoveries for understanding the basic organisation of the individual. Antonello Correale (1985) observes that the richness of Bion's thought on groups can only be understood in relation to the later elaboration in *Attention and Interpretation*. This is because many of the questions Bion poses in *Experiences* find their natural answer only in the subsequent development of his thought. Thomas H. Ogden (2009) finally admits that the radical reformulation of the psychoanalytic concept of thought introduced by Bion begins precisely with *Experiences in Groups*, thus re-evaluating a text long considered "pre-psychoanalytic". The theory of thought is, in fact, the only true theory formulated by Bion, a theory that runs through all his work, beginning with groups. The study of groups is, after all, a search for why the group does *not* learn. And this is the meaning of the division between the work and the basic group, where emotions get in the way of goals, but also of the group mind of the individual, split between collaborative and dissident internal objects.

As far as **complexity** is concerned, this also appears at the beginning of Bion's theoretical path, which starts from the group, arrives at the individual, returns to the couple, finds the group, the internal and external, even societal and cultural and scientific products, without ever forgetting the biological rootedness of the individual. To this must be added the systematic rejection of all linear causality and the introduction of concepts such as recursiveness, emergence, paradox and multiple points of observation, which already appear in *Experiences in Groups*. These are the aspects that place the concept of complexity at the centre of Bion's theories, a concept completely foreign to psychoanalysis at the time. The question remains whether Bion was familiar with the principles of systems theory that were beginning to circulate at the time. *General Systems Theory* appeared in 1969, but von

Bertalanffy published his first announcement in 1945, in German and in English in 1950. Nevertheless, his ideas began to be disseminated at conferences and symposia soon after the war, and in 1948–9 von Bertalanffy was a visiting professor at the University of London. Bion, however, acted as if he was familiar with the principles of systems theory; concepts such as recursiveness, Necker's cube, schism, paradox, organisation, emergence and even complexity are scattered throughout his group model. Some of these concepts have been known for a long time. The Swiss crystallographer N. A. Necker discovered multistable depth in 1832; Gregory Bateson published on schismogenesis in 1935; Albert Lautman (1908–44) had written about the links between the structure of the whole and the properties of the parts, although he was referring to mathematics and not to living systems. Other concepts, such as the role of the observer in the construction of observed reality, belong instead to second-order cybernetics, which was formulated later, while the concept of complexity was introduced in the 1970s by Edgar Morin (1977), in close connection with those of organisation and paradox in the theory of living systems. Nonetheless, these concepts already seem to be at work in the Bionian model of groups, at least at an intuitive level. In other words, these systemic concepts, although they never became part of Bion's system, are part of the conceptual tools with which Bion tried to come to terms with his experiences of groups. They are, therefore, part of Bion's epistemological tools, even if they do not make Bion an exponent of systemic theory.

Fractal structure is the third weighty feature of Bion's thought, a feature that some authors have begun to emphasise, albeit cautiously. The concepts of fractal, strange attractor, bifurcation, are complex and do not belong to the psychoanalytic tradition. Bion had an excellent knowledge of Henry Poincaré, who was the first to study the mathematics of bifurcations, from which the study of deterministic chaos and Lorenz's attractors originated. To this must be added Bion's surprising familiarity with logic and epistemology. And yet, Bion (1963) preferred models to theories, which are more effective in analogically grasping the immediate reality of the analytical situation. Models are the product of a process of abstracting an emotional experience, but they have the advantage of maintaining a minimum of particularisation. Models, however, must be able to articulate with each other, and converge into a scientific deductive system, but can be easily discarded when they prove no longer useful. Naturally, behind the models, there must be a metatheory, a set of premises that help decide which data to look for. All of this means that each model retains an aura of concreteness that refers back to the original situation, but also that the various models are interconnected and converge into a more general system that is increasingly abstract. Grotstein (2007) says he is convinced that the various Bionian models "are all synonymous", in other words, *containment, alpha function, transformations, grid, contact barrier, emotional ties L, H, K*, albeit with different names, identify related and/or enriched functions that together form a three-dimensional image, a "hologram", of perspectives of the same process seen from different points. Grotstein does not talk about fractals, but compares Bion's models to the chromosomes of organisms, in which each cell contains the genome of the entire organism. This means that each model contains the same structure as the global theory. This is a different way of referring to the concept of a fractal, which I recall is *a geometric figure that repeats itself identically at any scale*.

Instead, Civitarese (2012) speaks of a fractal structure in his analysis of the Grid. In fact, it is in the Grid that this fractal structure repeats, at each level, the complexity of the whole, starting from a basic structure, the selective membrane of the mind, the thought that interposes itself between stimulus and action. The same binary pair structure, separated/united by a bar, is found in the grid as a whole and understood as a contact barrier that separates and connects, but also in the second-order filters, the rows and columns, and the third-order filters as in the very lines that cut out the boxes. Civitarese considers slashes as semi-permeable barriers, or contact barriers, that simultaneously divide and reunite two dialectically opposed concepts. It is precisely this binary pair, obtained by selecting any two elements of the grid, separated by the caesura of a slash, that represents the mother-child relationship in its structure and functioning. In addition, needless to say, the analyst-patient relationship, A/P, was Bion's starting point. These relationships are represented in the two axes; the horizontal, where one finds the use of thoughts, hence the analyst and the oedipal function; the vertical, which represents the patient and the development of thoughts. In this way, the grid becomes a model of relationships that gives us an idea of how the container/contained mechanism works, which regulates the passage from box to box at all levels, and of which the alpha function is an expression. For Civitarese, it is precisely in this structural insistence, *depicted in the Grid*, that one rediscovers the duality (groupality) formed by each mind.

Civitarese therefore uses the image of the fractal as a metaphor that can help to visually understand the structure and dynamics of Bionian theory, in which each element repeats the complexity of the theory within itself and is connected to everything else in the theory. But more than a metaphor, the *fractal structure* seems to represent the intimate organisation of the Bionian paradigm, something like Bateson's connecting structure that gives the whole paradigm a basic unity based on beauty. The fractal element, which always shows the same structure at every scale, repeating at every level the basic analyst/patient, mother/child relationship, thus refers back to the aesthetic aspect of the Bionian Paradigm. Of this relationship, the ♀♂ model represents the most abstract form, but it is rooted in biology, which gives rise to life and which, from the very beginning, allows emotional growth and the development of thought processes or their involution, when envy dominates and the K and ♀♂ relationships become negative. Tabak De Bianchedi (1987, p. 91) describes the essence of ♀♂ in a dizzying exaggeration that pushes us towards complexity in its rapid passages:

It comes from the body, or rather from bodies in union: mouth and nipple, mother and child, vagina and penis, generating conception and growth when the medium is favourable; it develops towards the mind, where preconceptions join realisations, emotions join understanding them, words join meanings. It extends to the group, small and large, it extends to science, religion, art, to the history of being in its infinite possibilities of connections and realisations.[1]

The fractal structure thus makes the Bionian theory very different from the Freudian one, and also from that of any other psychoanalyst. Freudian theory, albeit with some limitations, can be represented by the archaeological metaphor, which unfolds in several overlapping layers, of which we can take one part and reject another, such as the structural model and drop the first topical. For Kleinian theories, however, what Bion (1976–9, p. 51) himself said in a seminar applies, they "bear a great resemblance to sin: everybody is against them, but everybody practises them in secret". In other words, Kleinian theories often creep into apparently very different theoretical systems, sometimes in a subterranean way, without being recognised. And this also applies to Bion.

Chaos and beauty in Bion

"Perhaps reality is the most complete chaos", says Lichtenberg to Einstein, in an imaginary conversation about causality that Cramer (1988) describes in his book *Chaos and Order*. Einstein prefers to think that in the objectively existing world, there is complete conformity to laws, and rejects the successes of quantum theory, to which he himself contributed, because such successes seem to reduce nature to a game of chance. Nevertheless, it is increasingly evident that in complex systems, such as living beings, quantum theory is indispensable, and the evolutionary path follows an indeterministic course, with discontinuities and bifurcations, which cannot be predicted.

We should not be surprised, then, that in his attempt to approach reality, particularly mental reality, Bion encounters mysticism. This is the paradoxical soul of O, in which mysticism represents one of its vertices, another vertex being brute reality, but there are many others. In "O", Grotstein (2007) sees the infinity, which as such requires religious, mystical and philosophical formulations. Still "O" is not only the infinite, it is also "reality", albeit unknowable and infinite, and precisely this paradoxicality is what makes *Transformations* puzzling, as if Bion found the point of maximum mystical tension precisely in the desperate attempt to approach reality, primarily the clinical one. Bion stretches to the breaking point the possibilities of formalising the psychoanalytic process, but in the end, he is forced to return to the original source of creativity, opening up to the mystical and ineffable experience as an immanent condition of the human being. The primary intent remains, however, to address the ineffability of mental reality, especially in its emergence, to describe change and growth, through the scientific method. This is why Bion (1965, p. 16) does not deal with psycho-analytic theories, but with theories of *psycho-analytic observation*, which as such seek to "bridge the gap between psycho-analytic preconceptions, and the facts as they emerge in the session".

It is, therefore, chaos that interests Bion, the reality that opens up in the psychoanalytic relationship and onto which he focuses his microscope, knowing full well that this relationship is an open window onto the primordial chaos of the birth of thought, of life, of the affective and social cosmos, and ultimately of the concept of time itself. To describe the origin of thought in this session is, therefore, to compress an entire expanding universe into a point of extreme density. It is from this point that the theory of attachment, emotion, the alpha function, the dream, the myth, the container/contained, the transformations, the grid and all the rest of the Bionian Universe originate. When Bion (1967, p. 105) hypothesises that "the link between patient and analyst, or infant and breast, is the mechanism of projective identification", in fact, he condenses the origin of the relational, affective and mental world into a "navel", which opens up extraordinary heuristic possibilities, but also the vertigo of the unspeakable. Equating the link between analyst and patient with the primordial and prototypical link between mother and child, Bion places projective identification at the theoretical foundation of the human relationship, and thus of development and therapy. From this mechanism, he abstracts the container/contained model, which he develops as a general model of the dyadic and group relationship on which emotional growth and the ability to think depend. Bion thus transforms projective identification from a very sensual and very Kleinian model of the mother/child relationship into a model of learning from relationship and experience, and thus into a complex theory. Alpha function, reverie, dream and transformations, are, therefore, all models linked to the container/contained theory in a circular, increasingly complex path that completes the theory of thought. The container/contained model is in fact linked to the alpha function and the dream and, as Civitarese observes, it is the most abstract and general of the mechanisms developed by Bion to describe psychic transformations. It represents the lowest common denominator between PS↔D, between negative capacity and chosen fact (CN↔FS), between projective identification and reverie, and it is the only one that, in its various declinations – convivial, symbiotic, parasitic, negative – can be applied to both the intrapsychic and interpersonal levels. Because of these container/contained characteristics, it seems to be the most natural Bionian model for the study of groups, couples, families and institutions. Although it has its origins in the analyst-patient and mother-child relationships, it in fact "alludes at macro and micro levels to the essentially interpsychic (bi/pluripersonal) nature of meaning and to Bion's radically social/political theory of how the psyche comes into being" (Civitarese, 2012, p. 348).

In his dizzying process of abstraction to an alleged mystical drift, Bion is thus always moved by the attempt to make the reality of psychic experience communicable, or rather to give form to the analytic experience, which in his case is always linked to the transformations associated with the patient-analyst relationship. In the models, in the evolution of the container/translation, in the transformative processes, up to the rarefied realms of "O" and mysticism, we may even lose sight of the origin of this expanding universe, but at its base, there is always a cosmic radiation, a penumbra of associations that give us a glimpse of the original experience, *the chaos of the session*. A similar path has been followed by contemporary physics, which has resorted to the "mystical" and "paradoxical" language to describe increasingly complex and unimaginable realities. In physics, classical theories are actually much more abstract than quantum theory, and yet they seem more natural to us. Newtonian theory calculates trajectories, but on the basis of abstractions and a Platonic idea of reality made up of ideal geometries. In the real world, however, there are no squares, circles, ellipses, etc., the real world has to do with fractals. Whenever we try to describe reality, we have to resort to fractal dimensions, i.e., "broken" dimensions that cannot be expressed in whole numbers. The point has dimension 0, the line has dimension 1, plane figures such as the square have dimension 2, solids such as spheres have dimension 3, but what dimension does a lightning bolt or a coastline have? The fractal dimension, between one and two, describing lightning and a rib, is, therefore, much closer to reality than the full dimensions of Euclidean geometry. Self-similarity is the shape invariant in the transition from a simple curve to progressively more branched and sinuous curves, Koch's curves, which have precisely to do with chaos. It is from chaos, therefore, that islands of order emerge, from which beauty is derived, such as the Mandelbrot set or the Fibonacci series and the golden number, which express the tendency towards spiral development in nature, noting the emergence of order at the frontiers of chaos. Fractals and strange attractors are indeed essential figures in the representation of the elements of Bionian theory. In other words, the Bionian model system is based on self-similarity, whereby the structure of the whole is repeated in each model, and each element attracts all the rest of the theory, and together they repeat the complexity of the theory. We can, therefore, think of the elements α and β as two strange attractors, separate and yet connected by a line that jumps from one to the other. Alpha and beta are separate, but they can also turn into each other; in any case, wherever we start from, our trajectories go towards alpha or beta, as in Lorenz's attractors. They are connected to everything else in Bionian theory, and each element repeats the whole theory in itself. So if we cannot deconstruct Bionian theory, isolate individual models – because they are all interconnected, we must try to see if there is an overall functioning of them, a final process towards which the various mental functions and operations tend.

How then is the mind constructed? The child is born with a rudimentary consciousness that lacks its unconscious complement. The child's unconscious is initially supplemented by the mother's reverie, which has the task of receiving and transforming the child's projective identifications and fears. The function of the maternal (and analytic) container is not only to process the infant's (and analysand's) proto-emotions but also to share with the infant (and analysand) the emotions, the β-elements, that come from O, the unknown and unknowable reality. The infant projects its emotions into the mother, who, thanks to a state of reverie and her α-function, absorbs, reclaims and purifies the projections. Growing up in a welcoming relationship, the infant begins to introject the mother's α-function, develops its own α-function and begins to think for itself. The container mother, through her alpha function, then dreams the child's emotional experience and her own, sharing it in a tuning relationship that gives form and meaning to the first sensory magma of emerging vitality. The container/contained model, therefore, also has a mirroring function, allowing the child to recognise itself and develop a sense of self, starting from the mother's gaze. This is why Grotstein (2009, v. 1, p. 306) speaks of a "lexithymic transactional experience", as it implies not only a digestion and detoxification of the child's emotions but also an emotional sharing and mutual awareness. The process of dreaming thus has an extremely important function in development, i.e., learning from experience, so that psychopathology itself can be understood as a failure of dreaming. The work of α-dreaming, or if we prefer the alpha function, enables the individual to bind together sensory and emotional experiences, thus making them mental and suitable for the processes of thought and memory, but also to remove and protect consciousness from the traumatic intrusion of reality, or as Grotstein (2007) puts it, from the "blinding glare of O". The Dreaming Ensamble concept thus condenses the general model of Bion's theory into a holographic image of a group of models at work, cooperating to construct meaning from emotional experiences that must be dreamed in order to be assimilated or mentalised. This ensemble, tuned like an orchestra to construct meaning, we should, however, add an anti-group to it, i.e., the same models operating in the negative sense, negative grid, -L, -H, -K, that are always present but at very different levels, and which tend to destroy meaning. Bion's theory can, therefore, be seen as a symbolic model of the relationship between our ability to feel and reflect emotions, and to learn through experience, in our encounter with

O. Internal and external reality, O, are thus like two arms that imprison the individual but at the same time nourish him, because contact with reality is absolutely indispensable for life. In this process, full of risks and dangers, *dreaming, thinking* and *becoming* are the path that Bion points to for individual growth, but also the only way out of barbarism.

To describe these complex processes, Bion used a difficult, perhaps even complicated language, burdened by a quest for formalism, not free of jargon. Terms and concepts such as α-function, α- and β-elements, transformations, O, grid, contact barrier, emotional bonds L, H, K, -L, -H, -K, $\male\female$, -$\male\female$, Ps$\leftrightarrow$D ... taken together, they run the risk of forming a cumbersome metapsychology with a vague metaphysical flavour. However, language is only an apparent difficulty, and the use of formalism and mathematics does not go beyond a kind of "Lewis Carroll" game. In fact, Bion himself tries to dispel the impression that he supports the idea that a discipline can only be considered scientific if it is formalised. Even so, Bion does not concede anything to simplification, he remains aware that the complexity of life and of relationships does not allow for discounts, and as Parthenope Bion (2013) recalls, he had no tolerance for anything to do with superficiality. That is why his works cannot be read in a linear way: in them lurks paradox, complexity, just as in life, in the clinic and in human relationships. Bion never addresses the reader. Grotstein (2007) writes that Bion did not go to the other, one had to go to him, to give oneself up to his movement and to trust. This was a characteristic of his personality. Of that human personality which Bion (1978) said in the Paris seminar could not be defined (labelled) in any way, but could only be painted, and evoked with coloured signs.

Approaching Bion's thought by avoiding the "Satanic Jargonieur"

The Symingtons (1996) state that it is more difficult to understand Bion if he is viewed through the lens of Freud and Klein. In other words, to approach Bion one would have to purge one's mind of the "dogmas" of the psychoanalytic faith. Approach Bion, therefore, as Bion said to approach patients, without memory, or desire, or theoretical prejudices. This method, paradoxically, can be indicated as the *simple way*, because it is a direct, intuitive approach, and it relies on the extraordinary internal coherence of Bion's theoretical system, which sooner or later catches the eye. But the easy way is not always the best way. To sever Bion's deep connections with Freud, Ferenczi and Klein is to isolate Bion, with the risk of reifying his jargon in a ponderous, contactless metapsychology. Bion was by no means an isolated thinker, he was a creative thinker, and his ideas did not emerge in a vacuum, but in an innovative and open environment such as the Tavistock Clinic, based on a deep knowledge of psychoanalysis and the epistemology of his time. For this reason, some authors, in particular Civitarese, have chosen the *difficult path* of describing Bion's thought in close dialogue with the thought of Freud and Klein. This way is difficult, and sometimes even impossible, because it has to deal with different epistemologies and languages, even if they have common conceptual nodes: to follow the different solutions, passages, differences, interweavings, and to grasp the evolutionary movements and possible hiccups and stoppages. But it is precisely for this reason that it can prove to be fruitful, and perhaps the only method that can account for the true paradigm shift that Bion achieved.

Following this method, I have chosen to interrogate Bion's thought on two fundamental themes: the *present* and the *past*; the *conscious* and the *unconscious*.

Both are central to psychoanalysis, and certainly to Bion, but they avoid starting from Bion's metapsychology, i.e., from that jargon which sometimes seems to isolate Bion's thought from the rest of psychoanalysis. Bion (1977c, p. 79), himself, in *A Memoir of the Future*, refers to psychoanalytic jargon as the work of "His Satanic Jargonieur", which forces him to seek asylum in literary fiction. Moreover, these themes cannot be isolated, neither from the rest of psychoanalysis nor from Bionian thought, nor, as we shall see, from thought in general: be it philosophical, literary or scientific. They thus have the advantage of placing Bion's thought directly within a wider debate that has always involved psychoanalysis and the philosophy of mind. Although ours is not a historical, but a clinical and epistemological point of view, it implies a prospective vision, because, as Meltzer teaches, the way to fully understand a subject and its problems is to follow the epistemological knots that continue to press and question thought because they are unresolved. And this implies a genetic and prospective vision that can see the knots, the transitions, the transformations and the paradigm leaps.

Present and past, conscious and unconscious in Bion's legacy

Present and **past**. This central and unsettling theme for any science, including the humanities, naturally also conditions psychoanalysis, which deals in the here and now with questions of origin, time, memory and traces of a past that is no longer there, but which never passes. In his works on time, Green (2000a) states that psychoanalysis has little interest in memory and that its real object is temporality, not only that, but that consciousness is nothing other than "consciousness of time".

However, Bion's relationship with this subject is more tortured than one might think, passing through seemingly contradictory positions: from a rigid defence of the here and now to the idea of a "past presented". For Bion, memories of the past are irrelevant in analysis, because nothing can be done about the past, and analysis looks forward. Not only that, but remembering hinders, blocks the emergence of new and dreaming memory. However, the concept of no memory, no desire, no understanding is often misunderstood and risks of being an empty slogan that hides the true complexity of the concept of the *past presented*.

The problem is to understand how the past affects us *here and now*, because it is only the past that we do not remember, and therefore a past that does not forget us, that matters. This opens up the concept of the "inaccessible state", which Bion postulates as a third state of mind alongside the conscious and the unconscious, and which does not coincide with Freud's concept of the not removed unconscious. Bion is convinced that we cannot do anything about the past, but he adds that we should not forget that, in addition to the sphere of the mind, there is "the body" through which the past persists as remnants, archaic parts, traces, which actively affect the present, as embodied memories or, if we prefer, as implicit memory. The problem that arises, then, is how to communicate effectively not only with the more developed aspects of the mind but also with the more primitive ones: the archaic and the traces of foetal life operating in the present, the split and dissociated states of the self, the generational horrors and truths, and the deep and confused states that draw on the proto-mental system. Indeed, the subject can only truly forget if it can bring to the surface these split and buried parts of the self that remain active and condition existence.

Other writers have described inaccessible areas of the mind. Hard-to-reach, dissociated areas related to early trauma, areas of non-life/non-death, crypts, frozen zones that manifest as an affectivity, isolation and withdrawal. Behind these situations, it is possible to perceive a deep state of pain that cannot be expressed in words or emotions, but from which the pain seems to emerge through a kind of negative thermal radiation, like from a steaming icy surface. In order to approach these areas embedded in the soma, to give representability to these primitive traumas inscribed in an "unconscious that is not made up of representations", Civitarese (2014, p. 12) postulates the necessity of a sensorial, corporeal reverie, conceived within the field theory. Intercorporeal communication, the body itself, starting with that of the analyst, has in fact proved to be an increasingly essential element in the process leading to the transformations of the field. The body "thinks", writes Civitarese (ibid., p. 62), postulating a "dreaming in the body", neither intentional nor conscious, which is already a first movement of awareness, a dialogue between postures, in the play of visual, olfactory, tactile, sound and proprioceptive sensations. The problem of the inaccessible unconscious, therefore, seems to go beyond psychopathology as we understand it, because part of our behaviour and everything that falls within the sphere of proxemic, i.e., gestures, mimicry, attitudes and ways of doing things, probably sinks into that part of us that goes by the name of implicit memory and that Mauro Mancia (1989) traces back to a primitive psychophysiological self.

Conscious and **Unconscious**. These two themes, which alone are synonymous with psychoanalysis and refer to the most mysterious antinomies, such as mind/body, interior/exterior and fantasy/reality, become in Bion a single complex system, in an unstable equilibrium, in which there is no conscious feeling that does not also carry the shadow of the unconscious. This is why Civitarese uses the term "un/conscious" with a slash, to indicate that the unconscious experience is contained within the conscious. Consciousness and unconsciousness are thus conceived as two dimensions of the psychic, separated by a contact barrier that makes it possible to see from both sides, in a binocular vision. There is thus a discontinuous continuity between conscious and unconscious experience, which can be represented by the topological model of the Moebius strip of a continuous surface in the shape of an 8. Consciousness and unconsciousness are thus like two surfaces that tend to slide into each other, in a paradoxical relationship in which what is internal becomes external and vice versa. This aspect of continuity between the conscious and the unconscious, this transcending of the caesura, whereby the conscious is also an expression of the unconscious, is one of the most revolutionary aspects of Bion's theory, perhaps the aspect that most undermines our certainties. It makes us realise that our way of perceiving reality is always conditioned by an unconscious vision that fishes not only in our past but also in that system between the physical and the mental that Bion calls the proto-mental, in which the individual sinks into a group and archaic, even mythical, dimension that can at certain moments burst into our individual and group actions and behaviour. Moreover, this turmoil can find its way through everyday images and words which retain traces of disturbing elements, whereby the archaic and the most disturbing primitive can suddenly emerge even in the most unthinkable situations. Archaic elements that often have to do with blood and sex, the sacred and myth, and that Bion (1992) summarises in the expression "blood everywhere".

Note

1 If not otherwise indicated, the translations are by the author (Ed), and the page indications refer to the works translated into Italian reported in References.

Part One

Present/Past

Chapter 1

Inaccessible states of mind

The wounds of Oedipus

Even before theory the clinic, life, poetry and art show us that the deepest wounds *remain*, eternally present, like irredeemable time in Thomas S. Eliot (1943). They are wounds that persist, like memory without remembrance, that can neither be forgotten nor remembered. Wounds that never heal, or fossils sealed in amber tears, these memories seared into living flesh are like timeless, inaccessible, yet ever-haemorrhaging pain. Even if we do not know it, each of us, like Oedipus, has a "swollen foot" bearing inscribed an unrepresentable wound, which in its invisible gore, determines for good and evil, the fate of the young Oedipus and that of his father Laius (Rugi, 1997).[1]

Jean-Pierre Vernant (1967), in his lucid naivety, argues that the Oedipus complex *does not exist*. Oedipus kills his father and possesses his mother precisely because he does not recognise them as such. However, things are more complex. In Sophocles' version, Oedipus and Laius meet at a *trivium* or fork in the road, "*schiste hodòs*", a place too narrow for father and son to avoid each other. Laius provokes Oedipus by forcibly pushing him out of the way or ordering him to move; Oedipus provokes Laius by arrogantly challenging his orders. Both behave as if they were father and son and at the same time deny that they are; the provocation refers to an unspoken, too cumbersome absence of the ghost of origin. Oedipus, the son of kings, is willing to acknowledge the superiority of his parents (or gods), but not that of an outsider, albeit a king! His father's denial is thus the culmination of the old king's provocation. In his reaction, he meets the fate foretold by the oracle: the son he has with Jocasta will kill his own father. Laius hits Oedipus on the head and on his swollen foot, marking his own death. Oedipus' foot is wounded for the second time, and for the second time, Laius tries

DOI: 10.4324/9781032655239-3

to kill his son. Striking the swollen foot again is to reactivate the physical memory of the secret filicide, of that unimaginable agony of one's origin, when Oedipus was exposed on Mount Cyton after having had his ankles pierced with an iron stake. The provocation, therefore, occurs precisely in the place of absence, in that mysterious wound where the agony has no representation, no words; that is why Oedipus can only act with a knowledge that is realised through death. The gaze that Oedipus and Laius exchange cannot lead to the recognition of father and son, but is directly the gaze that returns from death to birth, from the end to the beginning, whereby every destiny is made fatal starting from its end.

It is at the crossroads, then, that the forces of Ananke are at work, when the passage is too narrow and destiny can no longer be avoided. The episode of the crossroads is thus the centre of tragedy, the place where the tragic knowledge comes into being at the moment that denies it. After that, and only after that, can the narrative finally unfold according to the law of knowledge through suffering laid down by Aeschylus. Freud chose Sophocles, rather than Aeschylus or Euripides, precisely because Sophocles was interested in Oedipus as an individual hero. This allowed Sophocles to give greater prominence to the personal vicissitudes of a single hero and to trace the dramas and conflicts within the individual. This was his insight and it was also Freud's. It allowed Sophocles to move away from the fatalistic vision of his master Aeschylus, who was concerned with the transmission of violence and guilt between generations, but unable to see man as a being striving for fulfilment in his individuality. It allowed Freud to construct the subject of psychoanalysis, to have a model of psychic conflict centred on the individual, and a metaphor for the analytical work itself.

The Sphinx and the mystery of the past

Sophocles does not say why Laius and Oedipus meet. His focus is on Oedipus and not on his father's faults. Therefore, the Oedipus complex, as formulated by Freud, concerns only the relationship of the son to his parents, not the relationship of the parents to the son, nor the relationship between the generations. In the versions by R. Graves (1955) and J. P. Vernant (1986), however, Laius, who was on his way to Delphi to ask the oracle how to free Thebes from the Sphinx, is also taken into account. Another version makes the meeting even less coincidental. At the opening of Euripides' *Phoenician Women*, Jocasta says that Oedipus, now a man, wanted to know who he was born from, because he had begun to have doubts about his origins. So Oedipus set out for the sanctuary of Phoebus, at the same time as Laius, worried about knowing whether the son he had had exposed on Mount Cithaeron was still alive. Therefore, father and son try to avoid each other, but they also seek each other out. Oedipus flees from his parents, whom he knows, but he searches for his origins, which he does not know. Laius, who is trying to become a good king again by correcting his mistakes, is searching for the ghost of his "murdered" son. The encounter between Laius and Oedipus, which Haydée Faimberg (1993a) traces back to an event under the banner of a patricide-filicide relationship, must, therefore, be re-examined from the perspective of predestination. The presence of the Sphinx in front of Thebes is not accidental. It represents a returning past, in the memory-less repetition of trauma, and has a precise purpose, that of punishing its inhabitants for the sins of King Laius. The Sphinx, sent by Hera, furious at Laius for his abuse and abduction of Chrysippus and the boy's subsequent suicide, thus has the questioning and deadly gaze of a past that cannot be transmitted, but which nevertheless acts, just as the unspoken act: the violence between generations and the transmission of guilt that lie at the bottom of the field and plague it. The Sphinx's question, then, is not aimed at the search for truth, as Bion had understood it, but rather manifests a lack of content and qualifies as a trace of a vanished truth that can no longer be transmitted. This is why Sophocles does not mention the reasons why the Sphinx is in that position, repeating his question endlessly. The Sphinx sign is pure repetition, without motive. The fundamental question posed by the Sphinx cannot be answered, "it can only be repeated endlessly, and in this continuous repetition it will be transferred to the protagonist, who, like the Sphinx, will embody it" (Tonelli, 1984). In other words, the content of this repetition is nothing other than the tragic necessity for Oedipus to dismantle the representational or rhetorical mechanisms not of the gods, but of their absence, because to clarify, to understand, to discover is the exact opposite of solving an enigma. That is why Nietzsche can say: "Who are you? [...] I do not know, perhaps Oedipus, perhaps the Sphinx. Let me go!" (ibid., p. 39). The Sphinx kills herself after Oedipus has killed the enigma with a clear and unequivocal answer, but the enigma does not disappear, it is transferred to him, who now has the tragic necessity of discovering the truth. Who is the man? Now, he is the Sphinx.

It is, then, the path of painful knowledge that expresses the encounter with the Greek Sphinx, a heroic knowledge in that it involves the encounter with the deep, dark layers of the self that we would rather do without. Not only that, but the knowledge to which the Sphinx obliges us, implies an awareness of our finitude, of the vanity of all triumphalism, in the face of death.

We can think, then, that the "monstrous" knowledge that the Greek Sphinx compels us to acquire has to do precisely with the "monstrous" complexity of human knowledge, which is being constantly forced to put together impossible elements: good and evil, happiness and unhappiness, love and hate, life and death, but also the present and the past. This is our only knowledge; hybrid, layered, where there is no passage except through pain, where present, past and future contaminate each other, where light and shadow alternate, in the mystery of a mind and a body that we inhabit essentially as strangers and that calls us to an unaware, gloryless heroism. In this sense, the Greek Sphinx differs from the Egyptian Sphinx, who, in her silent power as the guardian of the infinite, appears instead as the image of a self-founding and silent knowledge. Like a compassionate mother in her safe and protective bearing, rather than a sinister interrogation, the Egyptian Sphinx in fact expresses the dimension of a sacredness, mysterious and pacifying in the face of death. Freud, on the other hand, identifies himself with Oedipus, the solver of riddles, whom Molinari (1981) calls Oedipus 1, who focuses on fantasies of power, leaving out the real issue of tragedy, which is obviously related to the pain of knowledge. The medal that his students gave him had on the back the image of Oedipus in front of the Sphinx, with the final lines of Sophocles indicating Oedipus as the most powerful of men because he knew how to solve famous riddles. Freud himself had thought of this verse for a bust of himself at the university, curiously forgetting the ironic and admonitory nature of the entire speech of the chorus. In the last part, Sophocles warns that no one should consider him or herself happy before the last day of his or her life, without having suffered anything painful. By this time, Freud had moved away from the hypothesis of hysteria as suffering associated with the recollection of painful traumatic memories, which was causing him too many problems, both personally and scientifically, and was, in fact, preparing to abandon the traumatic theory of hysteria. "I no longer believe in my *neurotica*", Freud (21 September 1897) wrote in a letter to Fliess. Freud, who loved the archaeological metaphor, therefore, had good reason not to worry too much about the wounds of the young Oedipus. He had even realised that the central problem of hysteria was the splitting of consciousness, but he preferred to take the path of repression, abandoning the splitting that carried the shadow of the trauma and of Janet: "Psycho-analysis, however, was not in any way based on these researches of Janet's", Freud (1923b, p. 193) admitted some 30 years later.[2] The proof is in the same case of Elisabeth von R., who, while caring for her sick father, began to experience pain in her right thigh. Freud (1892–5, p. 163) hypothesised that her duties as a daughter were incompatible with the content of her erotic desire, which concerned her brother-in-law: "she repressed her erotic idea from consciousness and transformed the amount of its affect into physical sensations of pain". Freud (1892–5, p. 166) speaks of an incompatible representation that causes a split in consciousness and, through conversion, physical pain:

> In place of the mental pains which she avoided, physical pains made their appearence. In this way a transformation was effected which had the advantage that the patient escaped from an intolerable mental condition; though, it is true, this was at the cost of a psichical abnormality – the splitting of consciousness that come about – and of a physicall ilness – her pains, on which an astasia-abasia was built up.

Freud, therefore, states that the incompatible representation is excluded along with its associations to form a "separate psychical group" and that "It is these moments, then, that are to be described as 'traumatic': it is these moments that conversion takes place, of which the results are the splitting of consciousness and the hysterical symptom" (ibid., p. 167). When he chose to privilege repression at the expense of splitting and to abandon the theme of pain and trauma in favour of the theory of the Oedipal complex, Freud thus gave a radical twist to psychoanalysis, developing an intrapsychic and one-person psychology that has accompanied us for a century. The past he began to look at were the desires buried in the unconscious, emerging through the gaps in the speech texture: deviations, discordances that involuntarily present what consciousness cannot voluntarily represent. The founder of psychoanalysis devoted himself to following the metamorphoses of the experience of satisfaction, as the fulfilment of desire (dream), as the formation of a compromise (symptom), and finally as pleasure hidden in suffering (perversion), unconsciously sought by the individual. Psychoanalysis thus developed as a theory of unconscious representation, under the illusion that the unconscious could fill the gaps in consciousness. Freud was astonished to discover that mysterious infantile amnesia prevented the reconstruction of the first years of life, and he later understood that there was also a "not repressed" part of the unconscious, a part of the ego and superego which remained on top of the id, from which it was structured by differentiation and not by repression.[3] At the end of his work, Freud (1937, p. 252) admitted that his analytical and reconstructive work, centred on representation, could not go beyond the "underlying bedrock" of biological sexuality. All this may seem strange for a genius who, from the very beginning, had intuited not only the power of trauma but also the existence of a form of defence far more effective than repression, directed at parts that should have been accepted (*aufneh-men*, registered) but were instead previously "rejected",[4] so that they could only leave a trace (*eine spur*) in the *id*. Thus rejected elements, never accepted in the ego, and leaving no representations but only traces, that Freud (1938a), however, did not want to distinguish from the repressed, as if he himself had fallen victim to the doctrine of repression. Freud (1915b, p. 180) also intuited the creative capacities of the unconscious: "The Ucs is alive and capable of development, and maintains a number of relations with the Pcs, amongst that of co-operation". Even so, the aim of Freudian analysis remains that of undoing removal, of making the unconscious conscious, of increasing insight, of reconstructing pieces of past and forgotten history, in the belief that through the analytic method, consciousness could finally come to know the ultimate expression of psychic reality. In other words, as Green acknowledges, Freud always remained faithful to his own initial intuitions, which saw the purpose of analysis as filling in the gaps in consciousness and thus overcoming the infantile amnesia that remains linked to repression. What about pain? What about unrepresentable pain? Green admits that Freud leaves out the experience of pain, and Pontalis (1977) argues that Freud "stumbled" on the problem of pain and only with difficulty tried to fit it into his system, where it remains relegated to an appendix of *Inhibition, Symptom and Anxiety*. But Freud had not actually stumbled on pain. Rather, pain is a central, even original, theme that periodically returns to haunt him, in theory and in life. A problem he knew he could not solve, so much so that for years he resorted to cocaine and, in the final agony of the tumour in his jaw, to a pitiful dose of morphine. In fact, after addressing this subject in *The Project*, Freud put it aside, having chosen a theoretical path in which reality and the biological are placed in parentheses. And with it pain, which is set aside and repressed, although it will return periodically as a symptom of this repression of reality, filtered through the dream model. Pain, therefore, inevitably returns, along with the problem of trauma and the compulsion to repeat (Rugi, 2011, 2015).

Deleuze (1968), in his text *Différence et répétition,* captures the fundamental problem of repetition at the root of his insistence on questioning. Moving from Freud to Leclaire and Lacan, Deleuze sees the question as a living act that invests the unconscious, so that he associates the conflicts of Oedipus with the question of the Sphinx, conflicts that nevertheless remain linked to sexuality, to the difference between the sexes and to the phallus in its eternal disguise and transformation as a virtual object. Following Leclaire, the notion of the question becomes a fundamental category of the unconscious, configured in the hysteric as "am I a man or a woman"? and in the obsessive as "am I alive or dead"? For Freud, however, the child does not ask questions but desires, and the core of the dream remains linked to infantile desire. The category of desire thus remains at the heart of both Lacan's and Deleuze's concept of the unconscious. In the question of the Sphinx, Deleuze continues to see the desire of the phallus, which never ceases to shift and disguise itself. In the disquieting repetition of the Sphinx's questions, however, it is not the desire for the phallus, as a virtual object with riddles always found in the place where it is lacking, that is pressing, but the problem of truth, of trauma, of pain, of an unrepresentable past, and thus ultimately of *time that returns* in its deadly and endless questioning.

The presented past

In his restless late career, Wilfred R. Bion does not seem to place too much emphasis on historical reconstruction, arguing assertively that in psychoanalysis it is only possible to work in the here and now of the session and on the shared emotional experience. More than the past, Bion (1967a, p. 206) is interested in the emergence of the new: "The only point of importance in any session is the unknown". Remembrance itself becomes an example of a "view as backward-looking and relating to what has been lost, and the ordinary view as forward-looking and relating to what can be found" (Bion, 1965, p. 77). Bion goes so far as to say that memory has no role to play in the conduct of analysis because, in fact, we exist in the present and cannot do anything about the past. The analyst's interest must, therefore, be focused on the material of which (s)he has direct knowledge – the experience of the analytic session – not only because this is the only way to promote transformation but also because "If he witnesses certain facts he is under an obligation to state his evidence; equally, he must not report what he does not see. Otherwise he is guilty of fraud" (Bion, 1971, p. 15). Knowledge in analysis is, therefore, never an end in itself, and knowledge about or of a patient is of little use if it does not enter into the process leading to trans-formation or change. The method of working on the *hic et nunc* is thus not only an epistemological choice but also an ethical choice in which Bion's psychoanalysis reveals its credentials.

However, Bion's relationship with the past is more complex than the mis-used and often misunderstood instruction to work without memory, desire and understanding. It is an indication that belongs to the method and not to the nature of the psychic reality that emerges; those mental phenomena that Bion (1992, p. 341) says in one of his last *Cogitations* that he cannot describe. Bion is wary of memories, desires and theories that can hinder the encounter with the emerging psychic reality, the true and hidden emotions that press at the bottom of patients and of each of us. He searches for a past that is alive and active in the here and now and is interested in fantasies, emotions and thoughts that emerge as dream-like memories, the very fabric of analysis, experiences of the not yet known, which can be obstructed by conscious attempts to recall memories. However, it is only in later works that Bion succeeds in giving a coherent theoretical framework to the crucial importance of the past in therapy and in life.

In *Evidence*, Bion (1976b) admits that the most disturbing and revolu-tionary theory of psychoanalysis is that nothing can be forgotten, in the sense of actually disappearing. This old Freudian echo, that the mind can-not completely destroy any psychic formation, implies that a child cannot truly get rid of unpleasant aspects. Bion (1976b, p. 130) then proposes the hypothesis that to the omnipotent fantasy of having got rid of something, in the child's mind "a layer" is added at the bottom of which remain "parcel of an archaic mentality, unconscious thoughts" which have never become conscious and which remain "extremely active". The idea that we cannot do anything about the past remains, but Bion adds that we should not forget that next to the sphere of the mind there is "the body" through which the past can persist as a remnant. Archaic parts, then, remnants that actively af-fect the present, as embodied memories or, if we prefer, as implicit memo-ries. Alongside the conscious and the unconscious, Bion (1997, p. 50) thus postulates the existence of a third state, which he tentatively calls the "*in-accessible* state of mind". The emerging idea is that "there might still be traces in the mind or character or the personality, *in the present*, of particles that have a long history [...] archaic states of mind, archaic thoughts and ideas, primitive patterns of behaviour" (ibid., p. 38) which, like gill slits, can develop into tumours or affect our behaviour. In other words, the past is important not for what it was, but for "the mark it has left on you, or me or us *now*" (ibid.). After the concept of the "caesura" that connects and separates, and of the "inaccessible state of mind", the *here and now* ends up showing its hidden connections with the *there and then*, suggesting that the relational experience of the encounter always also implies an intimate contact with the cores of the patient's past experience, which in fact persists and insists on the present of the relationship. This aspect of continuity, this overcoming of the caesura, implies that the conscious is always also an expression of unconscious thought, so that our way of perceiving reality is always conditioned by an unconscious vision that fishes not only in our past but also in that system between the physical and the mental that Bion called the *proto-mental*, in which the individual sinks into a group and archaic, even mythical, dimension that at certain moments can unexpectedly burst into our actions and behaviour. In addition, this turmoil can find its way through everyday images and words which retain traces of disturbing elements, whereby the archaic and the most disturbing primitive can suddenly emerge even in the most unthinkable situations. Archaic elements that often have to do with blood and sex, the sacred and myth, which Bion (1992) summarises in the phrase "blood everywhere".

Old problems and new insights

Seemingly there is nothing new in these concepts. They are already implicit in the Freudian concepts of compulsion to repeat, transference, the repressed unconscious and that non-representational aspect of the unconscious, those elements which the ego rejects (*Verwirft*) and which only leave traces in the *id*. The novelty, however, lies in the way Bion deals with these old problems, and this way resembles the concentric deepening of the analytic process itself, in which at each turn nothing is the same as before. The "old problem", as Bion calls communication with the patient, now becomes more complex because it is actually about accessing inaccessible states of mind.

The question Bion asks is: how do we see the invisible? The real "phenomena of mental life which are shapeless, intouchable, invisible, odourless, tasteless" (1970, p. 70). But above all, how is it possible to communicate with "a whole, a complete person", a "he" and a "she", and not with a separate "body" and "mind", because we often do not know whether the source of discomfort is physical or mental, and this is a problem we will have "tomorrow and all the other tomorrows" (Bion, 1977b, p. 135). In fact, it is no longer a question of conscious or unconscious, of making assumptions about what lies behind or underneath the manifest contents, gaps in consciousness or behaviour, but of *seeing the inaccessible*. Beyond the hypothesis of the inaccessible unconscious, the root of the problem then becomes how to communicate effectively not only with the repressed aspects but also with the more primitive ones: the archaic and the traces of fetal life operating in the present, the split and dissociated states of the self, generational horrors and truths, and the deep states that draw on the proto-mental system. Indeed, the subject can only truly forget if he can bring to the surface these split and buried parts of the self, "feeble ideas but powerful emotions" (Bion, 1973, p. 33), for these archaic aspects of the self remain extremely active and condition our existence.

In the second volume of the trilogy, *A Memoir of the Future*, Bion uses a paradoxical title, *The Past Presented*, which seems to indicate the presence of the past in the present of the here and now, but also the dense network of events that preside over interpersonal conflict; a Joycean stream of consciousness that is actually a continuous flow of concatenations. The title is probably taken from one of Milton's sonnets: "Restless thoughts, that deadly swarm / of armed hornets, as soon as I am left alone / on me they descend in throng, to make present / the past, who I was, who I am now".[5]

In this text, Bion (1977c, p. 3) inserts time from Roland's first words: "What's the date?" To which Alice replies: "No idea; does it matter?" And time, the past, is present everywhere; time and reality. The story – if one can speak of a story, because it is above all the staging of a psyche at work, in a kaleidoscope of images, characters, events, relationships – is present from the very beginning, because it all takes place on the ruins of an impending past. There are the ruins of war, which Bion sees on the side of the losers, the ruins of relationships in which everything is reversed, the ruins of civilisation and, needless to say, of psychoanalysis. However, this story is always event, reality, personal memory, it is never history. The commitment to reality, on the other hand, is constant and is underlined by the fact that the title in English is not "Memoir" but "A Memoir", which, as Sara Boffito (2020) points out, is a more autobiographical genre, centred on the narration of personal memories. The description of reality and truth, the "facts", are thus the essential themes that underpin the relationship between the characters and testify that Bion, like Francis Bacon, throws the highest card on the table: that of the relationship with the real (Rugi, 2015). A "real" which, even for the painter, was closer to psychic reality than to realism, and which has nothing to do with the "absolute truth" on which P.A., the ubiquitous psychoanalyst who replies to Roland-firing heavy-duty arrows, defining it "a most ferocious animal which has killed more innocent white lies and black wholes than you would think possible" (Bion, 1977c, p. 22). Bion thus shows an extraordinary ability to ironise even his own theories, absolute truth, etc., and apparently, no new theoretical concepts emerge. Rather, it is an attempt to subtract the "idée mère" of psychoanalysis from psychoanalytic jargon: "His Satanic Jargonieur took offence; on some pretence that psychoanalytic jargon was being eroded by eruptions of clarity. I was compelled to seek asylum in fiction. Disguised as fiction, the truth occasionally slipped through" (ibid., p. 79). Moreover, one wonders if the little bit of truth that Bion manages to make us perceive through literary fiction is precisely the art of disguise of time, which, according to Proust (1954), has the effect of a masquerade, because to become visible, time searches for bodies, and wherever it finds them, it takes possession of them, to show its magic lantern over them. Hence it is that time breaks up into a thousand relations, into a thousand events, it is dislocated and dispersed in space, it becomes space, its twin, "We were just coming to the twins, Absolute Space and Absolute Time" (Bion, 1977c, p. 23), says P.A., who, after invoking Cartesian co-ordinates, even dares to speak of beauty, although the "Doctor" hastens to say that "but it isn't at all clear what we mean by it", mathematical, athletic, religious beauty? (Bion, 1977c, p. 26).

Notes

1 This part on Laio is a review of a work previously published in the magazine Psicoterapia e Scienze Umane, N.1:41–55, 1997. I thank the publisher for permission.
2 The page indications of Freud's works always refer to the Standard Edition (S.E.).

3 For the concept of infantile amnesia, see Freud S. 1899, p. 435 and 1901, Chapter 4; for the concept of the unrepressed unconscious, see Freud S. 1915b and 1923.

4 Freud S. 1894, p. 58; "There is, however, a much more energetic and successful kind of defence. Here, the ego rejects (*verwirft*) the incompatible idea together with its affect and behaves as if the idea had never occurred to the ego at all".

5 Milton J., *Samson Agonistes*, vv.19–22 (1671).

Chapter 2

The inaccessible and the uncontainable in the clinic

The psychiatrist Bion

Does the concept of the "inaccessible state" apply to the work in the psychoanalyst's consulting room, where he is confronted with ever more primitive states of mind, or does it have parallels in the wider psychiatric clinic? In this chapter, I will try to show how this concept goes beyond the space of analysis and actually belongs to the more general psychiatric clinic, at least the one that maintains a phenomenological and dynamic point of view, and as such already being nuanced in the work of other authors. Bion is a sophisticated psychoanalyst, but he never refused to deal with psychiatry, nor with the social problems typical of Western society. His almost forgotten work, *Psychiatry in Times of Crisis* (1948), refers not only to the crisis of post-war London, but to the fundamental crisis that never leaves society, that always reappears in our lives, in barbarism, in the oppression of minorities, in the indifference to major social problems, and especially in the indifference to emotional problems. Bion points out that unconscious emotional impulses operate within groups and communities, which he associates with the psychological unknown that Means and Toymbee placed at the basis of the growth and decay of civilisations. Bion is pessimistic about the possibility of resolving these primary unconscious tensions with organisational solutions and external rules, going so far as to hypothesise an inverse relationship between technological progress and emotional development. These unconscious emotional impulses can be dealt with in the psychoanalytic relationship, but in society and institutions it is much more difficult to promote emotional development: "no method of communication of emotional development has yet been found which is not hopelessly limited in its field of influence" (Bion, 1948, p. 50). Bion, therefore, associates the acquisition of technical skills with a kind of ape-like ability, which

DOI: 10.4324/9781032655239-4

is easy to transmit through mimesis, but which does not serve emotional development. His conclusions are that in the social group, the destiny of technical development is in the hands of the technically gifted, while that of emotional development is in the hands of those who are "underdeveloped" in the emotional sense, even if well equipped in the mimetic sense. It is the task of the psychiatrist to develop a technique of emotional development, a technique which he seems to identify precisely in the group. Bion thus recognises the frustration and helplessness that reality imposes on us every day at the mere opening of a newspaper, and observes that in fact no one could have foreseen the personal catastrophes and the abysses of barbarism into which humanity has plunged. Bion, therefore, wonders whether this abyss of barbarism is not part of a mechanism of denial of pain itself, because in fact man prefers to flee from the problems of reality, both internal and external. It is at this point that Bion introduces the idea that pain has a function in the development of society, with a quotation from the poet John Donne that still sounds like a punch in the stomach: "affliction is a treasure and scarce any man hath enough of it. No man hath affliction enough that is not matured and ripened by it" (ibid., p. 53). Bion seems to locate this pain in the action of unconscious emotional impulses and thus in the problem of interpersonal relationships, which technological development and the passage of time are likely to make ever more urgent. He then recalls that, according to some, there has been some progress in the knowledge of this unconscious factor thanks to the contributions of Freud, Jung and Adler, but in the previous pages he had distanced himself from this by making a new epistemological proposal:

> There is no corpus of knowledge that does for the study of the group what psychoanalysis does for the study of the individual. The material that is relevant for our study is embedded in the information amassed by several at present widely separated disciplines.
>
> (ibid., p. 47)

The "pre-psychoanalytic" Bion is thus already a revolutionary thinker who realises that the social problem he feels called upon to address requires theoretical tools other than those offered by individual psychoanalysis. Therefore, his bewilderment is not surprising when in early 1948, the Technical Committee of the Tavistock Clinic asked him to set up groups for therapeutic purposes, in line with his wartime group experiences: "It was disconcerting to find that the Committee seemed to believe that patients could be cured in such groups as these. [...] However, I agreed" (Bion, 1961, p. 29).

The diagnostician Bion

We know the clinical, epistemological, mystical Bion, but we rarely speak of a diagnostician Bion. The lack of interest in Bion's diagnostic work goes beyond psychoanalysis' well-known inattention to the problems of diagnosis. More recently, psychoanalysis has attempted to bridge the diagnostic gap with psychiatry through important works such as OPD-2 and especially PDM-2, edited by Lingiardi and McWilliams.[1] These psychoanalytic tools succeed in giving us a refined and complex picture of the patient: his personality structure, his mental functioning and his subjective experience of symptoms, all of which converge in the formulation of the clinical case. Current diagnostic tools, whether psychiatric or psychoanalytic, therefore, propose a single knowledge: that of an objectified disorder, in the case of the DSM, and of a single history, in the case of the PDM and the OPD. In other words, they are concerned with the knowledge of an "object", be it a disembodied disorder or a "subject" represented in its relevant functions and behaviours. What is abstracted is always something that belongs to the subject; its way of responding to favourable or unfavourable stimuli from the world. The questions that psychiatric and psychoanalytic diagnoses fail to answer are precisely those that Bion sought to provide a solution to. These are on how to include in the diagnosis the relationship with the other, and even the diagnostic evaluation of the therapist. It is this last aspect, in which Bion deals with the therapist's difficulties in containing the patient, that is still a source of "scandal", but it is the most valuable legacy of *A Memoir of the Future*. The diagnostician Bion thus proposed, alongside a very refined phenomenological description of the psychotic world, the basis for a relational diagnosis and even a diagnosis of the therapist. Proposals that still seem both revelatory and provocative.

In Bion's approach to diagnosis, we can distinguish three phases which only partially correspond to a temporal scansion, since they tend to overlap. More properly they must be considered points of view, or even levels of approach. The first is *phenomenological*, in which Bion describes the psychotic parts of the personality up to the limit of the uncontainable; the second is *relational*, in which he analyses the patient-therapist relationship through the study of the various container/contained configurations; the third level concerns the *pathology of the diagnostician* and, more generally, the functions of the analyst.

Phenomenological level. The psychotic and non-psychotic personality, alpha and beta areas

Bion's ability to describe the fragmented and chaotic world of psychotic thought is "visionary". The meticulousness, precision and vividness with which he succeeds in describing the most primitive and pathological aspects of thought are such that unprecedented scenarios of madness emerge. Bion describes the psychotic as a patient who moves in a world of objects that have the characteristics of matter – anal objects, sensory stimuli, parts of the personality – objects that do not obey the laws of mental functioning and that can be expelled by projective identification. Bion, therefore, postulates that the psychotic's primary hatred of external and internal reality drives an excessive use of splitting and projective identification. The attack is launched against the perceptual apparatus, which is minutely split and expelled, against primitive thought as the link between sensory impressions and consciousness, and against the links between the various thought processes. Bion calls the expelled particles "bizarre objects" because they also contain fragments of the patient's personality. These elements have to be taken back in order to think and "become painfully compressed on being taken back", together with fragments of consciousness of sensory impressions, so that the patient feels "intruded upon, assaulted, and tortured" (Bion, 1967, p. 63). This is often "the explanation of the extremely painful tactile, auditory, and visual hallucinations in the grip of which he seems to labour" (ibid.). Alongside a psychotic personality, Bion always postulates the existence of a non-psychotic personality, and what counts is their proportion, although the ego always maintains a certain relationship with reality. The psychotic personality prevails when destructive instincts predominate, when there is hatred towards inner and outer reality and towards that part of the personality that allows contact with it, namely, consciousness. The patient presents a fear of imminent annihilation but also tends to form early and hasty object relations, and thus an early, fragile and tenacious transference, which can therefore allow a therapeutic approach to psychotic patients, contrary to what Freud thought.

This initial model, highly psychiatric and highly Kleinian, becomes, over time, a general model of the mind, this is more abstract and refined, and capable of highlighting the complex movements of growth and the anxieties of change. In fact, growth always implies the idea of falling, of stumbling, of the negative, and the possibility of stopping and destroying everything. The struggle between the non-psychotic part and the psychotic part becomes the incessant work between the alpha and beta parts of the mind, a work that revolves around the alpha function, which implements the process by which the mind creates metaphors, myths and symbols to give meaning to experience. However, this process, which is associated with the transition from the schizoparanoid to the depressive state, is painful, so it can be stopped and reversed because of the pain involved. In this way, an inversion of the alpha function can take place, which, through the proliferation of beta elements, produces pathological phenomena in the personality. And these "failed thoughts", which cannot be used or stored, form a kind of "backwash" in the mind which the person must somehow get rid of. Bion hypothesises various ways of disposing of these residues or rejects. Meltzer lists these ways as: the *beta screen*, where there is a huge flow of verbal material without content, and which is nothing but a collection of waste; the *evacuation of beta elements* through the senses and their subsequent reintroduction through processes of hallucination and transformation into hallucinosis; group behaviour in *basic assumptions*, through which violent emotions that cannot be used are evacuated. Finally, beta elements can be discharged through the vegetative system and the striated and non-striated parts of the musculature, causing psychosomatic or *somatopsychotic* disorders (Meltzer, 1987; Rugi, 2014). Lia Pistiner de Cortiñas (2005) extends the concept of "beta area" to include thoughts that belong to the prenatal realm of the mind, i.e., "foetal" or "prenatal" thoughts that have not yet had a psychic birth. In the clinic, we sometimes find patients who develop "pseudo-adaptive" prosthesis through which they continue to divide vital, albeit primitive, emotional forces that emerge through somatic pathology or through relational crisis situations. This is what Bion (1970, p. 23) calls an "exo-skeleton", which takes the place of an "endo-skeleton", namely, a pseudo-adaptive prosthesis that does not allow the individual to come into contact with their deepest parts, which remain separated. In these cases, the individual is unable to understand the origin of his or her psychic suffering, just like the foetus, which receives stimuli without being able to understand where they come from. These prenatal emotions are not only archaic residues but also thoughts without a thinker, wild intuitions that remain split off, at least until the ability to cross the caesura is developed, disarticulating defensive jargon and empty shells, to give birth to a thought that transforms foetal ideas into metaphorical forms of creative thought.

Finally, Bion hypothesises that every positive transformation is matched by a negative one, which, like the "shadow" for Jung, is the inescapable counterpart to every luminous side of us. In fact, every time we have to make a choice in everyday life, there is a conflict between interpreting reality in the light of the positive influence of our good inner objects, or in the negative light of our delusional system, our destructive side. We must, therefore, add the functioning of this destructive part of the personality, to the beta area, which operates according to the negative grid, using what Bion calls negative links – less love (-L), less hate (-H), less knowledge (-K) – to build a parallel structure that creates a delusional system. In Meltzer's words,

> in the structuring of the personality, simultaneously the processes of the alpha function (dreaming, thinking) and the internal aspects of object relations, an image/mirror process operates, a destructive part of the personality which Bion defines as the 'satanic' part, in the sense of Milton.
> (Meltzer, 1987, pp. 80–1)

And this "satanic part", which is necessary and perhaps inevitable in the structure of the mind, seems essential to understanding what Bion describes as the catastrophic anxiety and fear of change that we experience in the face of the unknown and new ideas, the relationship of which to pain is as unclear as it is inevitable. In these passages, it is important to note a profound continuity between the initial interest in the diagnosis of psychotic and non-psychotic personality, primitive groupiness and the subsequent development of the alpha and beta areas. These passages imply a progressive approach to the primitive mechanisms of thought but maintain a phenomenological and dynamic view of the psychopathological process.

The relational level and the container/contained model

In the 1950s, some passages in *Cogitations* show a Bion who is indecisive and worried about what he is discovering. He describes situations in which the atmosphere of the session remains dominated by a kind of confusion, with fragments of images: friendliness combined with hostility, depression and incongruity; fragments of smiles, tears without depth, hatred and fragmentary ideas. The whole is dream-like, but with excretory functions, a kind of screen of incoherent material, incapable of connection and completely indifferent to interpretation. Bion seems to be torn between a Kleinian position and something new that he is struggling to grasp. In 1954, in *Notes on the Theory of Schizophrenia,* when faced with the difficulties of establishing communication with a patient, Bion (1967, p. 30) gives an interpretation that still has strong Kleinian connotations:

> I suggest that he felt he had a very bad and hostile object inside him which was treating our verbal intercourse to much the same kind of destructive attack which he had once felt he had launched against parental intercourse whether sexual or verbal.

A few years later, in *On Arrogance,* (1957), Bion (1967, p. 92) shifted his attention from the patient to the relationship between himself and the patient, and the "very bad and hostile" object which he had previously placed within the patient, he now placed within the analyst, as an "obstructive object" which impeded the patient's only means of communication.

This is the discovery of the *negative container.* A simple displacement of the bad object from the patient to the analyst, which marks the beginning of a new way of posing in the analytic relationship. In this displacement, there is, in fact, a shift from a psychoanalysis that judges and interprets *at a distance,* to a psychoanalysis that allows itself to be involved and welcomes the most disturbed and disturbing parts of the patient. The container/contained model thus originates from the discovery in clinical practice of a negative form of container, hence the hypothesis of the need for a positive container function, which was lacking in the primitive relationship with the mother. The situation is thus reversed in relation to that of the neurotic. The latter is afraid to make conscious what is unconscious, for fear that it might drive them mad; the psychotic, on the other hand, is incapable of eliminating something that remains as if in suspension, scattered and devoid of connections. Bion then begins to think that in order for experiences to be stored in the unconscious, they must first be dreamed. In other words, dreamwork is seen as a mental digestion process that symbolises and binds experiences, making them available for memory, learning and communication. This is enough to overturn Freud's theory of dreams. For Freud, the unconscious creates the dream, and for Bion, it is the dream that creates the uncon-scious. The psychotic is incapable of dreaming experiences, and of binding them symbolically and thus making them unconscious, as the psychotic's hatred of reality and everything that allows awareness of it drives them to attack the very ability to bind, rendering them incapable of thinking and feeling. The discovery of the obstructive object also has profound implica-tions for the psychiatric conception of mental disorder, since it implies the recognition of the importance of the environment and poor parental care in the genesis of mental health and illness. The same observations are made by Winnicott in the same years. The obstructive internal object is also con-ceived as a malignant, hypermoralistic, extremely harsh superego, which hates all personality development and places its supposed moral superiority above the search for truth and contact with reality. This superego, through its harshness and omnipotence, gives the child a sadistic sense of security and contributes in creating their masochism.

Bion thus creates the conditions for rethinking many self-destructive phenomena, such as Ferenczi's and Anna Freud's identification with the aggressor, Fairbairn's introjection of the necessary bad object, and the same traumatic and psychic refuge phenomena which find a relational interpreta-tive model in the concept of the negative container. In fact, after the dis-covery of the other pole of projective identification, nothing could ever be the same again. The heuristic model had to begin to consider the real relationship between analyst and patient, between mother and child, and to understand how the receiving pole of projective identification reacted. Bion had thus lifted the veil on what neither Freud nor Klein had dared to do, on the analyst and the mother, on the penis and the breast, which had remained idealised, untouchable and silent signifiers, while the emotions, especially greed and envy, had remained confined to the envious subject as an innate charge of destructiveness.

The development of the container/contained model will occupy Bion for many years and will end up incorporating a large part of his theory, so much so that it becomes the most abstract and most general mechanism. Here it is sufficient to observe that Bion (1970) reaches a definitive formulation of the various container/contained configurations only in *Attention and Interpre-tation*, in which he takes up and deepens with new elements the relationship between thought and the thinker. In the ***convivial relationship***, ♂ and ♀ are interdependent, with mutual benefit and without mutual harm. The mother benefits and develops psychically from the experience, as does the child.

Still, there is no relationship between thought and thinker, and therefore truth, though it exists, has not yet been discovered, so when thought and thinker approach it, or when there is a threat of discovery, then a critical situation arises. On the other hand, the relationship is *parasitic,* when one depends on another to produce a third that is destructive of all three. There is a correspondence between thought and thinker, but it belongs to category 2 of the grid, which means that the formulation is known to be false, but is maintained as a barrier against a truth that can destroy the container, or vice versa. In a *symbiotic* **relationship**, on the other hand, each depends on the other for mutual benefit. The thought and the thinker correspond and through this correspondence modify each other, the thought multiplies and the thinker evolves. Again in *Attention and Interpretation*, Bion succeeds in showing how the container/contained model lends itself to understanding the inversions of the relationship, between analyst and patient as between mother and child. The analyst contains the patient, but when (s)he gives their interpretation, it is the patient who becomes the container, just as the child becomes the container of the mother when she nurtures him or her. These simple observations are extremely useful in diagnosis when trying to understand the relationship between mother and child, and analyst and patient. One of my patients vomited the food her anxious mother had given her at inappropriate times, as is often the case with premature interpretations when they are used to explain away the patient rather than to nourish him or her with truth and affection.

The functions of the analyst and the pathology of the diagnostician

Bion's final diagnostic interest concerns the container, the diagnostician, the therapist's mind. Bion is concerned not only with its functions but also with its degradation. This is a daring challenge which he takes up with the same ability to deal with the psychopathology of the patient, with courage and coherence multiplied by a boundless need for ethical and professional rigour. Indeed, Bion seems to operate within certain ethical principles that are not negotiable, nor can they be integrated into psychoanalytic theories. For example, the idea that to regard a psychotic as a "hopeless" case is an impulse that gradually undermines the integrity of the analyst. In other words, a diagnosis of "psychotic" or "borderline psychotic" not only limits the patient's possibility of expansion, because it leaves no space for development and growth, but it can also erode the integrity of the psychoanalyst (Bion, 1977a, pp. 252–5). In this research, Bion begins softly. His observations are limited to the study of the functions of the analyst, who must of course be well analysed, must have a good understanding of his own Oedipus, must not pollute the analytic relationship with his own feelings of love and hate, and must be able to exercise good containment skills. The latter are the most important. They range from simply providing a boundary, to withstanding the shock of the projective wave; from the ability to hold projected fears long enough to make them more bearable, to giving meaning and form to the "formless prime"; from making thinking bearable, to the ability to "suffer" pain. Bion also speaks of the inevitable "loneliness" of the analyst, of the impossibility of resorting to any instrument of recording, of the need to maintain a setting isolated from the rest of the world, and yet to remember that the patient is never detached from a context, and that it is always necessary to keep in mind the legal, familial and even institutional implications of what we do in the session. At this point, we may already understand why Bion said that he was not a psychoanalyst, but that he was trying to *become* one. Fortunately, he admitted mistakes. Bion even thought that mistakes were inevitable and a necessary part of learning from experience.

With *Transformations*, and especially with *Attention and Interpretation*, however, the demands Bion seems to make of the analyst, and especially of himself, become more disturbing. When he gives his famous instruction to work without memory, without desire and without understanding, the psychoanalytic world reacts with discomfort to the point of rejection. Meltzer (1978) does not hide his mixed feelings of admiration and confusion. Like a pilgrim robbed of everything, he feels compelled to renounce the last five centuries of culture; to throw overboard the Renaissance, the Reformation, the Age of Reason and the triumph of the scientific method, but above all memory; the Christian desire to help one's neighbour, and the disciplined ability to understand. This is the price that Bion seems to demand of the psychoanalyst in order to free his mind from the bondage of the senses, to learn to see through a ray of darkness into the non-sensuous world of psychic reality. Only in this way, will it be possible for the psychoanalyst to "enjoy" the hallucinations and thus to understand the patient who "enjoys" the transformations into hallucinosis! Bion (1970, pp. 46, 48) himself admits that a state without memory, desire and knowledge is "akin to dread" and "a very serious attack on the ego", because it disrupts the sensory experience on which the individual's familiar reality is based. Bion thus approximates this kind of experience to what happens in regressed patients and warns of the danger of the analyst falling into a kind of stupor or sleep. He, therefore, recommends his practice only to those analysts who have some experience and have been led through their own analysis at least to recognise the schizoparanoid and depressive positions. Not unexpectedly, these demands are not the whims of a madman, but the coherent consequences of a rigorous epistemological and ethical path. First, the need to consider only what is shared by patients and analysts, because only *shared* and *emergent* knowledge has any chance of promoting change. This means that pain can only be interpreted when it becomes an intersubjective phenomenon, also shared and acknowledged by the patient, and after it has been clothed in a personal myth. Only in the here and now of the analytic session is it therefore possible to have a shared emotional experience, an "O" that is accessible to both, and yet the patient's transformations are always subject to distortion, i.e., to L, H, K, and it is "the nature of that distortion" that "is the O of the transformation that the analyst effects in his progress from observation to interpretation" (Bion, 1965, p. 49). The indication that the patient's transformation must always act as O for the analyst is fundamental to understanding the need to be in agreement with the patient; only in this way, will the analyst be able to perceive the hallucinatory state, but also to "see" the developed aspects of O that are invariable to the analysand, to the point of being able to contemplate its irreducible minimum that cannot be cured. In the shared O, the analyst must, therefore, come to terms with the inevitable deformations of the patient and, at the same time, avoid his or her own deformations, so it is assumed that they take L or H into account and exclude them from their bond, or at least excludes the distortions related to his or her countertransference, because this remains unconscious and untreatable. To be sure, it is necessary to take into account the analyst's observational apparatus, linked to the Oedipal theory, and his or her training. But that is not all. Bion knows that when the analyst works on the mental, the burden of criteria and means of correct thinking collapses entirely on the mind, which finds itself hyper-responsible in its precariousness. In other words, the analyst cannot avail themselves of external help, of extramental verification. The same renunciation of desire, memory and understanding become precise stages of what Furio Di Paola (1995) calls "deontological holding", a desperate search for ethics that accompanies Bion in the construction of his method and finds its most complete expression in the interpretative modality. Interpretation must do more than increase knowledge, it "should be such that the transition from *knowing about* reality to *becoming real* is furthered" (Bion, 1965, p. 153). Bion postulates that the interpretations that make the transition from being aware of O to becoming O are those that establish a "complementarity" in which there is a kind of meshing, a mutual harmonious adaptation between container and contained, until the need for "bonding" or "complementarity" is triggered (ibid.). Moreover, this kind of interpretation cannot come from above, neither from theory nor from the subject that is supposed to know, but from a lived and suffered experience of the analyst. That is why a correct interpretation always passes through a sense of depression, and the oscillation between patience and security is taken by Bion as an index of good work. Assuming an analyst resists so many demands, there remains the problem of assessing the therapist-container's fears and resistance to change, his blockages and what Bion calls the "rigid poverty" of an inadequate container incapable of plasticity. And this is one of the themes that dominates *A Memoir of the Future*. But Bion (1978, p. 165) does not dwell on the faults of psychoanalysis, his pessimism is radical, even cosmic, and ranges from psychoanalysis to power, from science to the establishment, to the very nature of man: "I think the disease is a mind", a mind that, among other things, does not like to be aware of the universe in which it lives.

The inaccessible

Before Bion, various authors described severe pathologies and difficult therapeutic experiences with subjects who seemed to lack the basic capacity to relate, even through primitive forms of attachment such as projective identification. Sandor Ferenczi is perhaps the first of these authors. An analyst of Melanie Klein, who in turn was an analyst of Bion, Ferenczi has only recently been re-evaluated, thanks in particular to the valuable work of Franco Borgogno (2004). Since his early work, Ferenczi re-evaluates childhood sexual trauma and postulates that the dissociated and fragmented child remains, waiting to be called back into existence by an analyst who can restore the infantile language that has been banished by too much pain. In his *Clinical Diary*, Ferenczi thus turns his attention to the frozen, petrified, autistic nuclei of the self that remain outside the shared symbolic order and thus outside psychic subjectivation itself.[2] These primitive nuclei of the subject, described as "dead zones" of the self, require a generous capacity for imaginative identification in order to be reached and revitalised. The analyst must be willing to play the roles that the patient's unconscious requires of him or her, humbly embodying both the feelings that the patient has not been able to experience and the potentials that (s)he has not been able to experience. The therapist has to know from within the events that produced the pathogenic suffering. The therapist has to become the patient and take upon himself or herself the patient's pain, by becoming the dissociated and fragmented child who, because of the trauma and the premature, inevitable, unconscious identification with the defaulting adult, has lost all voice in the personality of the traumatised subject. In these concepts, we can see not only the beginning of the study of early survival strategies in the face of unrepresentable pain but also important seeds of Bion's future thought, such as the concept of "becoming the patient" and the need to accept one's pain so that it can be transformed. After Ferenczi, other authors turned their attention to the splitting of the self. Donald Fairbairn (1943), in *Schizoid Factors of Personality*, argues that every person exhibits schizoid phenomena and that the splitting of the ego is a universal phenomenon that represents the basic position of the psyche. The dream, in which all the characters represent a part of the dreaming personality, is the clearest proof of this. Libido is also primarily a search for the object. Fairbairn assumes that the ego is original and innate, not a secondary defensive structure that, in the Freudian model, develops on the surface of the psyche to regulate the *id*'s drives in relation to reality. Fairbairn's attention is, therefore, not so much on the guilty drives, nor on the Oedipal situation, but on the bad objects that are internalised. The first defence that the ego adopts to deal with an unsatisfactory relationship is the internalisation of the bad object, which, contrary to what Melanie Klein postulates, becomes the fundamental element in the construction of identity. The bad object, introjected, is divided into an exciting part and a rejecting part, which constitute foreign bodies in the psyche and contribute to the constitution of dynamic structures. The egoic structure associated with the rejecting object is called the *internal saboteur*, a structure hostile to the libidinal ego, which remains persecutory and a source of anxiety.

From these early descriptions, other authors have described similar situations, referring to split-self situations. These split parts of the self are described in various ways: as parts enclosed in an "enclave" (Baranger & Baranger, 1969), in a "claustrum" (Meltzer, 1992), trapped in a "refuge of the mind" (Steiner, 1993), or excluded as a "forgotten self" (López Corvo, 2006). Recently, the theme of primitive states of mind has been the subject of an international volume edited by Van Buren and Alhati (2010), which brings together important work by J. S. Grotstein, A. Ferro, A. Chuster, C. Fix Korbivcher and others. Grotstein's work on resistance to change in hard-to-reach patients is particularly important. The author describes a kind of "burial of the child's psychic life" that weighs on the adult's life like a pathological enclave, trapping the individual in a persecutory, kapo-like custody, in a kind of identification with the aggressor. If the childhood experience is too painful, the lack of care actually buries part of the child's personality in a sort of "crypt", neither alive nor dead, as described by Abraham and Torok (1987). The negative therapeutic reaction is thus seen as a form of chronic resistance, resulting from a split pathological organisation that works against change and growth. This hypothesis opens up a conception of the unconscious as a divided system, composed of living subjects, supernatural presences, demons, homunculi or ghosts, acting as elements with a life of their own and in opposition to each other. Drawing on Frances Tustin's work on the autistic encapsulation of traumatic situations in neurotic patients, Celia Fix Korbivcher instead develops the concept of autistic transformations that impede the growth and development of affective life and thought. These transformations create a kind of autistic pocket, conceived as a hidden dimension, characterised by an absence of affective life and difficult to reach. These transformations, which are also present in neurotic patients when faced with situations of intolerable pain, differ from projective identification in that there is no separate object to project into, nor feelings towards the object.

In a more recent work, Civitarese (2014) also turns his attention to "autistic cores" in adults, present in a wide range of disorders. The author argues that in autistic areas of the mind, the analyst feels a strong pressure linked to a tantalising quality of the patient, who is moved by a desperate need to feel that he or she exists in the other's desire, to be recognised and to come to be. Civitarese links these situations of deficit in the capacity to symbolise the apparently opposite conditions of turbulence that occur in borderline or psychotic states, in which everything has a minus sign in front of it. The author speaks of the trapping of emotions, using the metaphor of the black hole that traps light. The presence of these black holes of memory, of areas of non-life/non-death, emanates an intense negative radiation, from which the analyst is sometimes tempted to flee with a symmetrical withdrawal, an escape into boredom and impotence, where instead a listening and vitalising presence would be required.

From another point of view, Russell Meares (2000) describes equivalent situations, a "traumatic memory system", a set of memories of similar traumatic events recorded in a memory system other than that of habitual consciousness. These unconscious memories, which persist in a state dissociated from the trauma, are linked by the author to Janet's unconscious fixed ideas as a set of dissociated cognitive aspects accompanied by a hypnotic state. The intrusion of this traumatic memory system may be transient and cause no harm, but in some people, it can cause alienation, a deep sense of estrangement from the basic sense of the self. These are unthinkable thoughts and unbearable feelings that erupt in the mind as states of intense fear, terror, loneliness and despair, or in the body as psychosomatic disorders. Along the same lines, Philip M. Bromberg (2006) rethinks the concept of dissociation as a defensive structure that controls traumatic affects that the mind cannot tolerate. In situations of massive or developmental trauma, this defensive structure severely undermines the intersubjective capacity of the person, who becomes unable to see themselves through the eyes of another. Bromberg (2006, p. 2) then describes his conception of the mind in an iconic formula:

States of the self are what the mind is made of. Dissociation is what the mind does. The relationship between states of the self and dissociation is what the mind is. It is the stability of this relationship that allows an individual to experience continuity as 'I'.

For Bromberg (1998/2001), mental health thus becomes the ability to "standing in the spaces", to feel "one in many", or rather to move from one space to another without becoming trapped in an area of dissociation.

Many authors, therefore, describe inaccessible, hard-to-reach areas of the psyche linked to repeated early traumas, areas of non-life/non-death, crypts, frozen zones, which manifest themselves as apathy, isolation and withdrawal, but behind which it is possible to perceive a deep state of pain, which cannot be expressed in words or with emotions, but from which pain seems to emerge through a kind of negative thermal radiation, like from a steaming icy surface. In order to get closer to these areas embedded in the soma, to give a figurability to these primitive traumas inscribed in an unconscious that is not made up of representations, Civitarese (2014) postulates the necessity of a sensorial, corporeal reverie, conceived within the field theory. Intercorporeal communication, the body itself, starting with that of the analyst, proved to be an increasingly essential element in the process leading to the transformations of the field. The body "thinks", says Civitarese, postulating a "dreaming in the body", neither intentional nor conscious, which is already a first movement of awareness, a dialogue between postures, in the play of visual, olfactory, tactile, sound and proprioceptive sensations. The problem of the inaccessible unconscious, therefore, seems to go beyond psychopathology as we understand it, because it is likely that part of our behaviour and everything that falls within the sphere of proxemics, gestures, mimicry, attitudes and ways of doing things, sinks into an implicit memory linked to a "primitive psychophysiological self" (Mancia, 1989). This implies that the impossibility or difficulty of accessing some dimension of the self, at some level, may belong to each of us, as Van Buren and Alhanati (2010) suggest. We must also bear in mind that the association of pain with consciousness makes it part of the enigmas of consciousness itself, starting with its ephemeral nature, which contemplates intentionality and the possibility of lying. Lying even to oneself. Bion (1997, p. 35) has no doubt that human beings have had a great deal of practice in lying to themselves, and in giving false information about themselves to "whoever else might be able to detect the supposed crime that the infant does not know about, although the infant can show any amount of guilt". Lying to oneself, evacuating the pain, does not mean, however, that we do not bear the marks that remain embedded in the flesh. Freud observed that one who is silent with their lips speaks with their fingertips, and when we want to hide something from consciousness, it comes out from the body. Bion goes further and seems to suggest that in the body we can also find the pain of previous generations, of which we know nothing, but whose burden we carry, even if we do not know "the mental counterpart of these lies" (ibid.). Pain can thus signal loss, the encounter with death, the stumbling upon painful memories, but also the approach of traumatic areas without memory, which bleed like wounds that have never healed, or the presence of "alien" areas that cross generations and absorb all meaning like black holes.

It is, therefore, possible to think that the realm of hallucinosis, which Bion (1970, p. 17) sums up in the extraordinary metaphor of "a short-sighted 'view'", may have something to do with – or rather is closely related to – the pain buried in the inaccessible unconscious. These patients tend to evacuate the thoughts and emotions that they cannot tolerate, and the mental event is transformed into a sensory impression that has no meaning, but only gives pleasure or pain. Hallucinations are, in fact, sensory creations resulting from the patient's need to surround himself with a self-generated universe in which the senses take on the function of creating a perfect, albeit hallucinated, world in which perception is a function of avoiding pain at all costs. Hallucinosis thus arises from pain that cannot be tolerated and leads to the construction of a hallucinated world, which can sometimes drive the individual in search of a desperate, even ascetic aesthetic vision, as in anorexia, in which beauty is a delirious mask that has the function of embodying a perfect, immutable body that transcends the limits of a real body. At certain levels, however, hallucinosis affects everyone, closely, because each of us, in our own way, tends to flee from pain, that which we carry within us and which we do not know, and that which comes from the "pain" of the world with which we resonate. The inaccessible unconscious, our early experiences and our limited capacity to bear the pain, and therefore condition perception, as Merleau-Ponty (1964, p. 205) intuited when he said that "perception is unconscious", and T. S. Eliot, when in the *Four Quartets,* he wrote that humankind cannot bear too much reality!

The uncontainable

The inaccessible is, therefore, difficult to reach, although it is always present and able to condition our behaviour, because, as Pontalis (1977) reminds us: "the unthinkable makes the thought". Pain and deep anguish generally manifest themselves in turmoil, and therefore in drama, which is sometimes loud and tragic. This is the uncontainable, something that escapes our ability to contain it, either because it is inadequate or because it is confronted with an excessive traumatic force. In his pathway into the phenomenology of the psychotic indescribable, Bion goes so far as to describe the abyss, those marginal conditions in which the disruptive force of the contained reveals the limits of the container and its functions. In a few dense pages,

Furio Di Paola (1995) effectively sums up Bion's visionary effort to trace the extreme threshold of the psychiatric negative: (a) as an explosive, unlimited dispersion, due to the failure of the container's capacity to offer limits to the propagation of the projective wave; (b) as an overflowing, incessant bleeding, due to the failure of the container's capacity to absorb the violence of the projective wave and to restore a pacified experientiality; (c) the escalation of intolerable, self-reinforcing, impoverishing dissipation and annihilating envy, due to the failure of the metabolic function of the container; (d) the impossibility of access to thought as form, symbol and even as dreaming image, due to the failure of the capacity of the alpha function to give meaning and form to the primordial formless, to the unthought, to the beta element.

All this is the *uncontainable*… situations to which no container can truly offer limits, absorb their violence, make them bearable or give them meaning and form. The uncontainable thus describes situations of excessive projective identification, the extreme threshold of the psychiatric negative, the abyss of mental pathology that undermines the containment capacity of the subject, the therapist and sometimes even the institutions.

Lia Pistiner de Cortiñas (2009), therefore, proposes an interesting distinction between patients with an excess of projective identification and patients with a *detention* of projective identification. Pistiner de Cortiñas thus contrasts the *disturbing presence* of patients with an excess of projective identification with that of patients with a *silent presence* that evokes frozen zones of the mind, or dead, non-living parts, where immobility and emotional isolation prevail, which can provoke a reaction of disinterest or boredom in the therapist. In other words, *positive excess of,* or *negative* projective identification, are situations that are apparently opposite, but both of which create turbulence in the therapist, who finds themselves exposed to a haemorrhagic pain or trapped in a feeling of impotence. Excess of projective identification, can be seen in borderline or psychotic patients, or detention of projective identification, in autistic withdrawal states or dissociated, frozen, non-life/non-death states of the self. In both cases, the analyst is caught in a situation of turbulence, which mysteriously occurs even in patients who claim to feel no emotions, because tolerating a state of near death, of agony, can be even more difficult than tolerating states of intense turbulence.

Notes

1 For an analysis of the epistemological problems of diagnosis and of the Bion diagnostician, see Rugi G., 2019; for psychoanalytical diagnosis see OPD-2, 2009; PDM-2, 2017.

2 Ferenczi's *Clinical Diary*, written in 1932, was not published until 1985, due to much opposition from the psychoanalytic mainstream, particularly from Ernst Jones. Aron and Harris, 1993, p. 1, write that after being banned and ostracised, Ferenczi was finally recognised as the prescient innovator of all modern trends.

Chapter 3

Recognising unrepresentable pain

Premonition and signs of catastrophe

Bion (1970, p. 45) seems to oscillate between the idea that the psychic world can indeed be evacuated into the "sensible world", and the idea that completely freeing oneself of psychic parts is only a fantasy, so that we cannot truly be free of anything, because everything remains, the wounds of the self and "These old ghosts, they never die" (Bion, 1897–1919, p. 296). In the second part of his autobiography, Bion uses poetic imagery to describe how emotional turbulence can cool and solidify into superimposed layers of crystallised residue that swell like lava to the surface. Memories of grief remain recorded as fossils, bound by emotional quality rather than chronological factors. These memories can emerge, even if they are confused, but a sufficient level of awareness is required to be able to identify them and thus think about them. The skill of the analyst is then to grasp the painful emotion when it is still in the state of premonition, "before it has become *painfully* obvious" (Bion, 1963, p. 74). *Premonition* is the equivalent in the realm of emotions of pre-conception in the realm of ideas. It is thus a kind of precursor of the emotion that must be grasped in order to avoid the onset of "unnecessary" pain that can lead to disintegration. The premonition of pain is experienced by the analyst as anxiety, an "unsaturated element", which Meltzer (1978) links to the Kleinian distinction of psychic pain into persecutory and depressive anxiety.

Bion's research, however, is concerned with the potential representability of experiences and traumas that cannot be represented because they are embodied, inscribed in the so-called implicit memory or in the inaccessible unconscious. It is in the body, in aesthetic experience, that the deepest emotions emerge, in that negative emotional background that conditions our experiences and actions. It is, therefore, to the emergence of the sign, the

DOI: 10.4324/9781032655239-5

premonition, as the precursor of the painful emotion, that we must turn our attention. In addition, these signs, which are not yet real signs, appear in the voice, which becomes weak and trembling; in mimicry, which becomes expressive; in gestures and interjections (*pre-verbal*), and between words that are full of silences, and within words that become charged and animated with emotion (*infra-verbal*).

Van Buren and Alhati (2010) note that the concept of "wild thoughts" and "thoughts without a thinker" actually describes a mental function at a level beyond familiar signs and symbols and introduces a profound shift in the understanding of how thoughts arise. Wild thoughts have an essential function in mental growth. Sleep, dreaming, states of ecstasy, music, art, even certain accidents, etc., are the particular conditions under which the individual can come into contact with these strange thoughts which Bion invites us to respect and welcome. In *The Past Presented*, Bion (1977c, p. 143) introduces a new character, "Apparition", who addresses Rosemary, the maid, with these words: "Dreams, apparitions, hallucinations may indeed be friends of yours … if you dare to admit the acquaintance. So far you have at least permitted yourself to admit my existence. You may be right to think that I am both the herald of impending disaster and a sign of that disaster". Bion uses the term "disaster", as in *On Arrogance*, where he refers to a psychic disaster that has already occurred, of which arrogance and stupidity are the scattered and fragmented traces. Although in the concept of catastrophe, which is linked to that of catastrophic change, Bion also seems to incorporate the original etymological meaning of the Greek word χαταστροφη, which indicates a reversal, with different outcomes, from the most benign to the most tragic. Furthermore, the sense of catastrophe, as Michael Eigen (1985) writes, underlies Bion's description of psychic birth and remains a kind of cement that holds the personality together, a universal forming principle. The birth, development and dissolution of the ego take place in a climate of catastrophe. The beta elements are primordial pre-thoughts that claim a birth and at the same time are signs of an ongoing catastrophe, "objects compounded of things-in-themselves [...] linked by a sense of catastrophe" (Bion, 1963, p. 40), whereby the psychotic personality is a "catastrophe in the making" (Eigen, 1985, p. 217). However, the Bionian vision goes beyond the psychopathological aspects. The sense of catastrophe pervades our being even before birth: "emotional life bears the imprint of the universe in which it grows, oscillating between combustion and preservation" (ibid.). Bion (1963), therefore, points to the production of signs as the earliest stages in the development of thought through PS↔D and argues that primitive language is based on the sign with an emotional charge, which refers to raw, undifferentiated elements, the beta-elements, so that the birth of thought appears as a kind of writing out of the chaos of a primordial catastrophe.

The evolutionary process, then, resembles a painful creative process that takes place through the courage to welcome and express our wandering thoughts, whatever they may be, dreams, flashes of dreams and even hallucinatory elements. This is why the birth, growth and development of knowledge are situations feared by the individual and the group, because they imply "the crossing of the thick screen of common sense, rationality and consensus (including that constituted by psychoanalytic theories) and the catastrophic impact with the true experience of the self" (Riolo, 2009, p. 32). By introducing "O" as a reality in becoming, Bion thus evokes a concept of the unconscious as a container of emotional truths that are difficult to reach because they are often buried in the deepest and most inaccessible layers of our minds, but also a concept of the unconscious as a process in continuous creation and expansion. Evolution and growth happen through the ability to reach these split denied and isolated truths, which push for a pre-representation, usually in the form of behaviour and somatic signs, which one must be able to grasp and welcome, knowing that the encounter with buried but extremely active truths is always painful and catastrophic. Bion's thought thus finds a timely connection with the ideas of other authors who have emphasised the need to regain contact with the split parts of the self. Winnicott (1974), first of all, shows how certain patients can present a current fear of collapse due to traumas that occurred at a time when they were too immature to experience them. Pontalis (1977) argues that at the heart of being there is what escapes any possibility of memorisation, so that unimaginable pain, without representation, is precisely what most conditions intrapsychic and interpersonal relationships. Bollas (1987) describes the effects of the "Unthought known" on adult life. Kristeva (1993) notes that the so-called new pathologies – wounded narcissisms, false personalities, borderline states – are precisely related to the difficulty of mentalising and representing one's own emotional states, or symbolising unbearable traumas. It is in these pathologies that pain can appear as a central and sometimes specific element, a pain that escapes inexorably, like a haemorrhage, but which does not express itself in mental suffering; rather, it takes the way of the body and behaviour, because it is expelled from the psyche, kept outside, in the failure of representation. The human mind, writes Joyce McDougall (2003), is capable of eliminating all traces of the representation of pain through processes of splitting, projection, denial and exclusion, but at the cost of disarticulating the psychosomatic unity. The same happens in severely deprived patients, whose sensations of psychic death and non-existence, as Borgogno (2003) shows, can be seen as radical defensive manoeuvres to survive unbearable pain.

Is the body, then, the proper route to pain when it is neither bearable nor representable? How then can we understand: the emergence of the sign, the premonition, as the precursor of painful emotion; the signs of the soma, which are not yet real signs, when they appear in the voice, in mimicry, in gestures and interjections? That is, in what we call the preverbal; between words, full of silences, and within words, charged and animated by emotion, that is, in what we call the infraverbal.

Seeing the invisible

The problem of how to see "the invisible", how to hear, see, smell, feel emotionally what the patient is trying to communicate to us, has always been present in Bion. However, the question of how to transmit an unconscious emotion from one body to another or from one mind to another becomes more urgent and complex after the concept of the inaccessible unconscious. Freud (1932) understood that the unconscious communicates with each other, but his idea remained an intuition, unnecessarily burdened by the problem of telepathy. With Bion (1977b, pp. 134–5), the problem becomes more precise: how do you feel unrepresentable pain, how do you perceive the patient as a whole, and what do you need to see in order to grasp the pain of a patient of which he is unaware, in his whole situation, body and mind, and then "formulate what we see in such a way that the patient can see what we want him to see". In psychoanalysis, recognition must also take place on the part of the patient, and what actually counts is the emergence of the unknown, because if it is already known by both, it is obsolete, and if it is only known by one or the other, a defensive process is underway (Bion, 1967a, pp. 205–6). For Freud, unconscious phenomena are usually conceived of as something invisible or indirectly manifest. But what is this invisibility? Consciousness in psychoanalysis is well represented by the astonishment of finding Edgar Allan Poe's lost letter right in front of our eyes, where it had always been and where we could not see it. "I never thought of that!" our patients sometimes say when they finally see what they could not see before. Removal is like removing a veil, but it is also like seeing in a new way what you have always seen. Resnik (2006, pp. 31–2), who has written a splendid essay on the visibility of the unconscious, observes that "the world is what it appears to be, but we are not always allowed to see everything. Perception keeps its secrets, its veils. Every glimpse of the world, every possible visibility, requires a consensus". Contact with the thing, therefore, requires not only an agreement between the senses but also an internal agreement between the various instances. The superego, in particular, functions as an internalised god, opening or closing the doors of perception. The poets, of course, understood this. William Blake (1790), in *The Marriage of Heaven and Hell*, says that if the doors of perception were cleansed, everything would appear to man as it truly is: infinite.

Where then to look for the pain that consciousness cannot contain, or has never become conscious, how to observe something that has no mental representation, neither conscious nor unconscious, something that is missing? Does this absence leave traces? Traces that we can discover? How can we get in touch with deep truths, forgotten, divided, enclosed or, more radically, embodied, fossilised, petrified by pain?

The signs of the soma

The clinical problem, then, is how to grasp pain, how to perceive its signs, which are not real signs but can become so in a movement reminiscent of what Merleau Ponty (1964, p. 205) called the "retrograde movement of truth". In some dizzying notes, the philosopher, after recalling how he had intuited the meaning of some fleeting verbal exchanges in English with a taxi driver and a tobacconist, writes that signs acquire total value as signs, but it is necessary that the meaning be given first, and that this meaning emerges from a previous unconscious perception, as if the intuition of a fragment of the verbal chain projects the meaning back onto the signs.

Gestaltung and *Rückgestaltung*. "Retrograde movement of the real", a phenomenon linked to the fact that

> one can no longer undo what was once thought, that one finds it in the materials themselves... Sense is 'perceived' and *Rückgestaltung* is 'perception'. [...] And that means: perception (the first) is in itself the opening of a field of *Gestaltungen* – and that means: perception is unconscious. What is the unconscious? That which acts as a hinge, existential, and in this sense is and is not perceived.
>
> (ibid.)

These observations refer to Bion's idea of binocular vision, of the unconscious as a process, of a knowledge that must pass through caesura, conscious and unconscious, but they also imply complex problems related to the origin of sign and signification, which Bion addresses throughout his work.

Sometimes pain seems to disappear, swallowed up in inaccessible, alien places, even to the patient. Enclosed in these secret places, pain becomes an internal dead object whose weight and even smell is borne by the patient, who becomes stone, ice, or like a rotting walking corpse. More generally, we are dealing with the thousand faces of anaesthesia, from the chemical to the emotional. Resnik (2003) speaks of "glaciation" to describe the numbing of pain by the hibernation of body and mind, waiting for better times. In the groups with Resnik, I learned to have great respect for the times of glaciation and the long work of containment to avoid haemorrhagic defrosting. In these situations, projective identification seems to be suspended, ineffective, as if for this kind of pain even the handling of the evacuation mechanism is too vital. There is nothing in the therapist to indicate an emotional or mental state of compulsion, nor sudden changes in his/her own bodily being, nor perceptions of alienation or loss of freedom, as sometimes occurs in situations where projective identification prevails. Rather, the therapist feels exposed to the disturbing experience of an icy emptiness emanating from a person who does not resonate.

Freud had already intuited the problem when, in *The Neuro-Psychoses of Defence*, he identified a more energetic and effective form of defence, which he called *verwerfung*. In this defence, the ego rejects (*verwerfing*) the incompatible idea together with its affect and behaves as if the idea had never occurred to the ego at all. But from the moment of which this has been successfully done the subject is in a psychosis, which can only be classified as "hallucinatory confusion" (Freud, 1894, p. 58). The term "*Verwerfen*" has been translated as "to reject", "to refuse", "to repudiate", being used as synonyms, and confused with other concepts such as that of "repression", to which Freud initially intended to contrast it, only to assimilate it to repression again in the *Compendium*. In short, as Riolo (2010) shows, *verwerfung* has long been rejected (*verwirft*) by psychoanalysis, with the fortunate exception of Lacan, who, however, limits it to the concept of the exclusion of the phallic signifier and thus of the father's name in psychosis, where, as we know, it is kept out of the mother-child relationship. Riolo, therefore, associates the production of "hallucinatory confusion" of Freud with the process of hallucinosis described by Bion.

Without in any way diminishing Riolo's intuition and Freud's genius, it should be noted that Freud's discourse remains built on a nineteenth-century epistemological framework, with worn-out terminology such as libido, regression, autoeroticism, overinvestment, but above all it remains centred on a description of the intrapsychic drive. For Bion, transformation in hallucinosis is a complex relational process that occurs when there is too much pain, or when the subject does not have sufficient capacity to tolerate it. In these cases, a rivalry develops between the patient and the analyst, a rivalry linked to the patient's need to prove his or her independence from anything other than his or her own creations. The patient believes that (s)he can use his or her senses as organs of evacuation and thus surround him or herself with a perfect world, a universe created by him or herself. (S)he wants to be independent of any person or thing except what (s)he produces him or herself, and this makes him or her feel beyond rivalry, envy, greed, pettiness, love, hate. Yet the patient is not satisfied. The optical hallucinations tend to perpetuate themselves, producing pleasure and pain but no meaning. The process of transforming the perception of emotional experiences into symbolic form, i.e., into alpha elements, comes to a halt, and there remains an excessive stimulation that needs to be evacuated. In other words, when there is an inability to tolerate pain and frustration, the personality can react against the thought, which always imposes a limitation. Thus the mental event is transformed into a sensory, hallucinatory impression that has no meaning, only pleasure or pain. Meaning is lost, replaced by pain and pleasure, regardless of the object and frustration of the thought. For Bion, then, hallucinosis is a psychotic defence, but one that belongs to all of us to varying degrees, and above all an ideal state of mind that the analyst must enter in order to intuit the facts of analysis. This is why Civitarese (2014, p. 82) sees hallucinosis as a sophisticated technical tool of the analyst, an "emotional vertex that the analyst must reach in order to grasp the patient's psychic reality, to grasp something true, even if it is denied by the reality of the senses". So is pain perceived unconsciously? Is pain seen or felt? Does it come through contagion, empathy, resonance, intuition, or is it forced upon us as in projective identification? And if it is visible, what are the signs of pain?

"He who cries out in pain or says he is in pain", writes Wittgenstein (1958, p. 92) *"does not choose the mouth that says this"*, which means that the person of whom we say: "'He is in pain' is, according to the rules of the game, the person who cries out, twitches his face, etc.".

Consequently, pain is a signal, but also a sign, a sign of itself, of its presence, or, as Luca Vanzago (2016) says, in the subject's painful affectivity, the object that manifests itself is the subject itself, but in an inverted and alienated form. As a sign, pain retains an essential value for the integrity of the person and for the doctor, who will use it to orientate him or herself towards a certain pathology, but will hardly orientate the psychiatrist and psychotherapist, who will generally have to deal with a pain that refers back to itself. This is why, in psychotherapy, we need to be able to grasp the signs of pain more than pain as a sign of something, because in any clinical situation, we are dealing with the person and not with a collection of organs. Any objective pain necessarily involves the way the subject perceives and feels it, so there is no point in studying pain without dealing with the person who suffers. This should remind us that we are not so much treating diseases as we are treating the sick. Faced with a suffering person, it is therefore necessary to recover the intuitive, semiotic and empathic capacity to grasp the person in his or her phenomenal wholeness.

For this reason, it will not be useless to try to sketch a gestalt, a global image of the suffering person, which can signal the presence of pain even before the specific somatic signs.

So where do we suffer? If it is the person as a whole who suffers, where can we grasp the signs of the emergence of pain? According to Salvatore Natoli (1986), the discovery of the experience of pain requires us to grasp it where it is, to recognise it when we encounter it, and this encounter takes place first of all with the face of the sufferer. That is why, with certain patients, the vis-à-vis setting seems to be more appropriate to grasp the signs of pain. The pain is there. We see it in front of us, even if it is sometimes difficult to bear. We see it in the eyes, first of all in the gaze, which remains languid, watery, even if it does not always manage to dissolve into tears. In the facial expressions, swollen, already crying in the dermis, full of liquids, in the movements, slow and difficult, but sometimes heartbreaking, in the posture, painful and awkward. Naturally in the voice as well, which slips fades into silence, or, more rarely explodes into a scream, but which sometimes comes out like an unstoppable haemorrhage of words harder than a bullet. When looking at a person suffering from pain, we often find ourselves faced with something that recalls the characteristics that Jean-Luc Nancy attributes to a real portrait. These are the characteristics of a subject who looks at nothing, who sees nothing, but who allows him or herself to be seen, who places him or herself in the gaze. As in the portrait, the gaze of the subject never sees anything appear, nothing comes from the depths, all depth is already on the surface: "Intimacy is the game played by a depth that is found in no other depth than that of the surface, where it is played and stretched. What is stretched is again a passion" (Nancy, 2000, p. 47). Where then to look for the pain that consciousness cannot contain, how to observe something that has no mental representation, something that is missing? And does this absence leave traces? Traces that we can discover? Can the word truly give us back the possibility of getting in touch with deep, forgotten, split, enclosed truths or, more radically, withered, embodied, fossilised, petrified; can the word truly touch the soma, speak to the body, or, as Bion (1976, pp. 134–5) writes, "Is it possible to talk to the soma in such a way that the psychosis is able to understand, or vice versa?" Bion believes that artists have a considerable advantage over analysts "because they can resort to the aesthetic as a universal linguistic" (ibid., p. 133), and we know how often he has used poetry to express otherwise inaccessible truths, to distil O from Milton's "void and formless infinite", to recover feelings and affections that have been expelled, repressed, by projective identification, leaving in their place "the ghosts of departed quantities" (Bion, 1970, p. 128). This pain cannot be found in language, at least not in a language understood as a system of representation, as a system of signs expressing ideas. The signs of pain do not express ideas, but pain itself. Gargani (2008, p. 17), commenting on the last Wittgenstein, says that "crying or laughing, sorrow or joy, are not governed by rules, they are not governed by pre-established norms, and they do not even consist in the use of conventional signs to feel joy, sorrow, laugh or cry". This is because "feelings, affections, emotions are not translated by language, they inhabit language" (ibid., p. 18). For Wittgenstein, language has a gestural, expressive and physiognomic character, which means that the symbol does not indicate something outside itself, but is contained within itself, as Merleau-Ponty had already observed. For the French philosopher, the conventionalist conception of linguistic signs is insufficient and prior communication must be assumed. The word "inhabits things"; it is not the mere sign of objects and meanings (Merleau-Ponty, 1984, p. 33). What seems necessary, then, is to become "sensitive to those threads of silence with which the stuff of the word is interwoven" and to be able to grasp that "primordial familiarity" which lies at the bottom of the word itself (ibid., p. 66). It is necessary to return to the great silence of the world, from whose "flesh" the word explodes and to "describe the gesture that breaks this silence" (Merleau-Ponty, 1945,

p. 255). This vocal gesture has a very special originality: it is the first gesture that the child makes at birth, in the form of a cry and a scream. The scream thus manifests in the clearest way the absence of the object, its non-being in the presence. The first vocal gesture thus speaks to us of the primordial absence into which the child is born. "The original vocal gesture can thus be defined as the first scream of the self 'thrown' (as Heidegger would say), that is, placed at a distance, ex-pulsed" (Sini, 1991, p. 215). Is it then from the scream, as the original vocal gesture, that we must begin? "Pain can only be cried out", writes Pontalis (1977, p. 249) in his famous essay *On (Psychic) Pain* – a cry, however, that cannot be satisfied in anything, it can only fall back into silence, where it is confused with being. And this "alternation of silence and cry", the diastole and systole of pain, is an inevitable polarity of existence (ibid.). The cry, therefore, or silence, remains the last threshold between pain and death. But how to give meaning to shouting or silence? When the question is reduced to a cry of despair for McDougall it is necessary to follow other paths than that of free associations. This method, which is fundamental in bringing unconscious thoughts to consciousness, has little effect in pathologies where there is difficulty in representation. In these situations, it is difficult to trace mental functions, affects and even experiences. McDougall (1990, p. 224) argues that at certain moments the analyst is in the same situation as the mother, who has to learn to listen to the child's cries and signs of distress and to translate them into language, thus assuming the role of her thinking apparatus: "From the beginning it is the mother who has to interpret her child's cries and gestures and later to name them for him". The infant does not speak and cannot distinguish between physical and psychological pain because it does not have the capacity to represent its experience symbolically. Therefore, the very young child cannot think about his or her own body and its sensations, nor can (s)he recognise painful affective states as his or her own. The difficulties of the patient in expressing the deep, indistinct and unrepresentable layer of his or her own discomfort, and those of the analyst in understanding it, are thus not very different from those of communication between mother and very young child. McDougall is aware that the semiotics of analytic discourse always remains to be done and describes psychoanalytic semiotic research as "hesitant" (ibid., p. 163). Psychoanalysis has mainly relied on the self-reflexive capacity and symbolic modes of language, limiting itself to paying attention to narrative content and associative chains, following the model of a dream narrative. In this way, it was able to follow the course of thought, of what was represented, but it left out the layer of the psyche in which the denial, the splitting, the turning against oneself or the rejection outside oneself took place. When that which is the source of psychic pain has not been removed, but has been expelled, frozen, enclosed, it is necessary to follow other paths than those of free association. McDougall argues that in these cases pain is expressed through what she calls "soma signs" (ibid., p. 219). Signs that are difficult to identify. While the exclusion of phantasms and chains of ideas from consciousness is well known, the suffocation of affection or the disturbed perception of messages from the soma is little known. These patients do not tell themselves and it is likely that it is only through such signs that they are able to communicate what has been subjected to exclusion or evacuation. But what are these "soma signs"? For McDougall, they are actually pseudo-communications in which the patient, driven by an impulse to maintain a hold on the interlocutor, rather than trying to inform the therapist, tries to act on him or her regardless of the meaning of his or her soma-speech. The patient is as if compelled by the need to free him or herself from a distressing intrapsychic situation, and the analyst seems more affected by the *signs that permeate the speech* than informed by his or her associations. Emotions are aroused by primitive infiltrations, by sensomotoric indices picked up subliminally, communication is discordant, empty, lacking those associative links that generally characterise the texture of language. In these cases, it is feelings of disturbance, fleeting attention, irritation and boredom that the analyst can experience. This private language of signs attempts to re-establish the unity of mother and child in such a way as to make symbolic communication completely superfluous. It is the original or fundamental transference in which the patient tries to abolish the difference between self and other and at the same time (s)he fears its fatal fusion. In these cases, following only the associative chains, the significant threads of the discourse, in coherence with the decoding grid learnt in training, will lead to the blocking of the analytical process. The resistance wins, even if it is that of the analyst. In this attempt to approach the inexpressible, McDougall thus recognises the importance of an empathic and perceptive, or rather aesthetic, understanding, aimed at grasping the signs of soma beyond and between words. However, this is not enough. The analyst him or herself must maintain an imagoic role, that is, a role associated with a self-representation capable of attracting the emotions, desires and prohibitions once associated with the primary objects. The strength of this transferential image derives, as you would expect, from the fact that the analyst has the status of both an imaginary object and a real object. As if to say that it is not enough to be able to see, but that one must also learn to be looked at.

The language of achievement

In his desperate search for a more precise and effective way of communicating, Bion (1970) comes up with the concept of the Language of Achievement, a language capable of disarticulating defensive jargon, empty shells and undermining the rigid framework of meaning. This language, capable of penetrating barriers, should be able to reach archaic residues, prenatal emotions, thoughts without a thinker, intuitions that otherwise remain disjointed. In this upheaval, in this crossing of *caesura*, the word, beyond the symbol, becomes the language of efficacy, a vital juice capable of transforming pain and eliminating the psychotic scars what the patient can only manage to divide. The language of effectivity is thus a language capable of capturing and transmitting emotions before they can be represented as concepts or ideas, and this word often inhabits the spaces of poetic creation, where, in its incessant search for truth and the ineffable, of that *thread* between minds in which emotion becomes an emotional bond, the word becomes capable of opening a breach and communicating with the other world. The greatest danger to growth and spiritual development is, in fact, the burial of truth. Bion's psychoanalysis keeps truth as its central goal, to be pursued at all costs, because truth is the "food" of the mind. Bion (1977c, p. 62) is well aware that we prefer to remain in the "womb of our ignorance", that truth is "a threat", sometimes incompatible with our fragility; he is also well aware that most of us have spent a lot of time trying not to be ourselves, lying to ourselves, conforming to the expectations of others. Nevertheless, Bion trusts that the personalities of analyst and analysand can survive the loss of their protective shell of lying, subterfuge, evasion and hallucination, and can even be fortified and enriched by this loss. Healthy mental development thus depends on the truth, as the living organism depends on food, and when the truth is missing or incomplete, the personality deteriorates. Authors such as Grotstein and Civitarese agree that all of Bion's work is based on the concept of the truth drive, and that all of the ego's defence mechanisms are primarily opposed to the intrusion of unconscious truth. In other words, man is a truth-seeking and/or truth-avoiding individual, and the oscillation between truth and truth-avoidance characterises the two poles of mental health and psychopathology. Truth-seeking as mental health and growth and truth-avoidance as the poisoning of the mind and psychopathology in Bion thus have the same function as creativity and complacency have in Winnicott. However, Bion is pessimistic about the actual capacity of human beings to think. He sees thinking as a response to the pressure of thoughts on the psyche, a hypothesis he shares with Heidegger, together with the conviction that the activity of thinking is still in an embryonic state. There must be a correspondence between thoughts and thinkers, and not everyone is able to accommodate certain thoughts, especially those related to death, violence and loss. To accommodate the deep truths, the divided parts that have never been conscious, or that have had only a faint glimmer of consciousness, can thus be a very difficult task, and even an endeavour "beyond the capacity of the human mind" (Bion, 1977a, p. 281). The inability to tolerate frustration and pain takes the form of a fear of the void, whereby the individual prefers to remain in the comforting world of the known, avoiding contact with all that is beyond representation, even if this limits mental space. It is, as a result, essential to take into account the patient's, and of course the analyst's, ability to tolerate emotional truth. On the other hand, if the problem is configured as a fear of empty space, as a need to remain in the comforting world of the already known, even if this limits mental space, then it is necessary to deepen the relationship between space and thought, and therefore between thought and time, which Bion calls the twin of space.

Chapter 4

Time and space. Walking across the time, between Freud and Bion

God's writing and the tiger's coat

In this clinical-theoretical excursus on the relationship between the present and the past in Freud and Bion, there seem to be more questions than answers, more doubts than certainties. First of all, there is an inherent difficulty in separating the two authors' conceptions. Both arrive at the idea that the past persists, that it operates in the here and now, that the time of desire and the time of pain never pass. Nonetheless, there is a strong sense that the two authors' conceptions of time and space are profoundly different, and at the same time that it is not yet possible to define them. Naturally, talking about time, or saying anything meaningful about time, is daunting. Husserl warns that time remains the most difficult problem for phenomenology. A problem that has always divided thinkers. In addition, it continues to do so in our time, with theoretical physicists on one side and neuroscientists, philosophers and poets on the other. The former generally believe that time is an illusion, the latter that it is real and an essential dimension of life. After all, nothing seems to have actually changed since Augustine's time. Not only did the latter say: "If no one questions me, I know; if I wanted to explain it to those who question me, I do not know"; Augustine (*Confessions*, cap. XI) also said: "We cannot speak truthfully of the existence of time, except insofar as it tends not to exist". For the past is no more, the future is not yet and the present, in order to be time, must be translated into the past, otherwise it would be eternity.

How, then, can we speak of time in general, and of Freud's and Bion's time in particular? Of that time which, according to Proust (1954), is not visible, and to become such, it searches for bodies, taking possession of them to show its magic lantern. Borges (1952), in his extraordinary story *The Writing of God*, writes that time is measured by the secret, equal steps

DOI: 10.4324/9781032655239-6

of a jaguar. Locked in a hemispherical stone prison, Tzinacàn tries to decipher, in vain, the writing of god in the spots and black lines of the jaguar's fur. The magician of the Pyramid of Qaholom, Tzinacán, finally realises that it is impossible to decipher this text and he understands that in human languages there is no sentence that does not imply the whole universe. Each word implies the whole, so the word tiger implies the tigers that gave birth to it, the deer it devoured, the pastures that fed it, the earth and the sky. It is only when the union with the divine takes place, in the ecstasy that abolishes all symbolic distinctions, in the image of an infinite wheel of which each of us is but a miserable thread, that Tzinacán understands the mystery of the universe, which renders all notions of identity futile. How can we fail to recall *A Memory of the Future*, in which Bion (1975b, p. 107) states that "Psychoanalysis itself is just a stripe on the coat of the tiger. Ultimately it may meet the Tiger – The Thing Itself -O". So Bion, like Borges, thinks that psychoanalysis corresponds to the vain attempt to decipher God's writing on the tiger's coat, but it is only "an ephemeral phenomenon, betraying forces on the surface of which the human race flickers, flares and fades in response to the unrecognized but gigantic reality" (ibid., p. 106): the psyche it betrays.

For this reason, Borges' sharp intelligence continually resonates in Bion's texts, not because Bion quotes the poet, but because of that sparkling of sudden fires that their minds have in common, for their ability to remain in paradox, not to shy away from complexity, of getting dangerously close to the real, and sometimes of being the real. Even before being able to outline a Bionian theory of time, what surprises us is the same mental attitude that unites the two thinkers, the poet and the analyst, an attitude that belongs to *mystery* and *wonder* in the face of the reality of life and death.

In *The New Refutation of Time*, Borges (1960, p. 186), after reviewing the innumerable refutations of time, from Buddhist texts to idealism, from the empirical Sextus to Plutarch, etc., at first with astonishment, but with increasing perplexity and boredom, allows himself to utter this small truth, which seems to spring from a profound feeling of being rather than from enlightening cognitions of reason:

> To deny temporal succession, to deny the astronomical universe, are secret despairs and consolations. Our destiny (unlike the hell of Swedenborg and the hell of Tibetan mythology) is not frightening because it is unreal; it is frightening because it is irreversible and ironclad. Time is the stuff of which I am made. Time is a river that drags me, but I am the

river; it is a tiger that mauls me, but I am the tiger; it is a fire that devours me, but I am the fire. The world, unfortunately, is real; I, unfortunately, am Borges.

I, therefore, suggest a series of walks across time between Freud and Bion, a coming and going, between texts and thoughts, as if to grasp some analogies, associations, narratives, avoiding hypotheses that may not even come or that may appear as if by magic.

Freud, the timeless unconscious and broken time

For Freud, the unconscious is timeless. Desire is immortal, and especially the desire for immortality, on which all religion and philosophy are based. The illusion of being eternal is the common denominator of the best thinkers and the sad minds of contemporary gurus. Freud's idea of time comes from the clinic but, as we shall see, it also corresponds paradoxically to the idea of time in physics.

In the first topical "unconscious wishes always remain active [...] indestructible. In the unconscious nothing can be brought to an end, nothing past or forgotten" (Freud, 1900, p. 577). The timelessness of desire remains unaltered in the second topical:

> There is nothing in the id that corresponds to the idea of time: there is no recognition of the passage of time and – a thing that is most remarkable that awaits consideration in philosophical thought – no alteration in its mental process is produced by the passage of time. Wishful impulses which have never passed beyond the id, but impressions, too, which have been sunk into the id by repression, are virtually immortal, after the passage of they behave as though they had just occurred. They can only be recognised as belonging to the past, can only lose their importance and be deprived of their cathexis of energy, when they have been made conscious by the work of analysis, and it is on this that the therapeutic effect of analytical treatment rest to no small extent.
>
> (Freud, 1932, p. 73)

Desire on that account remains "immortal", "indestructible", in the unconscious as in the id. Similarly, the old idea of analytic therapy as overcoming infantile amnesia, filling in the gaps and aporias of consciousness, persists, even at the cost of discovering that memories are, in the end, only a "cover".

However, the concept of the timelessness of the unconscious does not imply a renunciation of the arrow of time or the awareness of death, which is relegated to consciousness, the only witness to the continuous flow of time. Consciousness, however, is condemned to live in the paradox of a timeless present that is already past the moment it is thought.

So what is the idea of time in Freud? Green (2000a) speaks of "shattered time", and in a few key texts shows its complexity. Shattered time, because from *Studies on Hysteria* onwards, Freud speaks of a time blocked by fixation, of strangled affects, of affective movements frozen in a path that instead evolves over time. In the fourth chapter, written without Breuer's collaboration, Freud mentions a transchronic time that emanates from archived mnestic layers, the famous hysterical memories. These are painful representations, buried in the deepest layers, which form the core of the pathogenic organisation; unconscious thoughts, of buried traumas, which are hardly recognised as true memories, even though they emerge in the synchronic time of psychotherapy, or more precisely in the false nodes of *translation*, a key term that Freud uses here for the first time. As we know, Freud abandons the traumatic hypothesis but does not give up the idea of a traumatic force that acts by undermining the psyche, perhaps *a posteriori*.

"The time in which ça happens is not the time in which ça is signified", Green (2000a, p. 43) writes, recovering the meaning of time and the trauma of the real in the *après-coup*. This double time of signification, which Freud introduces with the concept of *nachträglichkeit*, is already an aspect of shuttered time. However, the issue becomes more complex starting from the problem of repetition. In "Remembering, Repeating and Working-Through", Freud (1914) discovers that repetition takes the place of memory, of representation. Working-Through, on the other hand, is to bind, to represent, to postpone, to conceive and thus to change form in order to develop. The patient, however, tends to repeat, and the more (s)he repeats, the less (s)he remembers, indeed (s)he repeats in order not to remember, in order not to open him or herself to the meaning of what insists in him or her. Green (2000a, p. 53) understands that what insists is an unconscious that is not made up of representations and affections,

> but rather an unconscious that gives rise to a psychic pain or is possessed by a redivivus trauma that springs from immemorial depths and refuses to sink into oblivion. The only memory that remains is that of a drive that throbs, rhythmically, without end.

Acting, repeating, is thus a way of remembering that actually replaces memory; repeating is the opposite of representing, everything is repeated as if it were happening for the first time, time stands still. The subject suffocates in agony, in suffering, revealing the inexpressible character of the urgent, which yet remains in the order of the instinct. Transference is described as a means of harnessing the drives that pulsate and do not stop pulsating, showing a vitality that, nevertheless, empties the psyche. Freud contrasts remembering, which is the aim of analysis, with transference, which is repetition, acting without remembering. Transference and repetition are thus expressions of a forgotten past which cannot be remembered, and "the compulsion to repeat", an expression which appears here for the first time, becomes the patient's true way of remembering (Freud, 1914). In *Beyond the Pleasure Principle*, however, the concept of the compulsion to repeat takes on a more dramatic colouring, the transference is coloured by the incoercion of acting in the service of resistance. It is here that Green (2000a, p. 93) identifies the true relationship with time: "Temporary exhaustion in acting or representative reworking, this is the new dilemma that refers to *the economy of time*". In the insistent and stubbornly repetitive discharge of the drive, Green detects a paradox, the paradox that the repetition of the drive, which should be conservative, in fact preserves nothing, but creates a vacuum in the psychic apparatus. This is why Green calls the paradox of the discharge of the drive "a murder of time" (ibid., p. 94). The discharge does not conserve, but is a regression towards an ever more primitive state, which for Freud is the soma. This is the work of the death instinct, which for Freud triggers the return to the state of inanimate matter. A situation that Green likens to the Bionian dilemma between frustration modification or evacuation in the form of beta elements. The analogy may hold, but only at the level of the point relationship, not in the relationship between systems. What seems strange is that Green (ibid., p. 100) recognises that what is repeated, for example, in traumatic dreams, manifests something that, while belonging to the order of the psychic, passes into the act, and that this passage is equivalent to a "realising" statute, "it seems like a claim to inscribe oneself in the field of the Real, as if it depended on it". Nonetheless, neither Freud nor Green are prepared to reintroduce reality into the psychoanalytic field. Green senses, however, that with the introduction of the second topic and the more radical formulation of the *id,* Freud brings into play something that goes beyond the simple denial of time by the unconscious. The timelessness of the unconscious concerns not only the future but also the origin. The origin of desire goes beyond mnestic traces, experience, and is already inscribed in the desire of parents and generations. The out-of-time of the unconscious thus escapes both the destruction of time and the creation of time. It qualifies the human unconscious as it passes through it from one side to the other: "Stretched between a limit that is not an origin and another that is not an end, the unconscious endures" (Green, 2000b, p. 26). It persists as a resistance to change, as a refusal of extinction, and as a resistance to the unveiling of the organisation of the signifier, in its perpetual movement between generations. The heterogeneity of psychism, with the tripartite introduction of *Id, Ego and Superego*, increases conflictuality, which now extends to conflict with external reality and conflict between *Id* and *Ego*. Additionally, structural heterogeneity increases the fragmentation of time and, with the compulsion to repeat, the urgency of the actualisation of desire. This shift – which accepts Lacanian references to the crossed-out subject, a subject that is "spoken" – identifies a fundamental paradox of psychoanalysis, that while it must deal with what is more properly individual, it has to deal with a subject of the unconscious that always comes from elsewhere. This would make the Freudian unconscious not only a reservoir of desires unacceptable to consciousness but also an inexhaustible source of dynamism, tending towards the future, through the thrust of forces that decentralise the subject, always thrust towards an elsewhere. Moreover, these forces, which in the first topic are a mark of the past that never passes, in the second topic, with the passage from the unconscious to the *Id*, are coloured with the illusion of an unalterable youthfulness of *Eros*, of a desire that is still there and that can wait no longer. In Green's words, "The compulsion to repeat abolishes negation – it does not want to know about it and therefore does not even need to deny the passage of time; it is the foreclosure of temporality" (Green, 2000a, p. 183). Nevertheless, the task of Freudian analysis remains to bring the representation of these desires into consciousness, to make the unconscious conscious, to increase insight, in other words, the task remains to fill the gaps in consciousness, to overcome the infantile amnesia due to repression. Green concludes, however, that in order to rediscover the heterochrony of time as a source of enrichment and complexification of the psyche, it is necessary to recover the value of the object, neglected by Freud, and to propose an instinct-object pair which obliges one to take into account the time of the other. In this sense, Green sees in the introduction of the dualism of life instinct/death instinct Freud's extreme attempt to reintroduce the time of death into the time of life.

Freud and the time metaphor of thinking

Although Green (2000a) states that the image "thinks" in its own way and that desire is also a way of thinking, for Freud (1900, p. 507), the dream "does not think, calculate or judge in any way at all; it restricts itself to giving things a new form", and the dream work is in any case "completely different qualitatively" from waking thought, and therefore "not immediately comparable with it". The Lacanian idea of thoughts that think themselves, and of a thought of desire that becomes one with its fulfilment and realisation, is not enough to lay the foundations of a psychoanalytic theory of thought. Expelled from the unconscious, for Freud, time exists only for consciousness, in the work of thought, in the asymmetrical world, Matte-Blanco would say. Time remains bound to consciousness, and the onset of the function of thinking is traced back to the time factor; the ability to think is a function of the frustration of desire and allows the time of waiting to be tolerated. "Freud speaks of the capacity for thinking as affording relief from frustration, in that thought can fill the gap between the time when an impulse is born and its satisfaction" (Bion, 1965, pp. 98–9). This is Bion's icastic synthesis of Freud's position. Thought thus comes to represent a missing object that has to be constructed in the mind in order to make the deferral of action bearable. The development of thought is thus linked to the postponement of the discharge of instincts, and consequently to the transition from the primary to the secondary principle. The aspect that should interest us most is that with Freud the protagonist of the narrative is a psychic apparatus that already seems capable of thinking or desiring and, when it does not obtain satisfaction, retreats into hallucinatory satisfaction, as happens in the dream. It is only the non-fulfilment of the expected satisfaction, the disappointment experienced, that therefore leads to the abandonment of the attempt at satisfaction and induces the subject to turn to reality. In other words, in Freud, thought is *delay*, a way to achieve satisfaction, even in its deferred form, whereby one renounces a pleasure only in favour of a greater amount of future pleasure. In this way, the reality principle is established, together with the gradual expansion of consciousness, understood as the psychic counterpart of the sense organs. The principle of pleasure, however, is not abandoned, but only secured: "A momentary pleasure, uncertain in its results, is given up, but only in order to gain along the new path an assured pleasure at a later time" (Freud, 1911, p. 223). Thought, as a result, remains linked to the time factor. However, Freud does not forget the spatial factor, which remains the background against which he builds his work. Terms such as "psychology of the depths", "surface of the psychic apparatus", "projection", "introjection", "topographical point of view", "provinces and regions of the mind" show how the spatial metaphor runs through all his work. It is emblematic that in the last scattered notes, published posthumously, Freud (1938b, p. 300) writes: "Space may be the projection of the extension of the psychical apparatus. No other derivation is probable. Instead of Kant's *a priori* determinants of our psychical apparatus. Psyche is extended; knows nothing about it".

Until the end of his life, therefore, Freud reflected on the concept of space and, although he had not yet found a scientific definition of it, he already intuited from the *Interpretation of Dreams* its intimate relationship with time. In discussing the means available to the dream for representing the logical relationships between thoughts, Freud (1900, p. 314) wrote:

They reproduces logical connection by simultaneity; Here they are acting like the painter who, in a picture of the School of Athens or of Parnassus, represents in one group all the philosophers or all the poets. It is true that they were never in fact assembled in a single hall or on a single mountain-top; but they certainly form a group in the conceptual sense.

In order to describe what the dream does, Freud therefore makes a leap from a temporal metaphor, expressing simultaneity, to a spatial metaphor, expressing logical connection. Thus, in the dream, simultaneity (temporal) expresses logical nexus (spatial), and this shows the abolition of spatial nexus and the construction of a mental space in which space and time are intimately connected and interchangeable. Furthermore, in *The Past Presented*, Bion (1977c, p. 23) defines "absolute space and absolute time" as twins.

Bion and the spatial metaphor of thinking

"The domain of thought may be conceived of as a space occupied by no-things" (Bion, 1965, p. 106). This is the powerful metaphor with which Chapter 8 of *Transformations* begins, in which Bion takes Melanie Klein's concept of mental space to its extreme. The Kleinian inner world is the very place where meaning is generated, the notion of image is transformed into that of inner object, as a three-dimensional presence and living reality, assumed through affective experience and introjective mechanism. Splitting and projective identification, understood as an omnipotent fantasy of control over the object, are the basic mechanisms of this spatial conception of the mind. It is on these premises that Bion builds his theoretical apparatus, making radical transformations in the process.

Projective identification becomes a mechanism capable of communicating the most primitive emotions and, above all, a mechanism capable of emotionally relating two or more minds to each other. In this sense, it becomes a mental operation that induces real emotional involvement and creates a shared mental space, opening up the possibility of thinking "the mind as something that extends 'beyond' the limits of the subject" (Corrao, 1977). The focus of attention thus shifts from the individual to its field, and the container/contained model assumes the specific function of a fundamental analytical element. In short, this concept of projective identification, placed in relation to the container/contained model, takes on the value of a relational function deeply embedded in a "field" and, in particular, a field conceived as a shared state of mind. The spatial metaphor of the mind thus takes over.

Despite that what does it mean to imagine the field of thought as a space inhabited by no-things? What does Bion mean by "no-thing", "no-breast", which refers to the "non-existence of the breast", and not something that "is not the breast"? The thought represented by a word or other sign, if it has the meaning of the absence of the thing (no-thing), can be represented by a dot. This is when the child can tolerate a certain amount of frustration. The absent breast, the no-breast, is then represented by a visual image. This is the only way to develop an awareness of the presence or absence of objects, and thus of time and space, where the breast originally was. On the other hand, intolerance of the absence of a thing (of a nothingness) precludes the possibility of using words, circles, dots and lines to promote learning from experience. It is, therefore, the tolerance of frustration and pain that allows awareness of the presence or absence of objects and what a developing personality will later recognise as time and space. When tolerance is low, however, time and space are destroyed: "The factors that reduce the chest to a point reduce time to 'now'. Time is denuded of past and future" (Bion, 1965, p. 55). Dots, circles and words become a "provocation" to replace the nothingness with the thing, and the thing becomes a medium that replaces representations. So you have to look for the real murderer instead of the thought represented by these words, the real breast or penis instead of the thought represented by these words, and so on...

According to Bion, then, thinking is *making space*, being able to contain emotional truth and traumatic reality; for Freud, it is *delay*, but it remains a way of achieving satisfaction, even if in its postponed form. In Bion's work, on the other hand, thinking is at the service of truth, which must be contained, tolerated, and which serves the individual to understand himself and the world. This is why thinking is painful. Change and growth occur when the subject is able to deal with pain rather than run away from it. This means that for Bion, emotional growth takes the place of sexual libido, and motivation is based on the tension of the search for truth rather than the desire for pleasure or the avoidance of pain. Thinking thus takes the place of tolerated absence, thinking is making space, being able to contain, thinking *more of* reality. Apart from the mysterious Freudian note that the psyche is extended, we can therefore assume that the spatial metaphor is more indicative of thinking in Bion, and that the temporal metaphor remains dominant in Freud. And yet, when speaking of loss of object, scars, wounds of the self and a returning past, both Freud and Bion resort to the spatial metaphor. Whether it is the repressed unconscious or the beta element, desire or unrepresentable pain, the past always needs a body in which to leave a trace. The past, especially the traumatic past, is always a trace, an impression in psychic matter: body, matter, somatic unconscious.

The consciousness of pain in Freud

Pontalis understood well that the quality of pain is that of abolishing boundaries. A radical quality that it shares with the cry. The boundaries between the physical and the psychic, first of all, between the mind and the body, as in the cry, in which the psyche becomes the body and the body becomes the psyche, in the unfolding of chaos. Moreover, the boundaries of the skin, psychic needless to say, which is "pierced", in the bleeding of a wound, from which pain overflows, comes out, as the scream comes out from the holes in the body in Bacon's paintings. Pain ultimately abolishes the boundaries between subject and object, annulling the game of representation and renders the body itself strange, alienated in pain, just as it renders inalienable any object or thought of pain that never ceases, to haunt us. Pontalis tries in vain to reflect on the specificity of psychic pain, to circumscribe its concept and experience, but he knows very well that Freud uses the same model and the same mechanisms to explain physical and psychic pain.

Pain is always realised in an ego-body, in the breakdown of bodily defences or in the excess of instinctual excitement, as if in pain the psyche was transformed into the body and the body into the psyche. In his letters to Fliess, Freud (1887–1904, p. 102) points to a connection between melancholia, sexual anaesthesia and loss of libido, which leads back to "a psychic inhibition with impoverishment of the drives and suffering in this respect". Immediately afterwards, however, he speaks of pain: "The associated neurons must give up their excitation, which *produces pain*. The uncoupling of associations is always *painful*; there sets in, as though through an *internal hemorrhage*, an impoverishment in excitation (in the free store of it) – which makes itself known in the other instinctual drives and functions. As an inhibition, this indrawing operates like a *wound*, in a manner analogous to pain (see the theory of physical pain)" (ibid.). In describing the loss of drive-in melancholia, Freud thus speaks of an "internal hemorrhage", a "wound", a "psychic hole", just as in physical pain, passing from one register to another, by direct transference, not by metaphor. These ideas, taken up and developed in the *Project,* are visionary in their lucidity, but they will not be followed up, and the problems of pain, consciousness and perception will remain at the margins of Freud's work. Only in *Minute C* of *Inhibitions, Symptoms and Anxiety*, does Freud (1925b, p. 170) cautiously go so far as to hypothesise that "The transition from physical pain to mental pain corresponds to a chance from narcissistic cathexis to object-cathexis", recognising to pain a side adjacent to the trauma through the break-in, and a side contiguous to mourning through the loss of the object.

Pontalis does not forget that, in the *Project,* Freud had worked out the outlines of an original theory of pain. Had Freud forgotten this? Having set pain against satisfaction, he ended up devoting himself almost entirely to the study of the transformations of the forms of desire and pleasure. Nonetheless this pleasure-pain pair is inscribed at the very heart of the body and affective life, so much so that Green admits that the experience of pain in Freud refers back to the affective model in a far more explicit way than the experience of satisfaction. For the Freud of the *Project*, pain and affect would in fact result from an internal discharge of certain secretory neurons, equivalent to motor neurons for external discharge. Pain is, therefore, seen as different from displeasure, as a barrier-breaking phenomenon that occurs when excessive amounts of energy breach protective devices. Pain is therefore the consequence of a breach of the para-excitation device and acts as a constant excitation. What Pontalis seems to overlook in this model is the fundamental link that Freud makes between memory, crying and pain. With this link, Freud takes two essential steps: he introduces the distinction between psychic and external reality and inaugurates the birth of consciousness. A consciousness of pain.

> In the first place, there are objects – perceptions – that make one *scream*, because they arouse pain; and it turns out as an immensely important fact that this association of a sound (which arouses motor images of one's own as well) with a perceptual [image], which is composite apart from this, emphasizes that object as hostile one and serves to direct attention to the perceptual [image]. When otherwise, owing to pain, one has received no good indication of the quality of the object, the *information of one's own scream* serves to characterise the object. Thus this association is a means of making memories that arouse *unpleasure* conscious and object of attention: the first class of *conscious memories* has been created.
>
> (Freud, 1895, pp. 366–7)

The information of one's own cry thus serves to characterise the object whose hostility it underlines, so that the first category of conscious memories is linked to the perception of an object that causes pain and makes one cry out. Thus, for Freud, as for the poet, "at the base of memory there is always a cry of pain" (Pratolini, 1960). Consciousness, therefore, is born as a *consciousness of pain*. Freud is thus close to understanding that subjective time is born as pain, but he associates pain with the memories of the infant's rudimentary consciousness, memories of which he will experience invincible amnesia. Freud also intuited the communicative value of crying. Cries are first of all a motor discharge of internal excitement, according to the reflex pattern that constitutes the primary structure of the psychic apparatus. For this reason, the cry is understood as a signal and a primary form of communication between mother and child: "This path of discharge acquires a secondary function of the highest importance, that of *communication*" (Freud, 1895, p. 318). The next level has to do with the mental image of the object that brings satisfaction. This image, whether visual or motor, is the basis of the primary psychic process that aims at the hallucinatory realisation of desire through an experience of self-satisfaction. When he writes that the first conscious memories are those associated with the object that causes pain and makes one cry out, Freud anticipates what Anzieu (1985) will call the "zero level" of the structure of the psychic apparatus, which leads to thought through the articulation of verbal traces and the representation of things.

Psychic processes thus acquire quality through association with speech-discharge which equates thought with perception and makes memory possible. Thought processes, which are in themselves unconscious, only become conscious when they are transformed into perceptions. In this way, language takes on the character of a sign of mental reality, and speech, characterised as mnestic residue, can be traced back to sensory sources. Freud qualifies "cognitive thinking" as that in which attention is directed from the outset to the discharge signs of thinking, i.e., the signs of language. In other words, cognitive thinking is realised as an experience in which the subject reproduces within him or herself, a situation of discharge which enables him/her to know the object. For Freud, thinking is always characterised by the association of a perception (internal or external) with a motor activity (which serves to satisfy a desire or to reproduce the image of the object).

These ideas of the *Project* will remain unchanged in later works; thinking, which Freud (1925a, p. 237) identifies with representation, always remains linked to perception and differs from action in that it displaces much less investment energy, but

> all presentations originate from perceptions and are repetitions of them […] thinking possesses the capacity to bring before the mind once more something that has once been perceived, by reproducing it as a presentation without the external object having still to be there. The first and immediate aim, therefore, of reality-testing is, not to *find* an object in real perception which corresponds to the one presented, but to *refind* such an object, to convince oneself that it is still there.

The problem of pain, consciousness and perception, however, remains on the margins of Freud's work, as does the distinction between the inner and outer worlds, which remains embryonic and is only hinted at in some works as an inside/outside dialectic. In particular, and again in *Negation*, Freud argues that the inside/outside difference is constituted by an assimilation of good objects within the subject and an expulsion of bad objects without, and it is precisely this "spitting out" of the bad and the retention of the good that underlies the myth of the inside/outside. But this link between perception, memory and pain is already the subjective birth of the idea of time.

The traces of time

So what is the link between time and pain? The physicist Carlo Rovelli (2017, p. 105), having shown that the equations of quantum gravity do not have a time variable, but merely describe the world by showing how things change in relation to each other, asks what time is for us in existence: "Memory and Nostalgia. The pain of absence". This is time for us, writes Rovelli.

Furthermore, he adds that the pain of absence is also good and beautiful because it is born of love and nourished by what gives meaning to life. Therefore, even if we do not know what time itself is, if we cast our phenomenological gaze on subjective time, we are likely to find pain. Pain leaves its mark, even if the way in which it imprints itself on flesh and spirit remains a mystery. It is said that the body "keeps score", that it "takes the blow", to indicate a bodily memory, without remembrance, the trace of a reality that in its harshness marks the individual and sometimes generations and peoples. The signs of pain are thus traces, but of what? The language of the body seems to preserve the memory of the event, of a reality that rages. Every sign, however, is a sign of a present, a living present, of which the past and the future are the true temporal dimensions, because the present passes, it has no temporal dimension, even if only the present exists. This is the paradox of time.

Deleuze (1968, p. 105) reminds us that

the scar is not the sign of the past wound, but of the 'present fact of having received a wound', for which reason it is said to be a contemplation of the wound, and it contracts all the instants that separate me from it into a living present.

It is the Bionian idea of the past acting in the here and now, "the mark it has left on you or me or us *now*" (Bion, 1997, p. 38). And yet sometimes the time of suffering is the suffering of the passing of time, of the *temps qui ronge la vie*, which digs deep wounds that are not just wrinkles.

François Jullien (2009, p. 13) speaks of silent transformations, those in which the "subject", who thinks (s)he is the master of him or herself and able to maintain his or her self-consciousness, looks at one of his or her photographs from twenty years ago and realises with horror that (s)he is "a process" that absorbs and transforms him or her, inexorably, in which:

"'I'm this (one) 'growing old'". This is Proust's extraordinary lesson in *Le temps retrouvé*, in which time transforms people into unrecognisable puppets. In addition, Proust realises that these unwanted transformations have the effect of a masquerade, an art of disguise, which, when carried to the extreme, produces a complete transformation of the personality, so much so as to evoke the Kafkaesque idea that human beings can undergo metamorphoses as complete as those of certain insects. Recognising someone, or rather *identifying* them after not recognising them, means for Proust bringing together two contradictory aspects, the person who was there and is no longer there and the person who is there and who we have not recognised, is to penetrate a mystery almost as bewildering as the mystery of death, of which it is also the premise and the herald.

Death, then, is a link between pain and time. This is why Hans Belting (2013) writes that the "cybernetic turn", which freed images from the reproduction of reality, for example, in morphing, produced faces that no longer belonged to anyone. Without any correspondence with the world of the body, the mask-images refer only to themselves, they have lost the function of hiding and representing, because they are now free from all traces of the past and of death. The loss of the image's relationship with time and death is also the profound reason for the current confusion between virtual and real. If, in the process of virtualisation, we begin to perceive virtual reality as a real entity, the "spectacle of pain" of which Boltanski (1993) speaks, in which everything becomes a theatrical spectacle, then it is possible for virtual reality to be experienced as reality without being reality, to the extent that even "the perfect sadistic image of an immortal torture victim who can suffer endless agony without having the escape route of death available to him" can become real (Žižek, 2002, p. 17). Moreover, this brilliant insight of Žižek's succeeds in grasping the profound and dramatic link "between the virtualisation of reality and the constitution of an infinite and 'infiniteised' physical pain, much stronger than normal pain" (ibid.). It must, therefore, make us reflect every time we try to understand the withdrawal of our adolescents, the drama of the hikikomori, who wall themselves up at home in front of a screen, or of the more recent Johatsu, the evaporates, subjects who disappear without leaving any trace of themselves, a phenomenon that Enrique Vila-Matas (2005) had already described in his extraordinary book *Doctor Pesavento*, which deals with the disappearance of the subject, under the irresistible push to cancel oneself. Not only is this it. If the sign refers only to itself, what possibility do we have of distinguishing present, past and future? Do we live in an eternal present, in a past that eternally presents itself, or in a future that is already here but may never come? Reality is not external to us, it does not belong to our interpretations and representations, rather we are part of this reality. In the crisis of any representationalist notion of reality, cognition becomes an embodied action, but what if this body shows signs of progressive dematerialisation, of a constant state of fading? This means that we are not only makers of worlds, that the real is virtual and the virtual is real, but also that we are made by the world, of the world, a world that precedes us, that is in us, and a past that is always there, we only have to look at the starry sky, writes Roberto Bolagno, to see that we live on memories. Reality, then, is the Kantian thing-in-itself, unattainable, but also the abyss, the sinking into a past that does not fade, and into a depth that contains us, that contains our body and our vision, "narcissistic vision", Merleau-Ponty (1964) recalls, but this reality is now also a virtual network that imprisons us in endless time and pain.

The destruction of time and space

Bion did not have the problem of dealing with the virtual of the net, but he had an intuition that we live in a curtain of illusions and that the virtual is always with us. The "ghosts of the past" and the "ghosts of the future" are "facts" that create problems to be solved, and a character like Falstaff, who had no real existence, may have more reality than a person that actually existed (Bion, 1965, pp. 95, 103). In psychoanalysis, and therefore in mental life, a thing can be and not be, without any contradiction, and the analyst truly present can be felt by the patient as the place where the analyst is not, and vice versa the analyst truly absent it can be considered as a space occupied by the absent analyst. In *Transformations*, Bion thus links emotion to space, postulating that geometric constructions are attempts to represent emotion according to the progression sinus → emotion (or place where the sinus was) → place where the emotion was. "The - . and - -------- retain meaning, as does the nothing (because at least there is a trace of whatever it is that does not occupy the position) so long as time itself is not reduced to the moment without a past or a future" (ibid., p. 100). Bion thus indicates with the signs ←↑ a "violent, greedy and envious, ruthless, murderous and predatory, without respect for the truth, persons or things" (ibid., p. 102), or as "the ultimate non-existent 'object', the 'space' and 'time' annihilated object and its all-consuming greed for, and envy of, anything that exists, because it exists" (ibid., p. 104). Time and space are destroyed, the patient is afraid of empty space and feels that space and psyche cannot coexist. This theme of the destruction of time was introduced in *A Theory of Thinking* where Bion describes the clinical vignette of a patient who felt he was wasting time. Time is destroyed as in the tea scene with the mad hatter in *Alice in Wonderland* where the clock always strikes 4 (actually 6), a scene repeated in *Transformations*.

In the first essay, the destruction of time and space is associated with a general situation of intolerance of frustration, while in *Transformations* it is more specifically associated with psychotic states dominated by envy and greed, psychotic anxiety and psychotic stupor, when thought is attacked as indistinguishable from a nothingness. It is interesting to note that in *A Theory of Thinking* the intolerance of frustration is still placed in the patient and attacks are made against the consciousness of reality data. Thought is thus treated in the same way as concrete things, which are as a result "evacuated at high speed as missiles to annihilate space" (Bion, 1967, p. 113). In *Transformations*, this destructive object can instead be "within of either analyst or analysand", or inside any other object or being, felt as an ejecting force that can enter an existing object to eject its existingness (Bion, 1965, p. 112).

Bion thus seems to move gradually from a Kleinian psychoanalysis centred on envy and primary destructiveness in the patient to a relational and field-centred psychoanalysis. This does not mean that Bion abandons the concept of envy, but that the relationship and the analyst's response to it become increasingly involved and decisive in the course of the therapeutic process. In *Attention and Interpretation,* Bion subsequently provides an exemplary clinical vignette of the problem of the destruction of space and time in situations so severe that even the use of projective identification is not possible. In these cases, it is difficult to make an interpretation because there is no concept of an adequate container into which projection could take place. Instead of making a projective identification, the patient then makes an explosive projection, realising a mental space that is felt "as an immensity so great that it cannot be represented even by astronomical space because it cannot be represented at all" (Bion, 1970, p. 12). This is the "psychotic panic", which can be expressed by a sudden and absolute silence, which Bion compares to a surgical shock in which the patient can bleed to death in his or her own tissues due to the extreme dilatation of the capillaries. In these cases, the mental space is so vast that it cannot be defined in its temporal and spatial limits; an infinite space in which emotion flows away and is lost in the immensity, leaving the patient with the feeling of having lost the capacity to feel emotion. The realisation of this model of explosion, with its pressure waves expanding and deforming all around it, is exemplified in Munch's painting *The Scream*.[1] For Munch, the container that finally succeeds in collecting and transforming the explosive force of feelings is the realisation of the painting of that blood-red sunset. The blood-red vision is then a violent and sudden reinjection of something that has been expelled, hence the sudden explosion and external evacuation in *The Scream*. So when we look at *The Scream*, we see not just an image deformed by the explosion of sound, but precisely the outflow of the mind; in the swirling fluidification of memories; in the violent expulsion of a mental space that dissolves and expands without end.

Bion (1970, pp. 13–4) also refers to *the scream*, describing the extraordinary case of a patient in whom the very events of analysis are reduced to fragments of a moment, dispersed in space, simultaneously present. At first, the patient says that he could buy no ice-cream. After six months he says he cannot even buy ice-cream, three days later he says it is too late to buy ice-cream, and after two years there was no ice-cream. Then comes the theme of "I scream", and later "no I scream". So in this sequence, there is an attack on the link between patient and analyst, a link that was initially based on a nurturing relationship, the good breast, the ice cream and that envy and destructiveness had turned into a scream, but in time even this link had been destroyed, "no I scream". The fragments of this bond had thus been scattered in an infinite space, which is mental space, and the distance between one fragment and another could now only be measured in time. For the interpretation, it is, therefore, necessary to show that these fragments are scattered here and there over a long period of years, but this can be very difficult because the means by which the patient carries out his transformation is not language but acting out.

The analysis as a whole can then be seen as a transformation in which "an intense catastrophic emotional explosion O has occurred" (Bion, 1970, p. 14), in which personality elements and link have been expelled to vast distance, in the form of beta elements, which are produced again and again because the intolerance of frustration sharpens the boundaries of three-dimensional space. The analyst, unlike the patient, can use points, lines and space to explore this situation, including non-Euclidean geometries, and like the painter or musician, can also use silence and communicate non-verbal material.

> The ability to use points, lines and space becomes important for understanding 'emotional space', for the continuance of the work and avoidance of a situation in which two inarticulate personalities are unable to release themselves from the bondage of inarticulation.
>
> (ibid., p. 15)

This is of course a borderline situation, but Bion notes that the impossibility of communicating without feeling frustrated is so familiar that the nature of the frustration is forgotten. The problem is then to find similar configurations in order to be able to understand the transformation, to find patterns that make it possible to recognise "some relations of the self with itself" (ibid.), because in certain situations of misunderstanding, it may become necessary to destroy either the container or the contained. In the end, the individual cannot contain the impulses that belong to a couple, and the couple cannot contain the impulses that belong to a group. Hence the general hypothesis that "The psycho-analytic problem is the problem of growth and its harmonious resolution in the relationship between the container and the contained, repeated in individual, pair, and finally group (intra and extra psychically)" (ibid., pp. 15–6). Psychoanalysis thus expands the mental universe it explores, but everything can always collapse and we never know where the change will lead because we only see the reality that has become. That is why the passage of time is never linear. Pathology shows that subjective time can always be destroyed, frozen, annulled, reduced to fragments, pieces of a story that analytical work sometimes manages to recompose in a sequence of meanings. Birth, growth, life, death, this is the time, paradoxically, of the human being who, in order to feel truly alive and responsible, must be aware that (s)he is moving towards death. And perhaps this is *the first really great difference with Freud, who in the unconscious does not know death*. Bion builds his theoretical system on an evolutionary horizon dominated by chaos. The evolutionary character of reality, of all reality, biological, social and cosmological, is always present in his work. His conception of psychoanalysis and development is also entirely relational. Ideas such as the removed unconscious, not removed and even inaccessible do not help to fully understand the processes that occur in the analytic field because they maintain a substantial halo. Bion (1975a, p. 49) states that one must investigate "the caesura; not the analyst, not the analysand; not the unconscious; not the conscious; not sanity, not insanity. But the caesura, the link, the synapse, the (counter-transference the transitive-intransitive mood". Furthermore, in other statements, Bion gives a glimpse of this world of relations:

> mouth is one anchor, breast is the other. Both of these have been treated as if they were the essential features of the analogy. It is exactly this point that marks the divergence of the path of growth from the path of decay. The breast and the mouth are only important in so far as they serve to define the bridge between the two. When the 'anchors' usurp the importance that belongs to the qualities which they should be imparting to the bridge, growth is impaired.
>
> (Bion, 1971, pp. 26–7)

In *The Dream*, Bion (1975b, pp. 70–1) entrusts Rosemary, Alice's old maid who has become the mistress, with the task of reminding that "the factual exercise of a relationship is not the two objects related, like the cunt and the prick, but keeping one thing inside another. (*Laughs contemptuously*) The container and contained!" Evolution, relation, process, Bion's world is hence made up of events, happenings, transformations, it speaks to us of the incessant and turbulent flow of life, of its infinite potential, but also of its precariousness, uncertainty and absolute relativism. In this interconnected network of events, exchanges and relationships, in which objects and subjects lose their individuality and become a network, an emotional web, how can we conceive of the very idea of time and space?

Evidence of contaminations and insertions between the physics and psychoanalysis of Freud and Bion

We have mentioned that in Freud the idea of time of the unconscious corresponds to the idea of time of science. In particular, Newtonian mechanics, for which time is reversible. In Newtonian physics, space and time are given once and for all; time flows uniformly, independently of things and their movements, and space exists even when it is empty of objects. Newton's law links force and acceleration and it is both deterministic and reversible.

It is reversible with respect to time (t→ -t), describes a static universe, and contradicts the evolutionary view associated with entropy and the second principle of thermodynamics. Its formulation thus represents a triumph of being over becoming. Moreover, determinism and temporal symmetry are also Freud's basic ideas (and perhaps illusions). With Einstein, things become more complicated. Space-time is no longer absolute but is linked to the material content of the universe, to gravity, which becomes the source of the curvature of space-time. Time is, therefore, slowed down by mass and velocity. There is no single, absolute time, nor is there a single time in a single place, because it depends on motion. Starting with Einstein, theoretical physicists so claim that time is an illusion: "It is necessary to learn to think of the world in non-temporal terms, even if this is difficult at the level of intuition", writes the physicist Carlo Rovelli (2004). This is the idea of Einstein, but also of quantum physics, which reduces the division between past, present and future to a persistent illusion. The fundamental laws of physics, from classical dynamics to the theory of relativity and quantum physics, do not allow any distinction between past and future. At the level of the fundamental description of nature, for many theoretical physicists, there is no arrow of time, which of course cannot arise in a world in which temporal symmetry is assumed. Freud's conception of time in the unconscious seems to correspond to this ideal of science.

Given these premises, we should expect Bion's ideas about time to be quite different from Freud's, and perhaps even different from Einstein's ideas about physics. Einstein wanted to escape the curse of history. He dreamed of a science capable of "reaching beyond the observable real to a timeless, intelligible reality" (Prigogine & Stenger 1988, p. 35). His scientific ideal was that of a science freed from the traces of human subjectivity, an ideal of classical science that was paradoxically undermined by the very quantum mechanics that Einstein himself had helped to find. Einstein could not accept the role it assigned to the observer, who becomes responsible for the transition from potentiality to reality. In quantum mechanics, the wave function corresponds to a probability amplitude, so the trajectory of classical mechanics becomes a probabilistic quantity. The electron behaves like a wave, which Schrödinger labelled Psi. But how can the wave nature of the electron be reconciled with the fact that when it arrives somewhere, it always arrives as a particle? The Psi wave, therefore, evolves over time according to the equation written by Schrödinger only as long as we do not observe it. When we do observe it, it concentrates on one point and we see the particle. So the mere fact of observing reality seems enough to change it! It is the controversy between Heisenberg and Schrödinger over the corpuscular and wave nature of the electron that leads Einstein to say: "Does God really play dice?" This radical "discovery" of quantum mechanics has enormous consequences, not only for physicists. It also has a direct impact on psychoanalytic field theories. "The physical substrate that determines duration and time intervals – the gravitational field – not only has a mass-influenced dynamic, it is also a quantum entity that has no fixed values except when it interacts with something" (Rovelli, 2017, p. 81).

This remark by Rovelli resonates with Bion's ideas and shows his agreement with quantum theory. The last Bion, eliminating any substantialist residue, opens up to a concept of transpersonal and, I would even say, quantum field; psychoanalysis becomes a relation independent of the objects involved, and *A Memory of the Future* imposes itself as a "polycentric and polymorphous" narration of the field of mental phenomena, which, in Riolo's words, becomes "such as to render impossible and completely meaningless any distinction between internal and external objects, identifications and splits, but also between the single and the multiple, between the individual and the group" (Riolo, 1986, p. 199). Mental space expands, loses its egoic boundaries, which are redrawn as a mobile and permeable membrane, and becomes populated by kaleidoscopic constructions, dreamlike thinking and dreamlike phenomena. The analytic field thus becomes a co-constructed and illusionary field in which elements, subjects, functions and events are constantly produced; that is, they are realisations of the system and coincide with the transformations generated by the system itself. The transformative event is placed at the centre of change, and psychoanalysis itself becomes a system of transformations in which the truth and knowledge produced do not truly belong "to the subject or to the world, but always and only to the mobile relationship between the two, between the mind and the world, between the field and its elements" (ibid., p. 202). Emotions are placed at the centre of the theory of meaning, and the mind, as an apparatus for thinking, is conceived as a relational function capable of development based on the transformations of primary emotions and the experience of the other. In the psychoanalytic field, space and time, therefore, lose any character of Newtonian absolute reference, and become a "transpersonal space-time", a field of interaction, in which the elements are no longer primary, but secondary forms of organisation of experience.

Obviously, we could think that the similarities of the so-called Bion field theory with quantum physics are coincidental, but I am convinced that Bion was more familiar with quantum theory than we think, and not only because he read Heisenberg, to whom he refers in the projective transformations, but because he experienced it daily with his analyses, in the analytic field! In other words, it is possible that the so-called physical metaphor of the field is not so much a metaphor as a description, from another point of view, of the same phenomena which we call mental but which we still do not know what they are, and which Bion (1997, p. 29) believed to be "physical" in nature. In the real physical world and in the field of analysis, time dissolves into a network of relations, it loses all coherence, it dissolves into images of fluctuating, overlapping time-spaces, that materialised at intervals in relation to specific objects; it is not a single time, it has a different duration for each trajectory, it passes with different rhythms according to place and speed. "It is not oriented: the difference between past and future does not exist in the elementary equations of the world, it is a contingent aspect that appears when we look at things without paying attention to the details" (Rovelli, 2017, p. 81). In the vast universe, there is no present valid for all, no common time, but only a time that "jumps, fluctuates, materialises only through interaction" (ibid., p. 82). The loss of the concept of a single time, however, does not call into question that the world is a network of events, things *are not*, says Rovelli, *but happen*, the world is a set of events, of happenings, of processes, it is in constant transformation, it is not a set of things: "the electron is concrete only in relation to the physical objects with which it interacts" (ibid., p. 80). The quantum-physical world and the mental world can, as a result, only be understood in terms of relations between happenings, events that crowd into chaos, that do not proceed along the reversible line of Newtonian time. Evolution, becoming, a network of events, relations, processes, transformations, the influence of the observer on the observed object, etc., are the leading ideas of contemporary physics and Bion's ideas about the mental and analytical field.

The problem is irreversibility, the arrow of time which marks the life of man and of every living being, but which for many physicists does not exist. Nevertheless, when Gödel proposed a cosmological model that included the possibility of travelling into one's own past, Einstein was disturbed and suggested that the problem of irreversibility be reconsidered. In fact, physics does not yet have a unified concept of time, but since Ilya Prigogine's research, the possibility of a mediation between the irreversible time of life and the great theoretical systems of physics that deny the arrow of time has gradually seemed less and less improbable. Studies of irreversible processes associated with dynamic instability have shown that time plays a crucial role not only in life but also in the birth of the universe. Irreversibility is not only central to our existence, but also retains its role in relativistic cosmology. Irreversibility is associated with the very origin of the universe, and the arrow of time, essential to biological processes, becomes part of cosmology. The evolutionary character of reality, of all reality, biological, social and cosmological, is in fact increasingly evident at all levels. Lee Smolin, whom Guido Tonelli (2021) calls one of the most ruthless "time-killers", now says that cosmology should be a historical science. The recent confirmation of gravitational waves would be proof of an evolving universe, in which the emergence of the new is constantly repeated, not only in living nature. Evolution, says Smolin, is inconceivable without time. The primacy of becoming over being is universal. In this perspective, time becomes central again, eternal, without beginning or end, so much so that Prigogine (1996) writes on the wall of Moscow's Lomonosov University: "Time precedes existence". Rovelli (2017, p. 92) himself, another enemy of Cronus, finally admits that "if by time we mean nothing but what happens, then everything is time: only what is in time exists" Smolin states that time does not derive from other categories of nature, not even from space, which would become its by-product, a structure that emerges from time and acquires the characteristics of an illusion. Smolin starts from the phenomenon of entanglement, the quantum entanglement that couples correlated states of matter, which seems to suggest instantaneous action at a distance. For Smolin, entanglement, rather than a timeless action, would be the clearest evidence of a phenomenon that is indifferent to space, operating as if the spatial distance between the two particles did not exist.

Theoretical physics thus finds itself denying now time, now space, but all this should make us realise that these are hypotheses, evocative, but hypotheses, as Tonelli repeatedly points out. What we must understand, however, is that at the level of the paradox of time, of the opposition between the time of physics and the time of man, the fundamental problem of the relationship between mind and matter arises. Toraldo Di Francia (1979) defines this paradox as the deepest root of the scientific debate, in which he also includes other dichotomies such as existent/being, art/logic and unconscious/conscious.

In this chaos of events and relationships, we could easily get lost, were it not for Prigogine's extraordinary insight that the very paradox of the arrow of time is actually the necessary condition for all our communication with the physical world, as well as with other human beings: "A common arrow of time, a common definition of the distinction between past and future", which implies the inclusion of the evolutionary character of the universe in our fundamental physical description, is the true interface between mind and matter (Prigogine, 1996, p. 52). In a world governed by symmetrical temporal laws, the acquisition of all our knowledge becomes paradoxical in itself, because "every measurement presupposes an irreversible process" (ibid., p. 47). John von Neumann and Eugene Wigner evoke mystical ideas, such as the consciousness of the observer, which bring back to the centre of interest the relationship between mind and matter, a relationship which had obsessed Freud and, not unexpectedly, Bion, and which Paul Davies considers "the greatest challenge of the new physics" (ibid.). There cannot be an absolute opposition between mind and matter, as Descartes thought. Rather, there is an interface, which for Prigogine appears precisely at the level of the paradox of time, which does not imply that the observer is responsible for the transition from potentiality to reality, but rather that (s)he introduces the rupture of temporal symmetry and thus irreversibility.

Bergson's shadow

Wild' thoughts in Bion's library

Henry Bergson's *Matter and Memory* and Alfred North Whitehead's *An Introduction to Mathematics*, in Bion's library, are thickly underlined in pencil. Bion's library is still legally inaccessible, but Francesca Bion generously provided photocopies of these texts after Parthenope Bion Talamo's valuable work on the roots of her father's thought was interrupted by her untimely tragic death. *Bion's Sources*, edited by Torres and Hinshelwood, thus remains a valuable book for understanding Bion's cultural formation. Nuno Torres notes that references to these two works are implicitly present throughout Bion's work. Bion's concepts of intuition and the proto-mental seem to be strongly rooted in Bergson's work. Torres follows their traces carefully, and yet I believe that Bergson's shadow extends far beyond these concepts. It looms over all of Bion's work, particularly in the concepts of time and memory, the mind-body relationship, the binocular view of the unconscious, and the evolutionary conception of life. Bergson's thoughts resonate in Bion's pages as a series of image-perceptions and image-memories, which Deleuze describes as an endless cycle. My hypothesis is that Bion and Bergson were two thinkers beset by the same problems, two geniuses who throughout their lives continued to think the same thoughts, albeit from different standpoints: *how to overcome Cartesian dualism and how to think matter.*

For Bergson, intelligence has the task of ensuring the perfect insertion of our body into its context, of representing the relationships of external things with each other, and finally of thinking about matter. The same questions that the clinician Bion (1976b, pp. 134–5) asked himself when he wrote "Is it possible to talk to the soma in such a way that the psychosis is able to understand, or vice versa?"

The debt of philosophy and science to Bergson has never really been paid and too often his work is misunderstood and "reduced" to literature. It is no coincidence that Bergson received the Nobel Prize for literature in 1927, and that he was considered the greatest thinker in the world and at the same time the most dangerous man in the world, for his alleged anti-scientific attitudes and rash ideas. A fate similar to that of Freud, who received the Goethe Prize for literature. Bion perhaps avoided being "confused" with a man of letters, because he never claimed to be admitted to the scientific pantheon, and when he used literature, in the hope of leaking a little more truth through fiction, he did not ever allow himself the liberties of a writer. However, he did not avoid being admitted among the "mystics". Therefore, it is not a question of understanding whether Bion misunderstood Bergson, or whether he saw in him the "literary", the "spiritualist", the "vitalist" or the "irrationalist". Bion also read mystics, such as John of the Cross and Meister Eckhart. It cannot be stressed enough that Bion's use of other people's thoughts has nothing to do with a "prosthetic" use, aimed at supporting his own constructions, nor with a work of exegesis of theories not belonging to him. Bion used the thoughts he found in his library, just like the "wild" thoughts he found somewhere, inside or outside of himself; he was an "active reader", with thousands of books, of which, as Parthenope remembered, only two or three metres of shelves were books on psychoanalysis. What about the others? One day, someone will continue the work begun by Parthenope Bion, but we can be sure that those who think of reducing Bion's ideas to the sources of Freud and Klein will never be able to understand the richness and depth of his thought. Bion had considerable knowledge of history, literature, philosophy, epistemology, he knew the philosophy of Bergson and Whitehead, the physics of Poincaré and Heisenberg, and he certainly had knowledge of quantum theory. These insights and theories resonate throughout Bion's conceptions of thought and the unconscious. In Part Two, we will see that for Bion the unconscious is something much broader than the Freudian unconscious in that it is characterised by a dual movement: of repetition and expansion. In fact, the Bionian unconscious maintains a conservative movement of repetition of forms and at the same time presents a movement of expansion and creation. Psychoanalysis is a process that stimulates the growth of the field it examines, so there is a moment when one can say that the unconscious has been created, because what was there before has now expanded. In this sense, for Bion, the unconscious is "the infinite", it is "O". These ideas, together with the concepts of intuition and proto-mental, have an obvious reference to the concepts of memory, time and creative evolution, which as such are directly rooted in Bergson's thought.

The image in itself

In *Matter and Memory*, Bergson (1896) proposes the basic hypothesis that matter has the capacity to preserve a trace of the past, while at the same time attributing to time an intrinsic creative capacity. Bergson's aim is to overcome the opposition between idealism and materialism, the two poles between which Cartesian dualism will always oscillate, denying any mutual influence between body and mind and leading inevitably to "sacrifice freedom" (ibid., p. 227).[2] This is why the philosopher takes the hypothesis of dualism to the extreme, to the point of implosion of that apparently "impassable abyss" between body and mind, but only as "the only possible means of bringing them together" (ibid., p. 226). For Bergson, neither perception nor memory, nor the higher activities of the mind emerge directly from the body. In order not to fall into a Berkeley-like idealism that makes matter coincide with spirit, or into a materialism that reduces consciousness to an epiphenomenon, Bergson, as a result, takes a seemingly extravagant step. He ascribes to matter the quality of an image, "but a self-existing image" (ibid., p. 10), before that dissociation between existence and appearance which idealism and realism have worked on it. It is the material universe itself, as a totality of images, that becomes a kind of consciousness that goes in search of pure memories in memory, to progressively materialise them in contact with present perception. For the philosopher, "interiority and exteriority are only relations among images. To ask whether the universe exists only in our thought, or outside of our thought, is to put the problem in terms that are insoluble" (ibid., p. 25).

Bergson believes that there is a solidarity between consciousness and the brain, but "the brain state indicates only a very small part of the mental state" (ibid., p. 13). Exactly what the "neurologist" Freud (1891, p. 109) argued in his study of aphasia:

> The fibres that reach the cerebral cortex after being interrupted in the grey matter still have a relation to the periphery of the body, but are no longer able to give a current image of it. That is to say, they contain the periphery of the body as a poem contains the alphabet.

However, Freud's metaphor of the poem of the mind still implies a kind of functional parallelism, which Bergson considers to be an unintelligible hypothesis, and shifts his attention to memory, which he considers to be the true point of intersection between mind and matter. He is convinced that the body is merely an instrument of action and that "In no degree, in no sense, under no aspect, does it serves to prepare, far less to explain, a representation" (Bergson, 1896, p. 225). The nervous system does not serve to produce representations: "Its function is to receive stimulation, to provide motor apparatus, and to present the largest possible number of these apparatuses to give a stimulus" (ibid., p. 31), and the more it is developed, the greater the freedom it leaves to our action. For Bergson, everything is an image, images that are not in the brain, which is part of these images. The body is a centre of action and cannot give rise to representation. Our perceptions do not come from or translate states of our nervous system, they vary with the molecular movements of the brain mass, but these remain inseparable from the rest of the material world. Consequently, for Bergson, we have a system of images corresponding to our perception of the universe, which varies according to a privileged image: "*my body*. This image occupies the centre; by it all the others are conditioned; at each of its movements everything changes, as though by a turn of a kaleidoscope" (ibid., p. 25).

Introduction of time

For Bergson, there is no perception that is not impregnated with memories, perception always has a certain duration, and therefore implies an effort of memory which prolongs, one into another, a plurality of moments. It is memory, then, that provides the main contribution of individual consciousness to perception and the subjective side of our knowledge of things. But an image "may *be* without *being perceived*" (ibid., p. 35), and the distance between presence and representation seems to measure precisely the interval between matter itself and our conscious perception of it. For images, between being and being consciously perceived, there is a simple difference of degree, not of nature:

> The reality of matter consists in the totality of its elements and of their actions of every kind. Our representation of matter is the measure of our possible action upon bodies; it results from the discarding of what has no interest for our needs and, or more generally, for our functions. In one sense we might say that the perception of any unconscious material point whatever, in it instantaneousness, is infinitely greater and more complete than ours, since the point gathers and transmits the influences of all the points of the material universe, whereas our consciousness only attains to certain parts and to certain aspect of those parts.
>
> (ibid., pp. 37–8)

So what is perception for Bergson? Let us take a point P. The vibrations transmitted from it to the retinal corpuscles and carried to the subcortical and cortical centres, are converted into a conscious image, then externalised in the point P.

> The truth is that the point P, the rays which it emits, the retina and the nervous elements affected, from a single whole; that the luminous point P is part of this whole; and that it is really in P, and not elsewhere, that the image of P is formed and perceived.
>
> (ibid., p. 43)

It is as if "We all of us began by believing that we grasped the very object, that we perceived it in itself and not in us" (ibid.). Here we find again the Bionian concept of unison, of at-one-ment, and of intuitive knowledge!

However, the encounter with memory, conscious and unconscious, introduces time:

> *Practically we perceive only the past*, the pure present being the invisible progress of the past gnawing into the future. Consciousness, then, illumines, at each moment of time, that immediate part of the past which, impending over the future, seeks to realize and to associated it [...] it is in this illuminated part of our history that we remain seated, in virtue of the fundamental law of life, which is a law of action; hence the difficulty we experience in conceiving memories which are preserved in the shadows. Our reluctance to admit the integral survival of the past has its origin, then, in the very bent of our psychical life -an unfolding of states wherein our interest prompts us to look at that which is unrolling, and not at that which is entirely unrolled.
>
> (ibid., p. 150)

This long quotation resonates like a tuning fork in Bion's ideas about the here and now, and the idea that the past insists on us. It thus opens up the idea of time, which is fundamental in both Bergson and Bion.

Spatialised time and time as invention

Bergson wants to understand the intimate experience of time, which starts from duration, *durée*, and not from physical objects, which have always been privileged by science. Physical knowledge for Bergson is destined to oppose the world described and the person describing it, and thus to ignore the human experience of time, to study objects that affirm a repetitive time and to reduce becoming to the production of the same. The motion-related time of classical mechanics and quantum theory is for Bergson a "spatialised time", unsuitable for explaining the evolution of life because it is tied to things, and therefore an obstacle to intuition. He is convinced that time is an invention or nothing at all. In fact, the analysis of time shows that duration means invention, creation of forms, continuous elaboration of what is absolutely new. In *Creative Evolution,* Bergson (1907) hence tries to link the knowledge of the living to time as duration, understood not as the Heraclitean flow of time, nor as its disappearance in moments different from each other. The *durée*, for Bergson, is a "spiritual act" by which we synthesise the data of experience and preserve them in memory, in sensory-motor habits useful for life, in free acts and novel creations. Lived time does not oppose us to an objective world but translates our solidarity with the real, and Bergson intends to show that the theory of knowledge and the theory of life are inseparable, so the Whole is of the same nature as the Ego, and can only be grasped through a deepening of oneself. In the essay *Le possible et le réel*, Bergson (1930) thus speaks of the possible as richer than the real, and of time as an actual explosion of unpredictable novelty:

> What is time for? [...] time is what prevents everything from being given simultaneously. It delays, or rather it is delay. It must therefore be elaboration. Could it not therefore be a vehicle of creation and choice? Could not its existence prove that there is indeterminacy in things?
>
> (Bergson, 1930, quoted in Prigogine, 1996, p. 21)

Modern physics, however, has had its greatest successes in determinism, which denies change and the reality of time. How, then, to escape the antinomies of determinism and indeterminism, of order and chaos, both of which deny life and freedom? Into this conflict comes the thought of Alfred North Whitehead, a mathematical philosopher and ardent follower of Bergson, who had a great influence on Bion's thought, particularly on the concept of "O". Whitehead finds in Greek thought the two ideals that have guided our history: that of the intelligibility of nature and that of democracy based on human freedom, creativity and responsibility. Ideas that are so dear to Bion. Whitehead (1929), for example, in his *Process and Reality*, takes the possible as a fundamental category of cosmology itself. When nature is represented by physical-mathematical abstraction, derived from the study of bodies in motion, the concept of creativity no longer makes sense. For Whitehead, however, creativity remains a cosmological category, the ultimate principle of all novelty. In this sense, the world is also seen as organic rather than materialistic: a self-feeding swarm of integrated units involved in life processes. Echoing Bergson, Whitehead adopted the motto "Nature is a process", whereby "Nature is a structure of evolutionary processes. Reality is a process".

Nevertheless, how did the ideas of Bergson and Whitehead influence Bion's thinking? On his concept of the unconscious and especially of time? Bion always starts from experience, but his experience must also include the encounter with the "wild" thoughts of Bergson and Whitehead in his library and circulating in the Tavistock Clinic, which was very open and sensitive to novelty. Torres and Hinshelwood (2013) effectively summarise the areas of convergence between Bion and these authors in five points: (1) duration is a heterogeneous flux of becoming; (2) it is irreversible and always tends towards the future; (3) it constantly creates novelty, and is therefore intrinsically irreversible; (4) it is an inexhaustible source of freedom; (5) its living reality can never be communicated in images or concepts, but must be directly intuited. It is then clear that Bergson proposes a completely new concept of matter, which radically changes the understanding of the concept of reality, no longer conceived according to the model of inorganic matter, as in modern rationalism, but according to the notion of organic biological development, which envisages cumulative progress and internal growth.

These premises will not have been in vain if they make us understand why Freud's position remains tied to determinism, while Bion's is open to evolution, to infinity, to O. For Bion, thinking is the development of the capacity to receive and process thoughts, even the thought of the infinite. For centuries, philosophy had defended Aristotle's idea of a "potential infinity", unattainable and unthinkable, and the non-existence of an "infinity in action". Kurt Gödel even so, shows that George Cantor, with his system theory, conceives of the actual infinite as a measurable entity worthy of scientific value, and also demonstrates that there are different types of infinity. Ignatius Gerber (2022, p. 133) states that -in Bion

the Unconscious is the most striking example of the concrete existence of the 'Infinite in Act', which constitutes us as human beings and that the possible apprehension of his interference in the field of the 'conscious finitude' is given in an attitude of 'Intuitive Attention' of the analyst.

Notes on memory in Freud and Bion

Mystic writing-pad

If I distrust my memory [...] I am able to supplement and guarantee its working by making a note in writing. [...] I am then in possession of a 'permanent memory-trace'. [...] Thus a unlimited receptive capacity and a retention of permanent traces seem to be mutually exclusive properties in the apparatus which we use as substitutes for our memory: either the receptive surface must be renewed or the note must be destroyed. [...] our mental apparatus [...] has an unlimited receptive capacity for new perceptions and nevertheless lays down permanent even though not unalterable – memory-traces of them. [...] we possess a system *Pept.-Cs.*, which receives perceptions but retains no permanent trace of them, so that it can react like a clean sheet to every new perception; while the permanent traces of the excitations which have been received are preserved in 'mnemic systems' lying behind the perceptual system. Later, in *Beyond the Pleasure Principle* (1920), I added a remark to the effect that the inexplicable phenomenon of consciousness arises in the perceptual system *instead of* the permanent traces. Now some time ago there came upon the market, under the name of the 'Mystic Writing-Pad', a small contrivance that promises to perform more than the sheet of paper or the slate'.

(Freud, 1924, pp. 227–8)

Freud, in consequence, stresses the analogy between memory and Mystic Writing-Pad, a resin or wax tablet covered with two layers: a transparent celluloid film and a thin, translucent sheet of waxed paper on which one can "write" with a pointed stilus. At the end of this extraordinary work, Freud says:

I further had a suspicion that this discontinuous method of functioning of the system *PCpt. -Cs.* lies at the bottom of the origin of the concept of time. If we imagine one hand writing upon the surface of the Mystic Writing-Pad while another periodically raises its covering-sheet from the wax slab, we shall have a concrete representation of the way in which I tried to picture the functioning of the perceptual apparatus of our mind.

(ibid., pp. 231–2)

In this long quotation, the main epistemological nodes of Freud's conception of memory and time emerge: the relationship between consciousness and memory, the origin of the representation of time, memory as a permanent trace and its representational nature.

Perception, consciousness and memory

Freud links consciousness to perception as an active process that develops from the relationship of the sensory extremity to the external world. His problem is therefore how to connect consciousness and memory. Freud remained tied to Breuer's original conception for a long time. He had hypothesised that the perceptive apparatus and that of memory were incompatible: "the mirror of a reflecting telescope cannot at the same time be a photographic plate" (Freud & Breuer, 1893–5, p. 168). Freud takes up this concept several times, starting from *The Project*, where he hypothesises "permeable neurons", φ, which offer no resistance and hold nothing, used for perception, and "impermeable neurons", ψ, which offer resistance and hold, to which the task of memory is entrusted (Freud, 1895, p. 299). Becoming conscious and leaving behind a lasting memory trace are therefore regarded as incompatible processes.

> It is the *Pcpt*-system, which is without the capacity to retain modifications and is thus without memory, that provides our consciousness with the whole multiplicity of sensory qualities. On the other, our memories, not excepting those which are most deeply stamped in our minds – are in themselves unconscious. They can be made conscious; but there can be no doubt that they can produce all their effects while in an unconscious condition. What we describe as our 'character' is based on the memory-traces of our impressions; and, moreover, the impressions which have had the greatest effect on us – those of our earliest youth- are precisely the ones which scarcely ever become conscious.
>
> (Freud, 1900, p. 540)

In this extraordinary passage from *The Interpretation of Dreams*, Freud shows surprising insights, he alludes to deep unconscious memories that rarely become conscious, he speaks of intense impressions that determine our character, as if he were referring not only to desire but also to the traumatic aspect, which he does not mention. Nonetheless, we sense all of Freud's ambivalence about trauma. Later Freud (1923a, p. 150) will say that there is a "store of memories of earlier perceptions" which, as an "internal world", is a constitutive element of the Ego itself. Freud (1929, p. 125) believes that "in mental life nothing which has once been formed can perish – that everything is somehow preserved and that in suitable circumstances (when, for instance, regression goes back far enough) it can once more be brought to light". Indeed, having introduced the death instinct to explain the compulsion to repeat, it is trauma that makes its disturbing presence felt again in his writings. In 1925, Freud (1925b, p. 93) wrote that "Affective states have become incorporated in the mind as precipitates of primaeval traumatic experiences, and when a similar situation occurs they are relived like mnemic symbols". The relationship between memory and trauma, between consciousness and memory, between memory and the unconscious, is therefore, an essential knot that is difficult to unravel.

> In relation to the traumatic situation, in which the subject is helpless external and internal dangers, real dangers and instinctual demands converge. Whether the ego is suffering from a pain which will not stop or experiencing an accumulation of instinctual needs which cannot obtain satisfaction, the economic situation is the same, and the motor helplessness of the ego find expression in psychical helplessness.
>
> (ibid., p. 168)

In *Terminable and Interminable Analysis*, Freud even goes so far as to attribute the value of trauma to the threat of castration, in what André Hayanal (2004) sees as a posthumous attempt to reconcile his theory of the Oedipal complex with Ferenczi's ideas, and what we can finally regard as his definitive position appears:

> The aetiology of every neurotic disturbance is, after all, a mixed one. It is question either of the instincts being excessively strong– that is to say, recalcitrant to taming by the ego- or of the effect of early (i.e. premature) traumas, which the immature ego was unable to master. As a rule there is a combination of both factors, the constitutional and the accidental. The stronger the constitutional factor, the more ready will a trauma lead to a fixation and leave behind a developmental disturbance; the stronger the trauma, the more certainly will its injurious effects become manifest even when the instinctual situation is normal. There is no doubt, that an aetiology of the traumatic sort offer by far the more favourable field for analysis. [...] Only in such cases can one speaks of an analysis having been definitively ended.
>
> (Freud, 1937a, p. 220)

This position is not surprising. It contrasts with the traditional vulgate, according to which Freud ultimately preferred to trace conflicts back to unconscious fantasy, psychic reality and the power of sexual instincts, emphasising that any trauma does not act directly but by reawakening the arousal of the instincts or by activating earlier internal phantasms. In reality, Freud tried to maintain a role for trauma, arriving at confused and contradictory positions, but his ambivalence should be understood as an awareness of a paradoxical situation that he could not resolve. Freud did not have our present knowledge of memory and consciousness, which is still very partial, but which can make us realise that the hypothesis of representational memory is untenable. In *Beyond the Pleasure Principle,* Freud summarises his ideas about consciousness. The P-C system, at the boundary between outside and inside, is located in the cerebral cortex, consciousness remains an inexplicable phenomenon that Freud refuses to define. The real psychic is the unconscious. The phenomenon of becoming conscious is thus for Freud a transient, unstable, inexplicable emergence, which he, like many contemporary epistemologists, regards as completely indescribable. Freud's hypothesis is that this unique and indescribable phenomenon should replace the mnestic traces, which are instead the true psychic reality, inscribed in the individual in what he calls a "double fixation" (*fixierung*), that of the "conscious reconstruction" and that of "original inconscious state" (Freud, 1938a, p. 160). Memory, as a permanent trace, therefore refers back to the unconscious, as he had already understood in *The Interpretation of Dreams*, when he wrote that "our memories, not excepting those which are most deeply stamped in our minds – are in themselves unconscious" (1900, p. 539). Repression, as we shall see, *does not suppress the representation*, it simply prevents it from becoming conscious. Freud notes that memories are fragmentary, ambiguous, deformed images, like the fragmented, deformed images of dreams. They continue to exist, but deprived of affect, they become unrecognisable. The secondary process, however, must have all the mnestic material at its disposal in order to make its movements in the external world. Thinking, which Freud identifies with representation, differs from acting in that it displaces much smaller energies of investment, but

> all presentations originate from perceptions and are repetitions of them
> [...] thinking possesses the capacity to bring before the mind once more
> something that has once been perceived, by reproducing it as a presentation without the external object having still to be there. The first and
> immediate aim, therefore, of reality-testing is, not to *find* an object in real
> perception which corresponds to the one presented, but to *refind* such an
> object, to convince oneself that it is still there.
>
> (Freud, 1925a, p. 237)

Freud seems close to understanding the relationship between perception and memory, but his idea of representational memory as a repository in which inscription and archiving take place leaves open the question of how the mind can perceive and recognise something new. In his later years, however, Freud seems to have recovered many of the insights he had abandoned in an extraordinary burst of creativity. Freud had first discovered the phenomenon of so-called infantile amnesia, which concerns the first years of life, and had questioned whether it was possible to have real memories of childhood. Infantile memories do not show the first years of life as they really were, but as they appear to us later, when memory develops and inevitably distorts them: "It may indeed be questioned whether we have any memories at all *from* our childhood; memory *relating* to our childhood may be all that we possess" (Freud, 1899, p. 321). This is the basis of the concept of the "family romances", with which everyone tries to embellish their past history (Freud, 1908). In his later works, Freud then moves towards a more complex, reconstructive concept of memory: the analyst's task "is to make out what has been forgotten from the traces which it has left behind or, more correctly, do *construct* it" (Freud, 1937b, p. 259). Interpretation thus becomes a construction in which the analyst moves from being a blank screen to becoming an active subject. It is the passage from an explanatory paradigm to a narrative paradigm. This is not a painless change, and not all psychoanalysts accept it, because it undermines the explanatory aspect of psychoanalysis itself. Many years later, R. Horacio Etchegoyen (1986) felt the need to distinguish interpretation – as the attribution of a new meaning to the patient's material – from Jasper's primary delusional experience; interpretation, as a hypothesis, never devalues and can always be corrected.

The archaeologist and the analyst thus reconstruct the found material through integrations and recompositions, but the analyst is more fortunate because (s)he is assisted by the transference. The analyst's work then turns to the past, which survives in the present precisely thanks to the transference, which promotes the return of affective relations that are meaningful for the patient. Memory and dreams consequently become fundamental in the reconstructive process in analysis. The memory, reactivated in the dream, connects the experience of the current life with the representations of the older experience and of the most archaic object relationships, with desires, fantasies, but also anxieties and defences, which are activated in the transference. In the analytic process and in the dream, the recovery of affective memory thus becomes the basis for the mind's ability to relive old experiences and attribute new meanings to them by virtue of a retranscription of the memory made possible by the analytic relationship, just as occurs in *Nachtraglichkeit*. Freud's conception of memory is thus complex and less naive than one might think. The construction is in fact a reconstruction and should be understood as a process of emotional retrieval of past experiences and integration with current experiences lived in the transference. Mancia points out, however, that current neurophysiological knowledge suggests that memory should not be seen as an actual reactivation of historically definable experiences (Mancia, 1998). More precisely, Edelman and Tononi (2000, p. 113) write that memory is "a form of constructive re-categorisation of an ongoing experience, not a punctual reproduction of a past sequence of events". Freud thus recognised that memory is not simply an archive, but he lacked the knowledge that would have enabled him to move beyond the concept of representational memory.

Non-representational memory

This aspect can only be understood in the light of current conceptions of consciousness and memory, such as those developed by Tononi and Edelman in their theory of neural group selection (TSGN) or neural Darwinism. This theory is based on some basic concepts that we can only hint at: selection in development, selection with experience, re-entry, degeneration and values. In the early stages of development, the anatomy of the brain is determined by genes and heredity. However, the patterns of synaptic connections are determined by the somatic selection, so that initially myriads of branches form. Some will become stronger, others weaker, as those that discharge together become wired together. The specific behavioural experience will then produce selective *pruning*. This is why a two-year-old child has more connections than his or her paediatrician and an enormous capacity for learning, for example, languages, which fades with time. A very interesting aspect of this theory is something called degeneration. This misleading term actually points to a fundamental property, namely, that in a selective nervous system with an enormous number of neural circuits, there are components that differ in structure but can produce similar results or output signals. Moreover, this implies great advantages, since a "degenerate" system can take advantage of a large number of ways to ensure a given output signal. This aspect cannot fail to remind us of the famous metaphor of the poetry of the mind that Freud had already intuited in his book on aphasia, albeit using much more poetic language. In any case, for Edelman and Tononi, so-called degeneration becomes the very basis for overcoming the concept of representational memory. "Neither cell death, nor changes in one or two circuits, nor even changes in the contextual aspects of incoming signals are sufficient to erase a memory" (ibid., p. 118). This is why non-representational memory is extraordinarily robust.

Freud's idea that the brain is fundamentally concerned with representations, and that what is stored is itself a kind of representation, goes far beyond Freud. Bergson had tried to overcome the common notion that the nervous system serves to produce representations. Yet the idea of representational memory persists today. Edelman and Tononi show that this theory actually creates more problems than it solves. The signals that the brain has to deal with do not, in fact, represent coded input, but are "ambiguous, context-dependent, and not necessarily enriched by a priori judgments about their meaning" (ibid., p. 112). Representation in fact implies a symbolic activity, central to the semantic and syntactic activities of language, whereby recalling what appears to be a previously experienced image suggests that the brain is performing representations. In fact, however,

> there is no pre-coded message in the signal; there are no structures that can store a code with great precision; there is not even a judge in nature to make decisions about alternative patterns, and no homunculus in our heads to read the message.
>
> (ibid., p. 113)

For these reasons, our memory cannot be representational. It is more like immune memory, where antibodies are not representations of specific antigens, but are able to recognise the antigen. Memory "is not a representation, but reflects the way the brain has modified its dynamics to allow repetition of a performance" (ibid.). For Edelman and Tononi, therefore, repetition over time is "a form of constructive re-categorisation of an ongoing experience, not a punctual reproduction of a past sequence of events" (ibid.). With his metaphor of the poetry of the mind and his concept of construction as reconstruction in two, Freud had come very close to understanding the mysteries of memory.

Bion's position

What about Bion? What is Bion's position on memory? Much has been said and written about Bion's references to working without memory, without desire and without understanding. These references belong to the analytic method and have often been a source of misunderstanding. Bion (1970, pp. 70, 107) calls "memory", "memories" or "a memory" the experience of consciously recalling what has been said or done or the *intentional* need to remember; while he calls "remembering" the experience of remembering, and "dream-like memory" the psychic reality that develops in the session and that belongs to the psychoanalytic experience, in which an idea or a figurative impression comes to mind without having been recalled. As far as method is concerned, Bion really does no more than repeat what Freud (1912, p. 112) said in his notes on technique about the physician's need to maintain a *floating attention*:

> He should withhold all conscious influences from his capacity to attend, and give himself over completely to his 'unconscious memory': or, to put it in terms of technique: 'he should simple listen, and not bother about whether he is keeping anything in mind'.

Bion also recalls the letter to Lou Andreas-Salomé in which Freud mentions the method of artificially blinding oneself in order to concentrate all the light on a dark spot. So far, nothing new, or at least nothing to justify so much controversy. However, Bion seems to go *beyond* Freud, even rejecting desire and understanding. The therapist's desire can trap the patient in his or her expectations and prevent him or her from grasping his or her real needs. The distinction between desire and memory is then more difficult than it seems. Both depend on the senses, although "one is the 'past' tense and the other the 'future'" (Bion, 1970, p. 45), but the memory of a missed satisfaction must be classified as desire and still points back to the problems of possession and grievance. By delving into the most primitive mechanisms of thought formation, in search of the unknown, Bion also points to the need to get rid of all prejudices and anticipations, starting with psychoanalytic theories themselves. This is why he is particularly interested in psychoanalytic theories of observation, recalling Darwin's famous statement that thinking is fundamental, but thinking while observing is fatal. Thus, in his *Notes on Memory and Desire*, Bion (1967a, p. 206) says: "The only point of importance in any session is the unknown. Nothing must be allowed to distract from intuiting that". So Bion's position is the opposite of Freud's one? Bion does not observe to find something that has been perceived in the past, nor to find his own ideas, the confirmation of his own theories, but the unknown, the patient him or herself, "the tiger", "O".

In order to understand this aspect and thus Bion's ideas on memory, a step of *Attention and Interpretation* seems to be essential

In the primitive phase, which Freud regards as dominated by the pleasure principle and from which he excludes the operation of memory, this last being dependent on the prior development of a capacity for thought, the prototype of memory appears to reside in one of the aspects of projective identification. The mechanism, employed to fulfill the duties of thought until thought takes over, appears as an interchange first between mouth and breast and then between introjected mouth and introjected breast. This I regard as reaction between container ♀ and contained ♂ [...] The nature of relationship needs investigation. ♀, which may evacuated or retain, is the prototype of a forgetful or retentive memory. Pleasure may be retained if possession is the dominant concern; grievance if a store of ammunition is the main concern. Evacuation may be forcible as if to convert the evacuated object into a missile; introjection likewise as fulfilment of greed. Development of memory that are inevitable to the psyco-analyst are C category elements, the dominance of ♀♂, the primacy of pleasure-pain (in contrast with reality or truth), and 'possession' with its reciprocal, fear of loss; all have been acquired in close association with the senses. The impulse to be rid of painful stimuli gives the 'content' of the memory (♀) an unsatisfactory quality when one is engaged in the pursuit of truth O. The more successful the memory is in its accumulations the more nearly it approximates to resembling a saturated element saturated with saturated elements. An analyst with such a mind is one who is incapable of learning because he is satisfied. Furthermore, because of its primitive nature, his memory is believed to be filled only with objects giving rise to feelings of pleasure and to be empty of unpleasure components, or vice versa. The attitude toward the 'memory' or 'unconscious' depends on the idea that it is a container for the 'evacuations' of projective identification. Such a 'memory' is no equipment for an analyst whose aim is O, as may be seen by considering what is represented by this sign. It stands for the absolute truth...

(Bion, 1970, pp. 28–30)

It is clear from these pages that Bion is not so much interested in the nature of memory and its mechanisms as in its use in the clinic. For Bion, the idea of memory as storage and container/contained relationship is quite primitive and inadequate for the search for truth. A memory so conceived remains tied to the principle of pleasure and pain, hence the tendency to retain what gives pleasure and to evacuate what gives displeasure. Pleasure can be retained depending on whether the preoccupation with possession or its reciprocal, fear of loss, predominates, but it can turn into resentment if the dominant preoccupation is to accumulate a store of ammunition. Evacuation can also be violent, and the evacuated object behaves like a bullet, as does the same introjection under the pressure of greed. All this makes memories misleading and memory as a store totally inadequate for the search for reality or truth, because it remains tied to the senses and the functions of possession and evacuation.

The importance of these concepts can be better understood in the context of the clinic. Bion links the concept of memory as storage, and therefore representational memory, to *moral causality*. And moral causality is the invariant of psychotic transformations. Resentment, need for possession and fear of loss can indeed become dominant elements in borderline disorders and in certain psychotic and traumatic situations. These patients do not allow themselves to investigate, to search for selected facts that give coherence, because there is a conflict between omnipotence and investigation. In these cases, an omniscient and strict God dominates, and the causal chain is set up with the express purpose of preventing investigation. Such patients cannot bear the depressive position due to the dominance of a cruel superego and feel persecuted by feelings of persecution to which they tend to ascribe a causal value. The very feeling of persecution is supported by the need to find a cause, which is used not to understand but to prevent understanding. The patient's communication becomes a circular argument based on a causal theory, but used to destroy contact with reality, where the hated reality is above all the reality of an aspect of the patient's own personality. In fact, these patients live as if blocked by "memories", like hysterical patients of Freud, but with the difference that these memories of resentment are used to prevent the search for truth and growth. I believe that every therapist of a particular experience can count on a vast archive of patients who live in resentment of supposed memories to which they ascribe causal value. However, as Bion (1965, p. 73) reminds us, "Meaning is a function of self-love, self-hate or self-knowledge. It is not logically, but a psycho-logically necessary". These memories, therefore, function as causal theories bordering on delirium. I remember a patient who spent his life complaining about his loneliness, he had a book of missed opportunities, women who gave "signs" of availability, but from whom he always fled. His need to "possess" a woman was dominant, but his resentment against his mother prevented him from approaching woman, and if he did, it was to attack them. In fact, he lived in a continuous hallucinosis. These situations are frequent. Whenever a split creates an internal traumatic object, it creates split object relationships, characterised by the need-fear dilemma, but also by desire-destructiveness, which can be the basis of so-called negative transference, or of lives of suffering, of people who have a great need for love but who are unable to love or be loved because the object of love is at the same time an object of desire and a traumatic object. This aspect of memory as a store of resentment or ammunition is so important that we need to rethink the whole psychopathology of trauma, which the dominant tendency today tends to reify, making it difficult to overcome the position of victimhood. "The more my life is explained on the basis of something already in my chromosomes, something my parents did or failed to do [...], the more my biography will be the story of a victim", writes James Hillman (1996) in his *The Soul's Code*.

This is not to say that Bion's theory does not consider trauma to be a real and active element, for Bion all reality is potentially traumatic. However, Bion's theory allows us, better than any other, to see both sides of the problem and to move away from the dichotomy of idealisation/negation of trauma. For Bion, the use of a causal theory can be indicative of the operation of an "invalid" theory, but it must always be evaluated in the situation in which it appears. If it belongs to column 2 (defensive use of theories) then the assumption that it is pathological is strong, but if it belongs to column 4 (attention) it is instead compatible with healthy development. The issue then is the transformation process by which O is transformed into thought and the developmental processes associated with the links between thoughts. However, the concept of cause and the associated theory of causation do not refer to external reality, but to the psychic reality with which psychoanalysis is concerned. Nonetheless, Bion himself, in a seminar in Rome, raised the problem of the importance of facts and the difficulty of establishing the value to be given to the sensory component in analysis. He observed that we cannot afford to ignore what our senses tell us "because the facts are very few anyway" and complained that in his psychoanalytic training "all of it was verbal. Are we supposed to be blind and deaf to everything except what comes in through the ears?" (Bion, 1977a, p. 101) To the question of a seminar participant on the sign function of emotions and the possibility of feeling with all the senses, Bion gave this answer: "I think that what the patient feels is the nearest thing to a fact"... and it is precisely these "facts", which sometimes emerge as "paradoxes", to which the psychoanalytic "jargon", in vain tries to give a sense and an order (ibid., p. 106). These paradoxes, these "facts", for Bion are the emotions that are transmitted from one body to another, or from one mind to another.

Even so, the problem of facts in psychoanalysis goes far beyond that of emotional experiences, on which Bion dwells and recalls aesthetic knowledge as understood by Wittgenstein. The facts under analysis also imply the possibility and the freedom to speak of the immediate! Christopher Bollas (1999) wonders if today with all our attention to the here and now it is still possible to talk about the immediate. As an "excess of presence" – the immediate – reveals a paradox, as Maurice Blanchot is able to deeply grasp in *L'entretien infini*. The immediate always eludes representation: "The immediate is the presence to which one cannot be present [...] the elusive which it is impossible to get rid of" (Blanchot, 1969, p. 62). Talking about the immediate, about the everyday, is therefore like talking about a traumatic event, which has no meaning, or rather as Bollas (1995, p. 85) observes, "The meaning that arises from a trauma originates from precise facts of life (the so-called fateful moments)", it "imposes itself on the Self, instead of deriving from it". Faced with the story of a real trauma, any creative response is blocked, precisely because the irruption of reality opens up a void of meaning, which only the patient can fill. This corresponds to the Bionian idea, taken up by Civitarese, that in order to have meaning, a fact must first be made unconscious, as we will see more clearly in the next section. At this point, we are reminded of the film *The Past*, which Asghar Farhadi sets in Paris, but in the suburbs, in order to prevent the images of the historic centre, which are too laden with the past, from erasing the thought of the past, which instead had to emerge as memory, or as evolution and dream memory. This is why Bion (1970, p. 108) says that close relatives are unreliable judges of a patient's personality and unsuitable as analysts. They are too burdened with memories.

Nevertheless, the problem of facts, of trauma, which of course relates back to pain, is so complex that it requires a separate treatment and will be developed in a forthcoming volume, *Paradoxes of Pain*. This is an essential point where we are in danger of experiencing the same disappointment as Meltzer (1978) when he wrote that Bion keeps postponing the explanation of the source of hate for growth. This is manifested, together with -K and -L, in the intolerance of pain associated with catastrophic change, for the discussion of which Bion refers to Chapter 12 of *Attention and Interpretation*. But in this text the expression "catastrophic change" disappears, reduced to a faint trace in the famous sentence: "In memory, time is of the essence. Time has often been regarded as being of the essence of psychoanalysis; in the growth process it has no part. Mental evolution or growth is catastrophic and time-less" (Bion, 1970, pp. 107–18). Indeed, the time of growth remains mysterious, ineffable and naturally time is not always associated with growth, but also with decline. Rather than time, growth seems to refer to mysterious internal processes, in which the concept of expiation, one of the meanings of atonement, retains an essential role in the balanced development of the mind, because it is linked to the fear of megalomania, the fear of assuming a position of creativity, which unconsciously amounts to taking the place of the Creator (Bion, 1967, p. 145).

The ancient Greek word for cause, *aitia,* guilt, bears the indelible mark of a close connection between guilt and causality. The patient who can tolerate frustration is aware of objects, time and space, but the patient who cannot tolerate it is deprived of past and future, because the same factors that reduce the breast to a point reduce time to an hour. The source of the patient's anxiety is his/her fear of depression and the associated fear of using the PS↔D oscillation and the mechanisms of the selected fact necessary for the investigation. In psychotic patients and groups, therefore, the search for the meaning to be attributed to the constant conjunction through the PS↔D process can be destroyed by the need to search for causality linked to morality. In these situations, the solution to a problem is more easily accepted if it is attributed to causality with moral components rather than to free thought; in this sense, "causation, responsibility and therefore a controlling force (as opposed to helplessness) provide a framework within which omnipotence reigns" (Bion, 1965, p. 64). Anyone interested in psychosomatic or somato-psychotic problems can confirm the frequent association of serious somatic illnesses with moral components. Meltzer's hypothesis that piles of β-elements can embed themselves in the body, causing tumours and possibly other conditions such as mental deterioration, goes in this direction. Bion extends this to the group often dominated by morality, where it is reflected in controversies such as the war between Science and

Religion. In fact, this component of moral causality seems to be an almost automatic tendency of the human mind, from which it can only free itself with considerable effort. In this sense, Farhadi's beautiful film *The Past* is an extraordinary example of what moral causality means. In it, all the characters struggle to find the cause, and thus the guilt, of the unlivable drama in which they find themselves. This makes them prisoners of a past that they cannot forget, or even know, but only reduce to some concrete and factual reason, such as the search for a cause-fault, but behind a cause, there is always another, in an endless circular postponement, whereby a suicide can be linked to depression, and depression to cheating, and cheating to a depression-wracked relationship, and so on ad infinitum, until it becomes clear that the problem is just like freeing oneself from this mechanism of moral causality, and this can only happen through growth and love which suspend the search for guilt (cause).

Civitarese's hypothesis on the theory and genesis of time in Bion

In a recent work, Civitarese (2019) puts forward the hypothesis that in *A Theory of Thinking* Bion elaborates an original theory of time and its genesis. The work, dense and sophisticated, requires a direct and in-depth reading, but it deserves the risk of an attempt at synthesis, in the hope of being able to outline the many points of originality of this precious and complex work. Civitarese starts from the distinction between *conception* and *thought*, which Bion associates with the child's experience of fulfilment and frustration, respectively. The sequence that Bion indicates for the development of thought is known. The image of a newborn that couples his or her expectation of breast (pre-conception), with an absent breast, "no-breast", corresponds to the model of thought; the emotional experience of satisfaction, given by the encounter of a pre-conception with the real breast, instead leads to a conception. Thinking, therefore, develops when the newborn realises the absence of an available breast, so the ability to tolerate frustration, or pain, marks the fate of not meeting the real breast, "no-breast". If this ability is sufficient, the "no-breast" becomes a thought and the apparatus for thinking develops; if it is inadequate, the newborn has a painful emotional experience which (s)he cannot think, but only to evacuate as a beta element, through projective identification. In other words, the infant has the feeling of a bad object, and instead of developing the apparatus for thinking, it develops an apparatus for ridding the psyche of the accumulation of bad internal objects. And yet, if there is a good mutual adaptation between mother and child, even projective identification can be considered realistic and "an early form of that which later is called a capacity for thinking" (Bion, 1962, p. 37). In these rapid and dense passages, Bion thus outlines his theory of thinking, based on the clear distinction between thoughts and thinking activity, the latter understood as the development imposed on the psyche by the pressure of the thoughts themselves.

Civitarese's work meticulously deconstructs and reconstructs these passages without ever losing sight of Bion's text and thought, which he enriches with implicit and unspoken elements. His hypothesis is that "conception" and "thought" must be considered together in a dialectical relationship in which each term simultaneously negates and affirms the other. A matrix, then, that gives rise to a pre-reflective first temporal order, which only assumes the status of subjective time – both in terms of duration and abstract representation – when it is incorporated into the symbolic order through the function of language. For Civitarese, the encounter of a pre-conception of the breast with the mere alternation of its presence and absence cannot generate a concept of time until the experience is given a name. It is only through the effect of this essential concomitance that the dialectic of conception and thought organises the horizontal transition between the two opposing affective states of pleasure and displeasure and the vertical transition from the concrete to the symbolic. In this way, the subject temporally structures its existence in terms of past, present and future, and later on on the basis of a consensual and measurable time. This hypothesis is therefore consistent with Bion's theory of the mind, which is entirely relational, and thought without a thinker is possible because relation and sociality precede the emergence of the subject. The child is as a result spoken to by language, because it is subject to it, and speaks language, that is (s)he expresses him or herself and gives a meaning to things; two vertices of subjectivity, passive and active, which are, respectively, unconscious and conscious.

Civitarese observes that although Bion presents his concept of thinking as a reinterpretation of Freud, he is actually trying to solve the problems that Freud left unresolved. Freud and Bion both place frustration at the centre of the development of thought. For Freud, the development of the reality principle passes through the double frustration of hallucinatory satisfaction and the discovery that it is illusory. However, there is no reference in his theory to the ability to tolerate frustration, and the development of thought is configured as an autonomous process of the ego. Paradoxically, greater frustration should correspond to a greater drive towards the reality principle. Freud warns that his view of the construction of thought is a "fiction" which takes maternal care for granted, evoked as a simple supply of "warmth" (ibid., p. 184). It is therefore a solipsistic view that stages the fiction of a child who manages to overcome the frustration of the absence of the breast on his or her own. Despite the intuition of the birth of consciousness as awareness of pain and the idea of crying as the prelude to mother-child communication, the development of thought and the subject in Freud thus follows a drive-based, intrasubjective and phantasmatic path, which he calls a "fiktion". And in this narrative, there is no place for an analysis of the quality of the relationship.

Consequently, Bion is not just making a correction, he is building a whole new model of the mother-infant relationship. By introducing a concept of projective identification that considers both poles of the relationship, Bion actually opens up the possibility of observing the quality of the relationship. Civitarese points out that only post-Freudian psychoanalysis, aware of infant observation, the contributions of Winnicott, attachment theory and neuroscientific research into the early mother-infant relationship, could truly fill the gaps left by Freud. His analysis, though, shows that Bion's theory of thinking and the formation of the unconscious remains the most important attempt to show the importance of the quality of the relationship in the growth and development of the apparatus of thought.

Bion thus focuses the problem on the ability to tolerate frustration which, if insufficient, drives the child to evacuate the bad breast through the mechanism of projective identification. When this intolerance is high, there is evasion through destructive attacks on the perception and consciousness of reality data: "space and time are perceived as identical with a bad object that is destroyed, that is to say a no-breast" (Bion, 1967, p. 113). The prevalence of projective identification thus leads to confusion between the self and external objects, and to the destruction of time, as in the Mad Hatter episode in *Alice in Wonderland*, where it was always four o'clock.

The hypothesis that in *A Theory of Thinking* Bion actually introduces a theory of time thus appears in all his evidence from clinical work. Nonetheless, Civitarese is convinced that Bion was aware that he was about to engage in philosophical speculation, because from the very beginning, he seems to apologise for the similarity between his theory and philosophical theories. Was Bion afraid of coming across as an amateur philosopher?

Civitarese merely points out Bion's explicit references to Kant's thought. Following Kant, Bion makes the theory of knowledge coincide with the theory of becoming a subject, shifting his interest from the content to the development of the container, with enormous consequences for psychoanalytic theory and practice. However, Bion quickly distances himself from Kant's transcendentalism by rooting the process of thought in experience and the intersubjective process. The very pillars of Kant's conception of time and space as a priori forms of knowledge are thus called into question. When the infant, in order to reduce the sense of persecution that afflicts it, eliminates the bad breast through projective identification, it also eliminates from itself "the space of proto-subjectivity that is both private and common" (Civitarese, 2019, p. 190). In order to survive, the infant has no choice but to cling to the object, to identify itself with it. Time liquefies and space collapses, as in Salvador Dali's painting *La persistenza de la memoria* or *Los relojes derretidos*. Bion thus roots the origin of the form of time and space in experience and makes it coincide with the development of subjectivity. With a precise weaving and reference to other parallel texts such as *Learning from Experience*, Civitarese shows how Bion's point of view is entirely relational and even systemic, moving from considering the child's limited capacity to tolerate frustration to the "*the degree of receptivity denoted by the object's response*" (ibid.). The bifurcation between the path of avoidance and the path of frustration modification is related to the mother-child or analyst-patient pair, and the decisive factor is the measure of the quality of the relationship, which is related to the object's capacity for reverie. In this passage, Civitarese recognises the support of Winnicott's admirable description of the recursive process between mother and child, which in the transitional area allows the passage from omnipotence to the development of the child's ability to use the object. All this opens up the importance of the analyst's receptivity to the factors involved in treatment.

Returning to Bion (1967, p. 115), he writes that when the infant feels that its projective identification is not accepted, "the infant is reduced to continued projective identification carried out with increasing force and frequency. The increased force seems to denude the projection of its penumbra of meaning". Intolerance to frustration or doubt, as an element favouring the expansion of the psychic container, causes the infant to behave as if (s)he had inside an object similar to a greedy "sinus-vagina", which destroys the goodness of everything which (s)he receives or gives, leaving him or her alone with degenerate objects. Space and time are also destroyed. Tolerance, understood as a complex interpsychic and intrapsychic experience, is then the real factor that establishes the shape of time and space. Bion speaks of a "well-balanced-mother", capable of accepting projective identification, which at this point becomes "realistic", i.e., a normal form of mother-infant communication, which if it does not exist, leads to a failure to introject the alpha function (ibid.). Bion, therefore, hypothesises that Freud's theory of consciousness, as a sense organ of psychic qualities, is no longer satisfactory and introduces the concept of alpha function, which by giving rise to alpha elements, builds a contact barrier, whose function is to separate the conscious from the unconscious seen according to a binocular vision.

For this reason, Civitarese attempts an in-depth analysis of the birth of the form of time. The main idea is that the relational development of the subject does not reside in the mere satisfaction of the instinctual impulse, but in the development of meaning, which is lost when the object – mother/Other – cannot accept the infant's manifestations of pain. In the beginning, all sensations are conscious, which means that they lack meaning. Sensations only acquire meaning when they are rendered unconscious: "rendering unconscious is equivalent to immersing perceptions in the field of human meanings" (Civitarese, 2019, p. 194). At birth there is an exchange through the normal route of projective identification "between the rudimentary consciousness and maternal reverie" (Bion, 1967, p. 116), and only with time does the child learn to "unconscious".

Civitarese's central question, then, is whether the sense of time can truly arise from the mere juxtaposition of punctual events and their merely intellectual apprehension. "What would then be the origin of the essential aspects of the experience *of duration and the directionality of time?*" (Civitarese, 2019, p. 195). To explain the emergence of the sense of time, Civitarese so postulates that "a conception is *alive* in a thought and that a thought is *alive* in a conception" (ibid.). When it is claimed that thought arises from the ability to tolerate frustration, the essence of this dialectic is lost, as if the source of a thought could lie in an encounter with a mere void or lack – the *gap* – rather than in the controlled interplay of figure and background, of satisfaction and frustration. However, a thought cannot arise from mere frustration unless the frustration has been identified with the gradual fading of an experience of concrete satisfaction in the pale form of a psychic trace and under the impulse of an imaginative anticipation of a new experience of satisfaction. This point is essential. The coupling of a pre-conception of a breast with the mere absence of a breast cannot generate a thought if it is not preceded by the conception of a breast, preserved as a mnestic impression or as a hallucinatory anticipatory vision of the future. The frustration arising from the experience of the absence of a breast must, therefore, be imagined as the gradual virtualisation of the experience of the breast, according to the metaphor of the progressive thinning of an elastic band stretched to hold together the extremes of the past and the present. In this sense, a modicum of realisation persists in a thought, just as an element of negative realisation persists in a conception.

Thus what we imagine as a diachronic succession between discontinuous and antithetical segments is also a synchronic and simultaneous relationship. In this way, the quality of harmony and melody of the encounter with the object transforms a simple succession into a rhythm. The present appears as a controlled coming and going between implicit and explicit memories, between the past and the future, a pleasant meeting of fantasies between what has been and what one hopes will be. The stuff of time, which is the same as that of the psyche, can then only be formed in a dialectical relationship based primarily on the physical capacity to retain traces of memory of positive and negative realisations. The bond of metonymic/metaphoric contact connects two or more elements, in such a way that being in tension or of opposite sign, they affirm and deny each other. This mutual influence is conditioned by the existence of "proximity" relationships between the elements involved. In the absence of this proximity relationship, the dynamic situation of mutual involvement is lost till a complete dissolution. The matrix of the sense of existence therefore emerges when a set of synchronic groups deriving from the quantitative and qualitative aspects of the relationship are arranged along a diachronic axis, becoming significant.

Civitarese's hypothesis is that thought could be the very factor that directs lived time towards the future, "as an expectation" (ibid., p. 196), and the direction of the arrow of time can, therefore, be seen as an "avant-coup", as an anticipation, as a glimpse before the end of the melody, as the order of time allows. It is in this anticipation, in this foresight, that the advantage of a relative predictability of things emerges, and the course of events is set within a horizon of expectation and meaning. Civitarese's question is then crucial: "Now is this having-barely-in-sight [...] not a synonym of no-breast?" (ibid., p. 197). The meaning lies in the search for the object (pleasure) or, at a more primitive level, in the avoidance of pain (grief), but both situations contain the negative element of an absence that persists in the presence and vice versa. The equation of the dialectic "breast ↔ no-breast" can then be rewritten as "breast ↔ (no→breast)", in which the arrow in brackets, between a minus sign [-] and a direction sign [>], strongly suggests that the origin of "intentionality", defined in philosophy as the awareness of an object, is the direction of time (ibid.).

According to Civitarese, philosophical theories lack a convincing explanation of why we experience time as flowing towards the future, because they are biased towards abstract representations that do not take into account affects. His hypothesis is that the flow of time corresponds precisely to "*affective tension*" and that, despite conscious experience, it is not so much a "*directing-oneself-towards*", or a "*going-close-to*", or a "*being-attracted*", as a "*distancing-oneself-from*", or a "*being-driven*" (ibid.). For Freud, the object arises out of hate, and the narcissistic ego performs a "*primordial repudiation*" of the overstimulating external world. What, then, is being rejected if not pain? The common perception of time as a kind of metaphysical space in which we move then reflects a profound intuition. The container that comprises time, that *supplies* time, is the object as container for anxiety in the Bion's sense, the agent capable of performing the specific action of repressing that anxiety. Thought for Bion is thus not just a lack, or a "no". The expression, indivisible, is in fact "no-breast", where "breast" stands for the memory/concept of satisfaction and, in the state of deprivation, also for an appearance of presence that directs desire. No-breast, or crossed-out "no-breXast", would then be what Bion calls *nougthiness*, the state of nameless terror, the experience of an absolute emptiness of meaning, without even the memory of the concept of the thing. If the no-breast is reduced to a mere "no" or nothingness, then there is no reverberation space, no retina to intercept the vibrations of light from the multiplicity of memory traces of the real breast. What is time, then, if not an experience of echo, as when a sound hits an obstacle or a point of reflection, a perception in memory and then, infinitely, of memory in a new perception? As a matter of course, there would be no echo without the no, without an obstacle, as in the absurd situation of an infant who never leaves the breast, or when the obstacle is infinitely far away. What moves Echo is his unsatisfied love for Narcissus. The arrow of time (minus and verso) must also be supported by another element, that of "*intensity*", expressed from another point of view in the concept of proximity. Conception and thought, the experience of satisfaction and experience of frustration, cannot then be separated. The former flows into the latter and the latter is experienced in the former.

The two concepts are linked by a mutually inclusive, dialectical relationship. At the birth of the psyche, however, an adjustment of the distance between these two elements is necessary. Only when the intensity falls within a tolerable range can the two forms of experience remain in relationship, so that the elastic band holding them together does not break or collapse, as when time stands still. The concept of intensity can thus be related to the subjective sensation of time passing quickly or slowly.

What makes the alternation of "breast" and "no-breast", i.e., of conception and thought, not a mere succession of empirical data, but a dialectic, is thus the factor of time, which is hidden in the concept of tolerating frustration. However, Civitarese goes further and proposes the hypothesis that time, as a sense of being, is also the product of the rhythms of breast and no-breast presentation. In phylogeny, it is the intervals that allow the human species to gradually acquire language and, consequently, primary temporality, lived time and its abstract representation as linear time. In ontogeny, the sense and the concept of time are absent in the infant, but already present in the object (the mother), so that from birth the infant is immersed in a matrix capable of interacting with the dynamic structuring necessary to establish the order of time. The infant, therefore, acquires the concept of time from the experience of the primary relationship. What the mother gifts to her child is time! It is the mother who weaves the warp (physical, semiotic, implicit or procedural) of meaning, the threads of which will later be incorporated into concepts. In this sense, we can say that the mother gives time to the child and that the name (language) is the means of access to the symbolic level. From a genetic point of view, therefore, it is the rhythm of care that establishes the primitive structure of time in an infant. At first, there is rather a pre-conception of time, while a true consciousness of time (of the self, of being) only emerges later, when the name is added to the dialectic of realisation/non-realisation. At this point, the triangulation of *conception*, *thought* and *name*, which allows access to the symbolic level, has been internalised. Kant conceives of the transcendence of time and space as *a priori* forms of sensible intuition, while Heidegger attributes transcendence to primary temporality (*Zeitlichkeit*), from which the sense of experienced time (*Zeit*) and the abstract representation of measurable linear time derive. Civitarese asks whether this transcendence can be translated by means of psychoanalytic concepts into a present knowledge, especially a schematic or procedural knowledge of the body, bringing it closer to Merleau-Ponty's form of embedded temporality.

How then does lived time emerge? In the at-one-moment there is a state of complete oneness that corresponds to conception, which is an experience of complete satisfaction. The author invites us to think of this as a *fractal model* of what we call experience, a model in which the same structure is recursively repeated at different scales. This allows the mother to make connections between the breast and the no-breast, as in the game of spools, where repetitions and variations allow the infant to formulate thoughts and later to connect them into second-degree thoughts, represented by dream thoughts and waking thoughts.

At-one-ment, atonement, sacrifice and reconciliation with divinity suggest a sinusoidal curve related to atonement and guilt. With *at, one, ment*, Bion also seems to invoke the trinity, which can be seen as the coincidence of three moments, *conception, act of naming* and *thought*, i.e., the three ways of experiencing time: future, present and past. Cleverly playing with the word decomposed, Civitarese observes that the *at-one-ment* also indicates the temporal progression of a subject that is always outside itself, extending from the past to the future and vice versa. "At", from the Latin *ad*, is, in fact, an expression of position or movement towards; "one" suggests unity, union; while "ment" is a suffix derived from *mentum*, which added to word roots, indicates the result of an action. The "at" in the sense of "towards" thus expresses the future direction, the thought arising from the absence of the object, which is never absolute; the "ment" corresponds to the positive realisation, the experience of satisfaction, the concept or the past. The "one" expresses the present, because between an "after" (at), which comes first in the word, and a "before" (-ment), which comes after, it denotes the synthesis of being one with the object and thus united with the wider network of sociality. At the heart of the compound word, "one", thus significantly expresses the concept of oneness as a proto-concept that is initially emotional/affective and as a result the first emergence of self-consciousness. The central part of the word consequently refers to both processes of mutual recognition between mother and child, which at first can only be non-verbal or semiotic, and later includes the identification of the mother-child dyad with the divine aspect of language and community.

This aspect is barely hinted at in Bion's work, but Civitarese underlines its centrality. In order to arrive at the establishment of temporality and its derivatives, the naming of the thing is an indispensable factor. From the child's point of view, once the breast/no-breast dialectic (conception and thought) has been established thanks to the mother, this dialectic can be understood as the implicit primary matrix of time. The third stage, the naming of things, the *concept*, is, on the contrary, essential in order to arrive at lived time. The grafting of temporality into a child's body, a prelude to opening up to the world of life, takes place when the object fixes conceptions and thoughts, or when it gives a name to the infinite experiences of presentation and representation linked together in a relationship of mutual affirmation/negation. This is what gives the infant access to the *concept*. Only when the consciousness of the self is intersubjectively established can the infant begin to be, that is to have consciousness of time as experience or presence to itself. The present is subjectively experienced as the only thing that exists, since conception and thought are nothing but traces of the past and future, respectively. We are aware of the past and the future, but only in the present; we project backwards and forwards, but always from the present. At the same time, we must be aware that the present is the sum of something that is no longer there and something that is not yet there. The present, therefore, consists of "two no-things" (ibid., p. 200). The present does not exist in itself. The "now", which emerges from the dialectical relationship of elements that simultaneously negate and affirm each other, must subsequently be thought of as a paradoxical place that both exists and does not exist.

Civitarese puts forward a hypothesis about its nature. The *present*, the Cartesian experience of cogito, the unquestionability of being in the here and now, is the awareness provided by the name (concept, language, O/other), obtained by means of the moments of at-one-ment, in the differential play of psychic traces. Although identical in internal psychological structure and external/material/neurological terms, they differ in subjective content and direction. It is, therefore, to the awareness of the functional division between perception and representational activity – at the level of memory and imagination, respectively – that Bion's concepts of conception and thought can be traced. The "now" exists insofar as it is the concept of the self-derived from the abstractions of its infinite memory records. Returning to the problem of "name", we must recognise in it its nature as process and the coincidence of its structure with that of temporality. When we speak of name, concept or abstraction, we are referring to the dialectic of recognition and intersubjectivity. The present thus shares the paradoxical nature of psyche and language. Linguistic signs do not exist individually, but only as elements of the linguistic system. The relationship between the thing and the no-thing, between the inherent change of the real and its intuitions in the subject as time and space, is no different from the paradoxical relationship between every name and the thing it denotes, for example, the word cat and the animal cat. The *tending-towards* or *distancing-from*, of the arrow in "no → breast", can only be revealed to consciousness as it is *now*, by virtue of the *in-between* of language, the nature of which is radically intersubjective. Perception itself, on the one hand, is condensed into representations, while on the other hand, being conscious, it is a phenomenon of mediation in every event. The present can, therefore, only exist in the virtual space of intersubjectivity and language. That is why the name is indispensable. If the breast is a psychosomatic or somato-psychic breast, that is to say, an agent that firstly replaces the infant with bodily and semiotic meanings and then with more properly psychic (conceptual, linguistic) meanings, then without this second component, self-consciousness, temporality is incomplete. What is missing is the ego (-one-), which feels its effects and reports to itself the feelings of being moved in opposite directions owing to the simultaneous presence of conflicting affective tensions, towards the past (-*ment*) and the future (*at-*). The subject feels alive when the sum of these forces is directed towards the future, when the avoidance of pain coexists with the belief in the possibility of finding the object again.

In conclusion, although the origins of time remain a mystery, it can be said that a sophisticated conception of time emerges in the work "A Theory of Thinking" through the concepts of "breast, no breast, at-one-ment, conception, thought, name and projective identification" (ibid., p. 202). The primary structure of time is explored by Bion in the primitive relationship with the mother, in the intersubjective emergence of the infant's coming into the world in its relationship with the breast and the object. However, it does not derive from a succession of discontinuous elements arranged along an infinitely long timeline, but from the movements of an indivisible totality intersubjectively perceived in the consciousness of the self. Space-time, or time-space, cannot be thought of as a property or entity of the physical world, as absolute time exists in itself, independent of what makes us human. It is more reasonable to think of it as a form of human understanding of the world, determined by history and mediated by language, like subjectivity itself, with which it in fact coincides. In a word, Civitarese concludes, perhaps, a long, long time ago – to paraphrase Ian McEwan – time (the now) was begotten, and is over and over again begotten, by pain.

Notes

1 For the description and analysis of Munch's Scream, I refer to some of my works: Rugi G. 1989; 1996; 2011; 2015.
2 The page indications refer to the translation by N. M. Paul and W. S. Palmer: *Matter and Memory*, 1911.

Chapter 5

Stray thoughts. Philosophy and neurobiology in dialogue with Bion's theory of time and thinking

Philosophical counterpoints

Is Bion's theory of thought limited to psychoanalytic practice or is it a general theory of the development of the capacity to think? Bion seems to pose this question from the very beginning of *A Theory of Thinking*, pointing out its similarity to philosophical theories. Naturally, like any psychoanalytic theory, Bion's theory of thinking has practical aims and needs to be empirically verified, so its natural place remains in the space of analysis. However, the fact that Bion compares the patient-analyst relationship to the mother-child relationship inevitably places Bion's theory within a general theory of the development of the capacity to think. Not only is it that. When he states that his theory overturns current theories which conceive of thinking as a product of thinking itself, Bion seems to take his challenge directly to the philosophical level. The hypothesis that thinking is related to the development that the pressure of thought itself imposes on the psyche is *a reversal* that goes far beyond the realm of analysis and the mother-child relationship. It is a philosophical idea.

The similarity of Bion's theory to philosophical theories of thought is deeper than Bion himself would like to admit. Philosophers, clearly, have dealt with the same subject matter, and Bion's philosophical knowledge is often beyond our expectations, so much so that Meltzer himself was taken aback. However, as Civitarese observes, it is likely that the psychoanalyst Bion had some fear of coming across as an amateur philosopher, or of straying too far from the proper terrain of empirical psychoanalysis. This is why his incipit appears as an *excusatio non petita*. Bion, however, does not pretend to be a philosopher, but has no qualms about using philosophical thought *to think* his theories. This is also another mark of how he differs from Freud. In his theory of thinking, Bion makes extensive use of Kantian philosophy,

DOI: 10.4324/9781032655239-7

linking the development of thought to the development of the subject. The importance of this aspect in contemporary psychoanalysis has been widely emphasised by Civitarese. However, the author points out how Bion distances himself from Kant's transcendentalism. By rooting the thought process in experience and intersubjective process, Bion locates the form of the primary structure of time in the primary relationship with the mother, in the intersubjective emergence of the infant's coming into the world. The stuff of time becomes the stuff of the psyche, which can only be formed in a dialectical relationship based on the physical capacity to retain traces of memory of positive and negative realisations. The container that contains time, that provides time, is thus the object (mother) as a container of fear or rather of pain in the Bionian sense. Space-time or time-space cannot, therefore, be thought of as a property or entity of the physical world, as absolute time existing in itself, but only in relation to what makes us human. In this sense, Bion seems to remain Kantian. Like the Königsberg philosopher, Bion believes that time is not a thing in itself, that time does not exist in itself, but is a purely subjective state of sensory intuition, and that apart from the human subject, time is nothing. Civitarese shows that for Bion, time can be likened to an echo experience, and clearly there would be no echo without no, without an obstacle, frustration and pain. The arrow of time is as a result based on the ability of the maternal container to give the infant time, so that (s)he can learn to dream his or her pain. It is in the complex dialectical relationship between frustration and satisfaction, between conception and thought, in the happy rhythm between appearance and disappearance, that the infant acquires a proto-feeling of time, and therefore the ability to experience the present as a coming and going between implicit and explicit memories, between past and future, in a pleasant meeting of fantasies between what has been and what (s)he hopes will happen again. The confidence in the subject's temporal progression from the past to the future and vice versa is thus born from the numerous happy moments of at-one-ment.

The rhythm of care thus establishes in the infant the primitive structure of time, which is initially more of a pre-feeling, while a true consciousness of time only emerges later, when the name is added to the dialectic of realisation/non-realisation. It is only at this point that the triangulation of *conception, thought* and *name*, which allows access to the symbolic, can be said to be internalised. Civitarese thus attempts to translate Kantian transcendence in terms of present, procedural, bodily knowledge, bringing it closer to Merleau-Ponty's form of embedded temporality. This aspect represents an enormous step forward in understanding the origin of the form of time. Nevertheless, it seems to lend itself to the same criticisms that have been levelled at Kant's conception of time since Trendelemburg (Alweiss, 2002). For it is one thing to say that we can only know time from a human perspective, and quite another to say that it does not exist apart from the subject. Another critical aspect of Kant's theory of time is that while it gives time an essentially human dimension, an "I think" that guarantees the difference and unity of our experience, it is conceived from the point of view of eternity. In this sense, Kant adheres to the Platonic vision that defines time as "the image of eternity", a vision that in fact conditions all Western metaphysics, characterised by the desire to defeat time and mortality, to which the Freudian position of the timeless unconscious also corresponds. For Kant, it is necessary to distinguish between the (empirical) consciousness of time and the transcendental consciousness that corresponds to "I think", since any synthesis presupposes a consciousness of our synthetic activity, a consciousness that is distinct from the empirical self that changes through time. This "I think" is never something that is represented, but the formal structure that makes the representation of anything possible. For Kant (1787), time is thus "a pure form of sensible intuition", a constituent form of our thinking, inherent in it, through which we interpret the phenomena that arise at the moment of experience. The representation of time does not emerge from the senses, but is presupposed by them. For Kant, then, time is not an ordering structure that we learn to know through experience, but the condition of thinkability, an *a priori* form inherent in us that allows us to speak of a before and an after. In *Transcendental Aesthetics*, then, Kant posits time as a form of sensible intuition, i.e., the principle of *a priori* knowledge. In this sense, it is transcendent. Does Bion's conception, which distances itself from Kantian transcendentalism, rooting the origin of the form of time in the intersubjective emergence of the infant, also manage to renounce the Kantian idea of defining time starting from the idea of eternity? To understand how much Bion truly distances himself from Kant, however, it is necessary to delve deeper into the philosophical foundations of his thinking theory.

What does it mean to think?

Bion's question of what it means to "think thoughts" refers back to a philosophical work that is not usually taken into account. *What does it mean to think?* is the title of a famous text by Heidegger (1954) with which Bion's theory of thinking has more than a few points in common. Bion did not speak German, and Heidegger's text was published in English in 1968. It is, therefore, highly unlikely that Bion was familiar with this work. The differences between the two authors could not be greater, but this makes their affinities all the more significant. Heidegger distinguished four ways of approaching the same question as Bion: What does the word "thinking" mean? What does the traditional doctrine of thinking, logic, mean by thinking? What are the conditions we need in order to really think? What is it that requires us, orders us, calls us to think?

The German philosopher asserts that man does not yet think, that science does not think in the proper sense of the thinking of thinkers, but that thinking resides in the ultimate speech of poetry, that the poetic word resides in the truth of beauty, and that what impels us to think is thought itself. Heidegger distinguishes between *thinking, (Denken), thought, (Gedachtes)* and the thought, *(Gedanke),* and argues that myth is that which subsists in its original utterance, that the essence of man is not in science but in relation, that meaning is not perceptible to the senses: "the non-sensible in concepts is their sense, the meaning" (ibid., v. 2, p. 22). In these statements, we must then recognise that the way in which Heidegger approaches the problem of thinking has unexpected and surprising points of contact with Bion's theory.

Bion himself distinguishes between "thinking" and "thoughts" and, like Heidegger, overturns theories that consider thoughts to be a product of the faculty of thinking. The hypothesis of the precedence of thoughts over thinking is thus a radical gesture that Bion shares with the philosopher, together with the conviction that the activity of thinking is still in an embryonic state. Thinking becomes a consequence of the pressure exerted by thoughts on the mind, a response to the challenge posed by the very existence of thoughts. Thoughts are thus antecedent to thinking, and the development of thinking is linked to the need for a method and an apparatus for dealing with thoughts.

Bion's theory of thinking as a result contrasts with current theories that consider thinking as the product of an autonomous function of the ego. The ability to think becomes a function hardly conquered by the infantile ego starting from the emotional experiences lived by those who take care of the child; in other words, the ability to think becomes a *relational function*. With Civitarese we have seen the complex passages of the development of this function, in the relationship with the breast and the object, and in the importance of language and culture in which the child is immersed from the very beginning. The ability to think cannot therefore be assumed once and for all; it involves various steps and must continually be regained. The transition from technological thinking to thinking that assumes responsibility for thinking is essential, which implies the ability to assume one's own contents and in particular "the responsibility for thinking about violence, aggression, death" (Neri, 1995, p. 96).

This last aspect suggests that Bion was familiar, at least in its main lines, with *Being and Time*, (*Sein und Zeit*), published in German in 1927. An important text in which Heidegger expresses the thesis that time finds its meaning not in eternity, but in death, understood not as an event that is not part of our experience, but as a way of being, as an awareness of one's own mortality and sense of finitude. Heidegger rejects the current philosophical view that takes eternity as the starting point for understanding the meaning of time. For the philosopher, death and time are modes of being as being. Death is the end of being-in-being, and as an end, it is interpreted from man's-being-for-death. Time thus finds its meaning in the original temporality of *Dasein*, of Being. Heidegger thus radicalises our notion of freedom and responsibility, placing them in the sense of the finitude of being in the world (*Dasein*). The task of philosophy returns to that of Plato's Phaedrus, namely, to manage and contain the fear of death. Heidegger calls us to confront death because only by seriously considering our mortality and finitude will we be able to give meaning to our existence. Death is always present and as such grounds the possibility of all possibilities. Blanchot (1955), whom Bion loved to quote, therefore, states that *Being and Time* can be read as a desire to transform the fear of death into a passion; death, in the human perspective, becomes a task without which it is not possible to take responsibility for our time and our being in the world. In *God, Death and Time*, Levinas (1993) tries to overcome Heidegger's position, avoiding from the beginning to reduce the human questioning to the question of what being is, which would reduce death, although certain, to the alternation of being /nothing. Behind the anguish for his own death, Levinas sees the responsibility of the other, for the death of the other, and therefore his own responsibility as a survivor. "And then – asks Levinas – does not time perhaps require a different interpretation from the projection towards the future?" (ibid., p. 103). To overcome the sense of finiteness of *Dasein*, Levinas resorts to Bergson, the philosopher with whom Bion appears in a continuous secret dialogue. For Bergson, finiteness and death are not inscribed in duration, but in the degradation of energy. Life is duration, vital impulse, and creative freedom. Not only is it this. Duration becomes the very possibility of being able to launch an appeal to the interiority of the other, which in the role of saint and hero, leads to a religion in which death no longer makes sense. In any case, regardless of the thought of philosophers, human beings do not have the experience of their own death at their disposal, just as they do not have the experience of eternity, so that original time remains incomprehensible. For Heidegger, the primary phenomenon of authentic temporality is the future, and the human future is death, although paradoxically in *Being and Time* there is no death, at least not the experience of our death, which is reduced to the experience of anguish. For Heidegger, it is through the experience of anguish that one can access nothingness. For Bergson, it is impossible to think of nothingness, which remains linked to the degradation of energy, to a state of physical death, with no difference in potential. Entropic death.

These brief forays into philosophy should make it clear that Bion cannot be reduced to Kant, Bergson or Heidegger, but that he uses the ideas of these thinkers in a very subjective way to construct his own theory of thought and the genesis of time. Bion uses Kant to identify the theory of knowledge and the development of the subject (and time); Heidegger for the awareness of finitude that makes us human as temporal beings; he uses Bergson for the sense of time as duration, life impulse and creative freedom. However, all these ideas, like stray thoughts, only enter his elaboration of the concept of time after he has already encountered the time-wasting patient in the analysis room and many other clinical experiences of the destruction and creation of time and space. The result is something completely new, different, in which clinical experience, and therefore empirical work, always remains the true foundation, the true source, to which he always returns.

The time of neurobiology

The neurobiology of time has a mythical beginning. It began around 1850, when Herman von Helmholtz discovered *le temps perdu*. Between the electrical stimulation of the motor nerve and the contraction of the muscle, Helmholtz showed that there is a latency, a time that passes without us being aware of it, at least for consciousness. Marcel Proust probably heard this expression from his father, who was a doctor. Are literature and psychoanalysis perhaps sciences of lost time? Today, neuroscience no longer speaks of "lost time", but of "compressed time" and "retroactive referral time", as Benjamin Libet (2004) refers to the neuronal delay between event and consciousness, which means that we become aware of a sensory perception with a delay of about half a second. A long latency of which we are unaware, thanks to a complex dynamic calibration that unifies the perception of different stimuli and cancels out the time it takes the associative cortex to make the stimuli conscious. Studies carried out since the 1960s by the physiologist Libet show that what we are aware of has already happened half a second before. We consequently live in the past, or rather in a retrospective present, and not only that. Libet shows that there can also be a distortion of the content of perceived images compared to the real image shown to the subject. An unconscious distortion, especially in the case of embarrassing or distressing images, which protects the subject from an overly painful experience. These distortions would not be possible if our awareness of a sensory image were immediate, without the delay necessary for the brain to process and possibly distort the perceived image without the subject's knowledge.

Experiments therefore show that the fact of perception is always overlaid by an unconscious emotional valence, which is capable of influencing the conscious content of perception. According to the neurobiologist Arnaldo Benini (2017, p. 29), "the brain can only distort time because it creates it"; time is a conscious content created by brain mechanisms. We shall return to this concept. For the moment, it is essential to understand the consequences of this delay in the awareness of a sensory event. Well, this delay – argues Paul Valery – is the basis of psychology! In particular, we might add, it has radical implications for the study of the inaccessible unconscious and of pain.

In *Monsieur Teste* and in his letter to Pierre Louys, Valery (1946) shows how we actually live behind a curtain of illusions. Exactly as Bion writes at the beginning of the eleventh chapter of *Transformations*. The idea that reality is in the presence of the gaze, and therefore of consciousness, is definitively challenged, and with it the position on which Western metaphysics has based its naive certainties. Teste is an observer, a witness, but a third witness, standing between the ego and the world, is self-consciousness, which shows that there is no possibility of an immediate presence of reality in the gaze, because there is always a delay before it reaches consciousness, and this delay "is all psychology – which one could paradoxically call: what happens between a thing… and itself!" (Valery, 1930, p. 298). There is as a result no neutral, pure perception of reality, as Merleau-Ponty intuited, anticipating Libet's research, which shows that conscious perception actually does lag behind the unconscious response, so that perception is always influenced by the inaccessible unconscious, by one's own personality and history.

Libet shows that sensory inputs, such as pain, take only 100–200 msec to evoke an unconscious response. Before it can become conscious, perception is then influenced by unconscious inputs that last much less than 0.5 sec. Character and past experience can then alter the conscious content of any perceptual event. The discovery of a delay in the awareness of a perceptual event thus provides a physiological time interval during which other unconscious inputs can modulate the content of an experience before it manifests in consciousness. This makes the concept of "now" a perpetually delayed experience. There is also the possibility that the conscious content of any experience can be altered depending on the nature of past experiences and the character of the person. This means that each person lives in their own individual conscious reality and that there is no neutral perception of reality. On account of this physiological lag, each person has their own individual conscious reality, depending on their history and embodied memories (the inaccessible unconscious). Thus, the complex brain mechanisms leading to consciousness in themselves provide a solid neurophysiological basis for the concept of hallucinosis, according to the extraordinary metaphor coined by Bion of a "short-sighted view" phenomenon.

Libet's studies have caused a sensation and have been challenged by Daniel Dennet (2003) because they seem to imply the existence of a unique place in the brain where everything happens at the same time, vision, hearing, decision-making processes, etc., a kind of Cartesian theatre in which a *homunculus* observes with great delay the decisions that the unconscious brain has already taken, thus blowing up free will. Dennet concedes, however, that Libet does indeed show that conscious decision-making processes take time, at least half a second, so that it is precisely neuroscience that paradoxically places the unconscious in a central position in learning from experience, while the function of consciousness itself and the so-called *qualia*, the qualitative and phenomenal aspects of mental experience, remain uncertain and mysterious. Merleau-Ponty, moreover, had anticipated Libet's reflections on the influence of the unconscious with his extraordinary formula that "perception is unconscious", recovering precisely the lesson of the late Freud, who speaks of a somatic psychic, an unremoved unconscious, the somatic navel of being. The fact that we perceive reality as a function of our character and our earliest experiences consequently has profound implications, affecting not only our perception of reality but the very basis of intersubjective relationship. It is precisely in these phenomena that the importance of Bion's concept of hallucinosis, and more generally of the aesthetic dimension in the clinic and the relationship between unconscious pain and perception, becomes apparent.

Since Libet's studies, neuroscience has carried out intensive research into the neural mechanisms of the sense of time. These studies, often ignored by pure physics, which continued to consider time an illusion, "stubbornly stubborn", as Einstein put it, have in fact shown that time is not only peculiar to humans but also to creatures with tiny nervous systems from very remote times. Benini shows the complexity of the nervous organisation of time mechanisms, which in humans extends from the prefrontal lobes to the cerebellum, but which also exists in other less evolved animals: ants, birds such as the hummingbird, Clark's hazel and laboratory mice. Time is then divided into *government time*, GT, which is objective, measurable time, and is probably processed by the left hemisphere, and *personal time*, PT, which is processed by the right hemisphere and is related to the areas of emotion. "GT is a datum, albeit created by the brain, PT is an experience" (Benini, 2017, p. 40). According to neurobiologists, the development of the sense of time goes hand in hand with the development of the ability to walk, language and experiences that give a sense of the passage of time. The child acquires awareness of the present, of the now, by the eighteenth month. From 18 to 42 months, the child learns the sense of before-then-after; at around 30 months, the child learns the sense of the future; the word "tomorrow" appears before "yesterday" because it is a memory that becomes conscious at 30–32 months. Abstract reflection on time finally becomes possible from the age of 10 or 12. Personal, subjective time is naturally perceived differently according to circumstances, it seems to pass more quickly when the experience is pleasant, and more slowly when it is unpleasant or threatening, because, from an evolutionary point of view, it is more convenient to consider a possible threat for longer. The organisation of time is compared to language in terms of its extension and connections to the centres of memory, emotionality and rationality. Time is defined as a category of experience which, unlike space, is not perceived but felt. The sense of time is present even without the experience of the environment, while the centres of space only come into play with the maturation linked to experience. For neurobiology, time and space remain separate, although closely related. For neurobiologists, time is "real and does not emerge from other categories of nature, not even from space and number, although there is a connection between the three domains due to the partly common brain areas that feed them" (ibid., p. 87). The hypothesis that time is a real category of the universe would be supported by the fact that nervous systems, in humans and many other animal species, are components of the universe. Evolution, says Smolin, which would be impossible to imagine without time, has selected the nervous mechanism of time that allows consciousness to order the succession of reality. The question then is what is time? A real feature of the universe, which humans and certain animals have learnt to recognise and perceive, or a "scaffolding of the brain mechanisms in which reality, including that of mental life, is embedded?" (ibid., p. 34). Benini's answer is rather ambiguous in this regard: "The continuous manipulation of the sense of time by the brain confirms that time is produced by it, that it is not a perception of the external world, and that it is real" (ibid., p. 32). Benini states that time is not perceived in the same way as a sound, a colour or a pain, and is not referred to the out-side world, but is created, produced in the brain, without there being a central, circumscribed organ of the sense of time within it. Objective time is a datum, but it is also created, produced by the brain. Benini's position is a complex one, but at its core, it reveals a kind of confusion between meaning and real-ity. Bion (1965, p. 73) teaches us that meaning is "a function of self-love, self-hate, self-knowledge. It is not a logically, but a psycho-logically neces-sary". We only learn through our mind, and we know that there is no pain, no colour out there, "there is no whatever in the universe that we can access without first filtering it through the labyrinthine lumps of grey matter in our head" (Benini, 2017, p. 35). In this sense, Benini is right to argue that

> the time on which self-conscious humanity can reflect has existed since the brain forms it as a dimension of life and the universe. Nervous mech-anisms transmit it from one generation to the next and make it conscious around the third year of life, together with memory, which is one of the bases of time.
>
> (ibid.)

All this, however, has to do with the meaning not the reality of time. Even when Einstein states that all that is needed to make the concept of time objective is a repetitive physical phenomenon that signals the interval be-tween two events, we are referring to the meaning we attach to events. A meaning that in this case we can define as objective because it is "shared".

Nevertheless, all this has little to do with the time before us that can very well do without us, and will do so, given the depressingly stupid and immense destructive capacity of human beings. It is one thing to give meaning to something, it is another to create something. We do not create time, if anything, it is time that creates us. Perhaps we are time. The stuff of the mind, says Civitarese, is the stuff of time, but we remain a paltry, insignificant web compared to the evolution of the universe. In the end, the problem remains the one expressed by Borges (1960, p. 186):

> Time is the substance of which I am made. Time is a river that drags me, but I am the river; it is a tiger that mauls me, but I am the tiger; it is a fire that devours me, but I am the fire. The world, unfortunately, is real; I, unfortunately, am Borges.

"I am pain", writes Pontalis (1977). Time is for humans memory and nostalgia, writes Rovelli (2017), it is "the pain of absence". Although we can disappear, time cannot.

Returning to the problem of perception, and in particular to unconscious perception, in which the nervous mechanisms of time perception remain active, as in sleep, we can then try to understand more deeply the problem of meaning.

Our brain, Beau Lotto (2017) observes, uses only ten per cent of the information that comes from sight to see, the remaining 90 per cent comes from the other regions of the brain, an extremely sophisticated network of interconnections that gives meaning to the information that enters our brain through our senses. Meaning is, therefore, created by us as we interact with the world, but from our past experiences and from what we have called the inaccessible unconscious, which lies before us like an invisible pair of spectacles. Not only that, but our perception is a product of our evolution, and this does not have the aim of seeing reality, but survival, evolution itself. Seeing reality, in all its details, may not necessarily be an advantage for our survival. Perception is used to move in the world, to react and act in our environment, to survive. Although we cannot see reality itself, we can remember the interpretations we have made in the past and this can help us to behave appropriately in different circumstances. Perception is thus the physical embodiment of the perceptual automatisms of our ancestors, combined with our own automatisms and those of the culture in which we are immersed, so that our individual development and learning allow us to see only what we needed to survive in the past.

Richard L. Gregory (2009) states that the past remains in our nervous system, so that ancestral patterns of behaviour lie deep in our brains, even if some are now outdated and inappropriate. They are usually repressed, but when activated they can evoke primal perceptions and behaviours that are bizarre in our present lives. As behavioural patterns have been built up over billions of years, and only some of them have gradually become extinct, it is important to recognise them as symptoms. Gregory calls neuro-archaeology the study of behavioural patterns that have been progressively stratified in the nervous system over the course of evolution. The simplest organisms respond predictably to a range of, with tropisms and reflexes that were appropriate long ago, but may not be today. Higher animals and humans are less predictable, and so are the laws that govern their behaviour. Human behaviour can be so difficult to predict that philosophers and scientists have regarded human mental activity as alien to science. Among them was Descartes, who argued that matter and thought were so different that they could not be related. Gregory also speaks of "implicit knowledge", such as reflexes, patterns of behaviour and illusions, which show how we see with the eyes and brains of our ancestors. Much of our behaviour and perception is then controlled by our inheritance from the past and from human history before us. Gregory describes as "living fossils" those behaviours and perceptions from the deep past that persist, such as fears and aversions to enclosed, dark places, sudden noises, phobias of spiders and snakes, which are not related to our childhood experiences but are universal and transcend different ethnic groups. Such patterns are stored in implicit memory, where perception and memory are intimately linked, meaning that *the present is seen through the past.*

To conclude this brief dialogue with neurobiology, I would like to mention how Libet's research feeds directly into the concept of the mental field, which contemporary psychoanalysis now uses to considerable advantage. Libet poses the problem of how mind and brain can interact in both directions, and thus how the mental, the non-physical, arises from the physical and vice versa. The problem of transformations, of mind-body, which has haunted Freud, Bion, generation of psychoanalysts and scientists of the mind. Libet puts forward the proposal, experimentally verifiable, that subjective conscious experience could be considered as a field produced by appropriate, albeit multiple and multiform, neural activities of the brain. Such a field would allow a form of communication within the cerebral cortex without passing through cortical neural connections and pathways (Libet, 2004, p. 171). Such a conscious mental field (CMC) could constitute "the entity in which the unified subjective experience is present" (ibid., p. 172), in other words, the experience of the Self. It could also represent the causal substrate underlying the ability of the mind to influence certain neural functions. Libet speaks of a conscious mental field, much simplified compared to the mental field with which psychoanalysis works, which of course must also include the unconscious and the spatial aspects, the atmospheres, and yet it is interesting that his description corresponds to Corrao's description of the field as a field of phenomenological movements that cannot be observed. Libet sees the mental field as not reducible to neural processes, even though it is intimately connected to them. He cites the example of Sperry's split-brain studies and points out that the two separate hemispheres do not lead to a sense of two separate selves; the patients experience themselves as the same single person before the separation of the hemispheres. For this reason, the hypothesis is that there may be something in the mental field that can connect the two hemispheres, beyond the fibres of the corpus callosum.

Part Two

Conscious/Unconscious

Chapter 6

The problem of the Bionian unconscious

Bion's perplexities, silences and attempts at normalisation

Is the unconscious to which Bion refers the same as that conceived and constructed by Freud? Psychoanalytic literature appears very reticent on the topic of Bion's unconscious and its possible diversity compared to that of Freud. Bion's position, oscillating between open criticism and the refusal to abandon the concept of the unconscious, has not favoured an open discussion on the topic. Bion was bitterly aware of the reluctance of the psychoanalytic establishment to face a foundational taboo such as the unconscious and we know his tendency to preserve psychoanalytic theories consolidated by clinical practice. The unconscious, therefore, remains a burning issue even for a desecrating genius like Bion. In *Caesura* Bion (1975a, p. 42) writes: "I do not wish to abandon the idea of the conscious or the unconscious", but in the seminars and notes of *Cogitations* we find repeated perplexity on the usefulness of the Freudian concept of the unconscious. "I think there is a certain confusion in Freud's ideas of conscious and unconscious," (Bion, 1978, p. 350) he said in a seminar at St. Paul's, and in *Cogitations* he writes that: "'unconscious' and 'conscious' do not meet the problem. 'Unconscious' could sometimes be replaced by 'obvious but unobserved'" (Bion, 1992, p. 305). In summary, Bion thinks that "the whole question of unconscious and conscious, which has been useful so far, needs a great deal of reconsideration" (Bion, 1973, p. 67). One gets the impression, however, that Bion has left this "careful revision" to others. In his theoretical writings, he merely expresses his preference for the finite/ infinite relationship over the conscious/unconscious, although in a passage in *Transformations* he is quite emphatic in stating that he does not wish to introduce a differentiating factor between conscious and unconscious, but

DOI: 10.4324/9781032655239-9

between finite and infinite (Bion, 1965, p. 46). In fact, his real policy was to drop psychoanalytic theories and concepts that did not interest him, starting with the theory of neurosis and repression. Bion's theoretical ideas on the unconscious are thus confined to sporadic dissertations, but this does not detract from the fact that his radical and revolutionary conception of the unconscious permeates his entire oeuvre.

The psychoanalytic mainstream has preferred to ignore the issue for a long time or at most has tried to mediate between the Freudian and Bionian concept of the unconscious, creating inconsistent and sometimes confusing compromises. The problem is that it is not always possible to reconcile the Bionian paradigm with that of Freud's, because even with Bion we find numerous nuclei germinated from Freud, these end up taking on a totally different and even opposite meaning within his new paradigm. The same can be said for Kleinian theories, often introduced in parentheses and made much more abstract as to be unrecognisable, such as the theory of projective identification which is developed as a container/contained relationship.

In their Bion dictionaries, P.C. Sandler (2005) and López Corvo (2002) do not mention the entry unconscious. Hinshelwood (1989) asserts that the concept of the unconscious is one of the few that has remained relatively unchanged. The Symingtons (1996), on the other hand, asks the reader to free the mind from the notions of unconscious and conscious, because they would be an obstacle to the understanding of the finite/infinite polarity, with which Bion replaces that of conscious/unconscious. Grotstein (2009) seeks a mediation. He argues that Bion uses the concept of the unconscious in three different ways: as *unrepressed* (collective) *unconscious*, as the source of Platonic ideal forms and/or Kantian noumena; as *dynamic* or *repressed unconscious*, as the sphere of unconscious memories and fantasies; as *pre-conscious*, the seat of reverie. These subsystems would be opposed and affixed to consciousness, but not necessarily in conflict with it. Experiences cross the contact-barrier and arrive at the dynamic or repressed unconscious, after having passed through the pre-conscious, the room that houses the alpha function and dreaming, and which constitutes the search engine and command control unit of all unconscious and conscious mental activity. Internal emotional and drive stimuli can originate in the unrepressed unconscious as well as the repressed unconscious, and they too cross the contact-barrier to be processed by the alpha function and relocated to the dynamically repressed unconscious. Grotstein's synthetic capacity is admirable, but rather than clarifying the problem it seems to confirm the psychoanalytic establishment's need to *normalise* the Bionian unconscious and does not do justice to the profound revolutionary charge of the Bionian conception of the unconscious, which in the clinical work, in the notes of *Cogitations*, and in the folds of his work, emerges with a disruptive and corrosive force far more radical than much of psychoanalysis is willing to accept.

"Unconscioused" and "Identijected"

As often happens, to understand Bion's thought and above all the travails of Bion the thinker, it is better to start with *Cogitations*. In his scattered notes, he expresses great interest in the term "unconscioused" in reference to the German "unbewusst", and he complains about the lack of a corresponding term for projective identification, for example, "identijected" (1992, p. 325). Already in the search for terms Bion, therefore, expresses the real crux of the question, namely, the difficulty of describing his procedural, dynamic and relational vision of the unconscious. Bion is not interested in describing the personality as made up of structures – such as the *id, superego, ego* – which according to him have no clinical confirmation, and he does not believe in an unconscious as a place of the mind (1976–9, p. 55). Hence, Bion conceives personality "as a series of functions, of variables, in relation to other variables" (Symington & Symington, 1996, p. 108), and he develops a theory of psychic functions, which together have the purpose of enabling the individual to know the world, to allow the transition from sensations and emotions to thought, to learn from experience, and therefore to grow and become oneself. For Bion, thinking means passing from the infinite of O to the finite, from the chaos of reality to the concept, through a progressive subtraction of emotion. However, growth implies passing from knowing phenomena to being what is real, the same difference between knowing about psychoanalysis and being psychoanalysed. It is the transformation into O. A transformation compared to *incarnation* in the sacrament of the Catholic religion, to becoming the "Godhead" that is in us.

This position brings Bion's concept of the unconscious closer to Matte Blanco's concept of the unconscious as emotion and infinite sets, while remaining more clinical than logical. Bion's interest is in the process that leads to the formation of the unconscious, to "becoming unconscioused", and at the same time in the process that leads to thinking, to the transformation of sensory and emotional elements into alpha elements, images or ideograms that can be thought and/or become part of dreams. This immediately excludes a substantial concept of the unconscious in favour of a processual one, in which the conscious and the unconscious are no longer two separate, mutually exclusive places, but two co-implicated processes. One is contained within the other, and there is no conscious feeling that does not carry with it the shadow of unconscious feeling. There is, therefore, a continuity between conscious and unconscious experience, conceived as two dimensions of the psychic, separated by a *contact-barrier*.

Civitarese (2014) consequently uses the term "un/conscious" with a slash to indicate that the unconscious experience is contained within the conscious, that there is a single dynamic system that operates according to a double register, unconscious/conscious, symmetrical/asymmetrical. For Bion, therefore, the unconscious is developed as a function of the personality. It starts from the primal relation, which is differentiated as the psychoanalytic function of the mind, and is realised as the capacity to perceive reality, based on an integrated functioning, which, by bringing together different points of view – conscious/unconscious, but also one and multiple – leads to the capacity to make sense of experience. Consciousness and unconsciousness can thus be represented in an image like that of the Möbius strip: a continuous surface into which what is external slides inside and vice versa, what is conscious becomes unconscious and vice versa, according to a temporal gradient and the vicissitudes of the alpha function.

The unconscious "unconscioused", then, may correspond to Freud's dynamic unconscious, at least for the time being, in the sense that both refer to contents that have been conscious, that have had a representation, but what about what Bion calls "identijected", that is, what has been expelled by projective identification, "identiject[ion]", what has been split off? We have seen that with every omnipotent fantasy of having got rid of something bad, a layer remains in the child's mind, particles of archaic mentality, unconscious thoughts which have never become conscious and which remain extremely active. Archaic parts, then, are remnants that actively affect the present, as embodied memories, as implicit memories. This means that the concept of the "inaccessible state", which originated as a reference to the remnants of intrauterine life, the somitic memory embedded in the soma, the thalamic and subthalamic anxieties that never had access to consciousness, legitimately becomes part of the Bionian concept of the unconscious.

In other words, the concept of the inaccessible unconscious can be extended to all those situations that belong to implicit memory and that are inaccessible to declarative or autobiographical memory. In this sense, the Bionian unconscious also includes the primitive nuclei of the self, the autistic and psychotic nuclei of the personality, in which dissociation and splitting operate, separating and imprisoning parts of the self, parts that are not alive / not dead, areas of the mind that are enclosed, forgotten, outcast. This is why Arnaldo Chuster (2010) claims that the Bionian unconscious is something much greater than the Freudian unconscious: an unconscious characterised by a double movement of repetition and expansion. It maintains a conservative movement of repetition of forms and at the same time presents a movement of expansion and creation. Psychoanalysis is in fact a process that stimulates the growth of the field it examines, so there is a moment when one can say that the unconscious has been created, because what was there before has now expanded. In this sense, for Bion, the unconscious is "the infinite", it is "O".

The troubled path to O

Bion arrives at this conception of the unconscious through a tortuous process of rethinking which, beginning in the psychosis clinic, leads him to overturn Freudian formulations of the unconscious. The Freudian unconscious is formed by the repression of infantile sexual desire and is based on the doctrine of repression and the theory of neurosis. Bion is not interested in neurosis, he leaves Freud's theory intact, including his theory of night dream, and he does not speak of slips of the tongue, of the gaps in language, but he starts from the psychotic world, from the most primitive mechanisms, from that unfathomable background inhabited by partial objects, of unconscious fantasies, splits and projective identifications, which Melanie Klein described in disturbing scenarios of infantile analysis. To access these primitive states of the mind, it is neither necessary to descend to the underworld of the Freudian unconscious nor to make assumptions. The bottom is already all on the surface. Visible. It is enough to observe. To describe what can be observed from the outside: this is the simple and revolutionary idea with which Werner Heisenberg, at the age of 23, in the windy solitude of Helgoland, inaugurated the new quantum mechanics: "through the surface of phenomena I was looking towards an interior of strange beauty" (Rovelli, 2020, p. 26). Like the young Heisenberg, Bion observes and describes with extraordinary vividness and minutiae of detail the fragmented and chaotic world of the psychotic, who rather than an apparatus for thinking seems to develop an apparatus for evacuating internal bad objects through projective identification. The atmospheres of the sessions are animated by fragments of expelled objects, stuck in like bullets, word-things, bizarre objects, hallucinations, inarticulate sounds, discordant grimaces, etc. What emerges is a chaotic analytical field in which "concrete", noisy objects move, felt as "blows", "stabbings", a falling piece of iron, gibbering and babbling, clouds of "blue haze" (Bion, 1967, pp. 95–6). Events and materials that have to do with fragments of the Ego, functions of the personality, coming from the destructiveness that patients direct towards any kind of link, including their own faculty of judgement, which is split off and expelled, and therefore felt as a bizarre object. It is as if Bion were describing the corpuscular nature of the mind, in analogy with the *quanta* of light, the photons, which earned Einstein the Nobel Prize.

The psychotic that Bion describes, in fact, moves in a world of objects that have the characteristics of matter – anal objects, sensory stimuli, parts of the personality – objects that do not obey the laws of mental functioning and that can be expelled by projective identification, but that cannot be reintroduced to think, except violently. Bion defines these concrete objects as the "furniture" of the dream, because they are the material one uses to construct dreams, but which are not real dreams, because they lack mental characteristics (1992, p. 42). Bion describes sessions with psychotic patients as dream-like scenarios, because the hypothesis of being able to see the patient dreaming in a session is useful "especially with its counterpart of seeing the contrasting activity of hallucination" (ibid., p. 43). However, the easy accessibility of what appears to be the psychotic's unconscious turns out to be related to the patient's actual inability to make these elements unconscious and to benefit from the experience, which means that what is consciously perceived "can be mentally stored in such a way that it is susceptible of both concretization and abstraction" (ibid., p. 73). Bion's great insight is that this process, which the psychotic fails to do, is related to dreaming: Introjection ...Dreaming... "The process of introjection is carried out by the patient's 'dreaming' the current events" (ibid., p. 47). Sensory impressions and emotions, in order to be mentally *assimilated*, must accordingly be transformed into *mental images*, alpha elements, through dream work. The alpha function, as he later called this work, thus performs a process of abstraction on the concreteness of sensory impressions and emotions, offering a model of the transition from the non-mental to the mental, and so saying of the capacity to desensitise and mentally assimilate the stimulus, whether external or internal, through a process of transformation. Bion subsequently states that

> you cannot let something become unconscious if α is not done to that something. The inability to have visual images of what is taking place means that the emotional experience cannot be preserved either in the conscious or in the unconscious.

(ibid., p. 135)

The alpha elements, which correspond to visual images (ideograms), are the basic metabolites used for memory and learning, and therefore for conscious thought, but also for the formation of the unconscious and for dreaming. In other words, if the alpha function is not working, i.e., if we are not able to "dream" reality, we cannot really represse it. Dreaming is, therefore, a continuous process that creates and differentiates the conscious from the unconscious, forming a kind of *contact-barrier*, a membrane whose function is to allow selected elements to pass from one side to the other and to protect our alert consciousness from any mental phenomena that might overwhelm it.

To help us understand the meaning of his operation, Bion (1962, pp. 15–6) describes the situation of a man talking to a friend. In order to continue the conversation and not be disturbed by the flow of sensory impressions or emotions, the subject must be able to dream. That is to say, the dream is a kind of barrier against mental phenomena that could overwhelm the awareness and attention of talking to a friend. The α-function thus makes possible the distinction between the conscious and the unconscious, and the ability to dream preserves the personality from an almost psychotic (chaotic) state. Bion is aware that his hypothesis overturns the dream theory. The dream, in fact, becomes the way in which the psyche functions in the waking state, allowing the conscious and pre-verbal unconscious material to acquire the quality of being storable and communicable, through a process comparable to digestion. A true reversal of perspective, whereby it is no longer the unconscious that produces the dream, but the dream that produces the unconscious, while the opposition between daytime and nighttime thinking dissolves into a *continuum*. Conscious and unconscious then become the

product of a differentiation operated by the α-function, which "by prolifer-
ating alpha-elements, is producing the contact-barrier" (ibid., p. 54), which
marks the point of separation between conscious and unconscious elements
and generates the distinction between them in a continuous process of formation. It follows that the conscious and the unconscious cease to be two
psychic provinces and become transitory and reversible states of mental
experience; "the conscious and the unconscious thus constantly produced
together do function as if they were binocular, therefore capable of correla-
tion and self-regard" (ibid.).

The real novelty introduced by Bion is thus the continuity between conscious and unconscious experience, conceived as two dimensions of the
psychic, separated by a contact-barrier. This semi-permeable film acts as
an articulation area that makes it possible to cooperate, to see from both
sides of the caesura, in a binocular vision. Furthermore, this aspect of
continuity, this transcending of the caesura, whereby the conscious is also
an expression of the unconscious, is probably the aspect that most undermines our certainties, the most revolutionary aspect of Bion's theory. It
will come as no surprise that this aspect brings the Bionian subject closer
to Merleau-Ponty's subject, but in the next section, we will see that it
also brings the Bionian conscious unconscious relationship closer to current conceptions of neuroscience. The Merleau-Ponty's subject stands at
the boundary between the conscious and the unconscious, it inhabits the
margins of these concepts, it is their hinge: "This unconscious is not to
be sought at the bottom of us, behind our 'consciousness', but in front of
us, as an articulation of our field" (Merleau-Ponty, 1964, p. 197). This is
why Merleau-Ponty can say, in an extraordinary formula, that "perception
is unconscious", anticipating by 50 years neuroscientific research on the
influence of the unconscious on perception. He makes us aware that our
way of perceiving reality is always conditioned by an unconscious vision
that fishes not only in our past but also in that system between the physical and the mental that Bion called the proto-mental, in which the individual sinks into a group and archaic, even mythical dimension that can,
at certain moments, unexpectedly invade our actions and behaviour. In
addition this turmoil can find its way through everyday images and words
that retain traces of disturbing elements, whereby the archaic and the most
disturbing primitive can suddenly emerge even in the most unthinkable
situations. Archaic elements that often have to do with blood and sex, with
the sacred and the mythical, which Bion condenses into the expression

"blood everywhere" and which finds an extraordinary representation in Bong Joon-ho's film *Parasite* in the birthday scene in the garden, where violence explodes in Dionysian mode. In the party scene, with beautiful people, playing classical instruments, talking, walking gracefully on the lawn of a magnificent villa on a hill, i.e., a modern representation of Mount Olympus, when violence suddenly erupts, with confusion taking hold, and it is difficult to understand who is killing whom, whit a pool of blood spreading throughout.

What are we talking about when we talk about the Bion's unconscious?

Bion's vision of the unconscious is therefore processual, dynamic and relational. This makes it difficult to define, so much so that Bion himself questions whether the concept of the unconscious is still "valuable" (Bion, 1962, p. 16, note 1), betraying his intolerance of any static and substantialist position. To understand the revolutionary scope of this position, it is worth considering the possible similarities and differences between Freud's repressed or dynamic unconscious and Bion's unconscious, which Grotstein assimilates. Both deal with material previously represented at the level of consciousness, or in Bionian terms, material transformed by the alpha function. Apart from this, the Bionian unconscious and the Freudian unconscious have nothing else in common, neither the mechanisms of production, nor the functions, nor the temporal dimension. We have seen the mechanisms of production associated with the alpha function in Bion, and with repression in Freud. These mechanisms obviously imply a variety of functions. In Freud, repression remains linked to the need to free the ego from incompatible representations. Thus, it is the pleasure-displeasure principle, modelled on the escape from the source of pain, that initially causes the psychic process to move away from the memory of what was once painful and provides "the prototype and first example of psychical repression" (Freud, 1900, p. 600). Beginning with *The Interpretation of Dreams*, however, what is repressed are "only sexual wisheful impulses from infancy" (ibid., p. 60). In *Repression* Freud thus refers only to the repression of instinctual representations. Repression, as a result, rejects the translation into words of the first, authentic, object investments. These drives, subject only to the pleasure principle and unchanging in time, have mobile investments that can move from one representation to another, condense into a single one, in the absence of contradiction. The unconscious, the repressed, is therefore, for Freud, "unknowable" and "inaccessible" in itself, and only "with the help of a certain amount of work they can be transformed into, or replaced by, conscious mental processes" (Freud, 1915b, p. 168). For Freud, therefore, the unconscious is timeless. Wishes are immortal, nothing in the id corresponds to the idea of time. Although Freud intuits that the unconscious is "alive and capable of development and mantains a number of other relations with the Pcs, amongst them that of co-operation" (ibid., p. 190), his idea of the unconscious remains that expressed in a letter to Fliess of 9 February 1898, when he writes of a "first rough map" of the territory where the dreaming process takes place, where the "impulses of sexual desire derived from infantile material" simmer up (Freud, 1900, p. 605). Civitarese (2014) himself describes the Freudian unconscious with visual metaphors such as "Indian reservation" to show how it is inhabited by representations incompatible with the ego, which never had access to consciousness (primary repression) or which have been secondarily repressed (secondary repression). But once the id has become the great reservoir of instincts and the ego the real repressing force, the perspective of repression will tend to deal more and more with the instincts that emerge from the primordial unconscious.

In Bion, the hypothesis of the alpha function deprives repression of any function in the creation of the unconscious, leaving the correct functioning of the two systems to the alpha barrier, which remain in balance with each other. The work of the alpha function is then a transformation into alpha elements, of "the sense impressions, whatever they are, and the emotions, whatever there are, of which the patient is aware" (Bion, 1962, p. 6). In other words, the α function works day and night on the sensory impressions and emotions of our immediate experience, carrying out a desensitisation operation, a transformation into an image which represents the first act of mentalisation.

Becoming unconscious, thus becomes a necessary process that allows consciousness to function and maintain its tasks, in particular "attention". The subject can only repress, in the sense of becoming unconscious, material that was previously "dreamed", or rather transformed into alpha elements. There is thus a continuity between conscious and unconscious experience, separated by a semi-permeable film that, through continuous visual accommodation, allows us to see from both sides of the caesura, in a

binocular vision. For this reason, repression ceases to be the basic psychopathological mechanism and becomes part of the normal thought process.
This is why the psychotic part of the personality, which does not dream or
has a defective alpha barrier, is not able to repress, but only to split and project, whereas the so-called neurotics and the healthy part of the personality,
which dreams, can repress.

Bion's unconscious and neuroscience

This aspect of Bion's Unconscious is quite complex and not always understood, not least because it can be confused with the cognitive unconscious. By
the term unconscious, cognitive science simply means that most of what the
mind does takes place outside of consciousness. In this sense, the cognitive
unconscious does not involve the repression of experience in a dynamic sense,
but refers to forms of implicit knowledge that are not subject, or not very subject, to verbal processing, whereas the dynamic unconscious has to do with
content that has had access to consciousness but has subsequently been actively repressed. From this point of view, the Freudian dynamic unconscious
has a special status that does not sit well with the cognitive unconscious. The
cognitive unconscious focuses on the existence of mental processes that cannot be made conscious because their awareness would conflict with the need
for a fast and automatic process (Varela, Thompson, Rosch, 1991). It therefore refers to any physiological process of which we may never be aware.

The concept of the Bion's unconscious, insofar as it implies the need for
knowledge to be made unconscious in order to free consciousness to pay
attention without being invaded by chaos, e.g., talking to a friend and reading a book while listening to music, can come close to the concept of the
cognitive unconscious. In this case, the term unconscious tends to approach
the meaning of automaticity.

Within this limiting constraint, the Bionian concept of the unconscious
provides an unexpected link to neuroscience. Edelman and Tononi (2000)
assert that conscious and unconscious processes are in contact and that their
separation is by no means clear-cut, as Bion postulates. Most of our adult
cognitive life is the product of automated procedures such as driving, talking, listening, reading, multitasking operations such as typing on a mobile
phone, talking and listening to music at the same time. Of course, not all of
the neural processes involved in carrying out these procedures contribute

directly to conscious experience. Edelman and Tononi have, therefore, developed a theory to shed light on the possible ways in which conscious and unconscious processes interact. They are aware that there are many other aspects of the unconscious that are completely unknown from a neurophysiological perspective, e.g., unconscious expectations and intentions, conscious and unconscious regulation of attention and the substrates of the Freudian unconscious. However, their theory merely identifies a general neurophysiological framework for studying the relationships between conscious and unconscious processes. This theory is based on the *dynamic core* hypothesis. This hypothesis is based on the observation that only a subset of neuronal groups contributes directly to conscious experience at any given time.

More precisely, the hypothesis states, "A group of neurons contributes directly to conscious experience only if it is part of a distributed functional aggregate which, through interactions within the thalamocortical system, implements a high integration over hundreds of milliseconds" (ibid., p. 171). This aggregate must be significantly differentiated. The first to understand that consciousness is a process and not a property or place was William James. A dynamic nucleus is, therefore, a process, not a thing or place, and is defined by neural interactions rather than specific localisation. Even if it has an extension, this nucleus is distributed, changeable in composition, and cannot be located in a single brain site. The exact composition of the nucleus related to specific states of consciousness also varies from person to person. Edelman and Tononi so limit themselves to defining unconscious processes as those determined by neural circuits whose activity does not contribute directly to conscious experience. The example given is that of a hand reaching out to grasp a glass. This simple movement involves a large number of processes in specific structures: in the basal ganglia, cerebellum, subcortical motor nuclei and parts of the motor cortex. These processes are essential for the coordination of movements and their timing, but we are not aware of them, nor we would like to be. In fact, there is a continuous assistance of the unconscious to conscious life, such as when we drive a car, or simply talk, but only some of these processes are capable of becoming conscious through a complex interface with the dynamic nucleus:

The anatomy of the thalamic-cortical, therefore, favours the emergence of a diffuse coherence between distributed regions, an emergence caused by reentrant interactions. On the contrary, it seems that in the basal gan-glia, different neurons are organised in parallel rings that are independ-ent of each other and hence not involved in the kind of dialogue that we find in the cortex.

(ibid., p. 221)

This underlying theory of a nucleus underlying states of consciousness and connected to a series of unconscious but functionally isolated procedures is consequently a good theoretical and experimental framework for research on the unconscious. However, Edelman and Tononi so put forward an inter-esting hypothesis for the pathological aspects, which more closely concern our type of unconscious. They suppose that there may be a category of unconscious neural processes, linked to the thalamo-cortical system itself, which, however, are not incorporated into the dominant dynamic nucleus because they are disconnected for some reason. In other words, it is possi-ble that some neural processes of the thalamic-cortical system itself, which usually form part of the dynamic nucleus and which contribute to conscious perception, may remain functionally isolated under certain conditions. These "splinters" or "active thalamocortical islands" are then functionally disconnected areas because they seem to underlie pathological dissocia-tions. The authors wonder whether they can remain unconscious until they merge with the dominant nucleus and whether they could eventually be linked to repression and the Freudian unconscious. We should of course add the Bionian unconscious, also because Edelman and Tononi explicitly re-fer to pathological dissociations, to "splinters" that remain disconnected, at least until they merge with the central nucleus. A concept that cannot fail to refer to the concepts of splitting, dissociation, psychodynamic integration and Bion's idea of transcending the caesura. In addition, this "transcend-ing the caesura", this possibility of "penetrating the barrier", remains one of Bion's deepest suggestions: it is the idea that there are various caesuras and that it is possible to cross them, that an interpretation is like an idea *in transit* able to penetrate barriers, reach fears which "are buried in the future which has not happened, or buried in the past which is forgotten" (Bion, 1975a, p. 38). In other words, the most primitive states, the archaic, the traces of fetal life acting in the present, the split and dissociated states of the Self, generational terrors and truths, the fear of the future and the deep states that fish in the proto-mental system, which are all part of Bion's unconscious, could find an interesting and reliable neurophysiological basis in the theory of the dynamic nucleus of Edelman and Tononi.

However, the links between Bion's unconscious and the neurosciences go beyond this hypothesis. Psychoanalysis and neuroscience find common ground in the field of psychic wounds, of those traumas which not only condition the mind of those who have suffered them, but which can also have transgenerational effects. Today, it is increasingly evident that traumas and negative situations during early childhood can adversely affect adult behaviour due to lasting changes in brain biology. Epidemiological studies support the evidence that mental distress has its roots in childhood dynamics, for which there is a clear relationship between early experiences, brain function and behaviour, but not only. Epigenetics shows that early traumas produce alterations in the expression of genes with transgenerational effects (Oliviero, 2018). In other words, the phenotype, i.e., the characteristics of the brain, are determined not only by the inherited genotype, but also by the superimposition of an experiential "imprint" which influences its expression. A history of negative early experiences, therefore, leaves an "imprint" on the gene that regulates cortisol production, thus amplifying reactivity to subsequent stresses, so that children of parents who have suffered severe trauma may be more sensitive to stress. From a neuroscientific point of view, the discovery that there is not only one system of long-term memory – declarative and explicit, verbalisable and rememberable – but also an underground, non-conscious, implicit, non-rememberable and non-verbalisable memory, therefore represents a fundamental point of contact between psychoanalysis and neuroscience. The identification of the implicit long-term memory system, which Bion calls the inaccessible unconscious, hence opens up new perspectives and extends the concept of the unconscious. The implicit system is in fact the only memory that develops precociously. It is present and active already in the last weeks of gestation and it is the only memory available to the newborn in its first two or three years of life: its procedural dimension (recording and perform movements) and emotional-affective, linked to the pleasure-pain system, allows the child to "archive", or rather to "inscribe", in embodied procedures, his or her first experiences connected to actions, voice, maternal and paternal language, to the internal and external sound rhythms, to the environment and to the emotional vicissitudes in which (s)he grows.

Chapter 7

(Mythical) origins of the unconscious

The Freudian origin narrative

In a work on the origins of the unconscious, Arnaldo Chuster (2010) states that there is very little literature on the subject, since priority has been given to the investigation of the contents of the unconscious. For Freud, moreover, the priority problem was to demonstrate the existence of the unconscious and not its origin or formation. In our age, the existence of the unconscious is taken for granted, even by neuroscience, which instead fails to get to the bottom of the phenomenon of consciousness. However, the question of origin, any origin, remains disturbing, having to do with birth and death, creation and emptiness. In the case of the unconscious, this question also risks confusing the ontological level with the operational level, it risks forgetting that the unconscious is a hypothesis, which determines a praxis. In fact, it is different to ask oneself about the origin of the unconscious in clinical practice, from asking oneself about the origin of the unconscious as an ontological subject. The concept of the unconscious that should interest the psychoanalyst is, therefore, the one that generates and sustains analytic practice. Hypothesising a coincidence between the two levels, or even just a link, is a passage that Freud could not face, given his concern to demonstrate the existence of the unconscious in order to give a scientific basis to the analytic method. The transition from contents to processes, from the "discovery" of the unconscious to the formation of the unconscious, required a paradigm shift, which occurred with Bion and Winnicott. Thomas H. Ogden (2022) indicates this passage as the shift from an epistemological psychoanalysis, relating to knowing and understanding, to an ontological psychoanalysis, relating to being and becoming. With Bion the analyst-patient relationship becomes symmetrical to that of the mother-child and goes to create a basic model for understanding how the quality of the relationship

DOI: 10.4324/9781032655239-10

can or cannot favour the growth and development of the unconscious as a psychoanalytic function of the personality. Origin and formation of the unconscious become equivalent, the analysis of the unconscious becomes formation of the unconscious, epistemology becomes ontology. However, the discourse on the origins of the ontological unconscious remains on a mythical level. Green (1966) writes that the primitive level of the unconscious, the one prior to repression, is in fact a completely inaccessible if not mythical layer. Furthermore the myth of origins goes far beyond the problem of the unconscious. "When it comes to the question of origins, the discourse of a science is no purer than that of a myth", recalls Isabella Stengers (1991, p. 41). The origin is basically a story about the very origin of thought that questions itself, and for Paolo Fabbri (1991) to tell is always to transform actions and passions by signs. For this Lorena Preta (1991, p. 229), in a now distant interview with Matta, writes that "we can only see the origin in the moment in which things are transformed [...] there is no origin in the past".

It is, therefore, possible to describe two mythologies of the birth of the unconscious, the Freudian and the Bionian. Melanie Klein was not interested in the origin of the unconscious, which she assumes as already given within the system of unconscious drives and fantasies. Two mythologies, consequently, different in their narrative, and which allow us to observe the profound difference in method between the "speculation" of Freud, and above all of the Freudians, and the use of imagination and myth in Bion and the post-Bionians.

In *Freudian narration*, original repression, whose object never became conscious, remains the true creator of the unconscious, because there can be no repression except through attraction by a repression already present. But what is the mechanism of the original repression? Freud (1925b, p. 94) links the original repression to a single mechanism, which he calls countercathexis, and which he traces back to quantitative factors such "as an excessive degree of excitation and the breaking through of the protective shield against stimuli". For this reason, in the auroral moment of the origin of the unconscious, we therefore find break-ins, wounds, incorporations of too much excitement, such as images of the representation of the living vesicle under the action of external forces. The model of pain, elaborated in the *Project*, hence returns every time Freud has to do with reality, trauma, but also with the origin of the unconscious and primary repression. The relationship between pain, instinct and reality remains an inextricable knot. The archaic and non-conscious core of the ego has its roots in the biological and bears the imprint of the first relationships and of everything that was traumatic and painful. In this nucleus automatisms and the compulsion to repeat are condensed, and we find those ideas on pain and trauma of the *Project* that Freud had set aside for the theory of repression and oedipal fantasies. Reality knocks again, forcefully, but the solution will again be intrapsychic. The compulsion to repeat is referred to a drive force, "dae-monic", which inevitably casts its shadow also on the transference, and tears apart psychoanalysis: the death instinct (Freud, 1920, p. 34). Trauma and pain are a door to external reality that Freud could not open. Psychoa-nalysis and the theory of dreams were safe, albeit with a visible laceration. When large masses of stimuli overwhelm the Pcpt-Cs system, overcoming the protective barrier, the pleasure principle is put out of action and the task of the psychic apparatus becomes that of "mastering the amounts of stimulus which have broken in and of binding them, in the psychical sense, so that they can be disposed of" (ibid., p. 29). In this ingenious idea, which Freud links to the work of the "anticathexis" and to the "preparation con-nected to anxiety", it is possible to intuit the true origin of Bion's concept of alpha function. However, Laplance and Leclaire take the Freudian lesson on the compulsion to repeat literally and trace the origin of the unconscious to the emergence of the death instinct. The specific energy that allows the anticathexis necessary for the original repression, true creator of the uncon-scious, is the death instinct, which presents itself as a radical and immobile force, or the opposite of a force, a void. The representatives of sense of thirst, scar, trace and mark, are for the authors what constitute the primary unconscious, which exists only in the primary repressed stage. From these primary unconscious representatives, from this primordial text – insepara-bly linked to the emergence of the death instinct – it is structured what can truly be called the subject's desire:

> More generally, we can say that language, like the unconscious, is pri-marily place and inextricably linked to the emergence of the death in-stinct so long as it remains precisely that foundation of the world of desire which one cannot, in life, either see or name.
>
> (Laplance & Leclaire, 1966, p. 54)

Speculation, we will say, a term that Freud (1920, p. 24) often uses, as in his reflections on consciousness "What follows is speculation".

Nevertheless, this speculation is supported by a basic question, which could be reformulated as *to what*, starting with Freud, is at stake in the concept of the unconscious. Starting with Freud, because it is only thanks to Freud that this concept becomes the object of systematic study and takes on a special status in psychology.

What is at stake in the concept of the unconscious

To understand what is at stake with the concept of the unconscious, it may be useful to start from a incisive statement by Lacan (1966a, p. 93) which has the merit of placing the unconscious in the place it really deserves:

> The unconscious is a concept forged on the traces of what works to constitute the subject. The unconscious is not a species that defines in psychic reality the circle of what does not have the attribute (or virtue) of consciousness.

The Freudian narration of the origin of the unconscious finds its climax in the historic colloquium on the unconscious held in 1966 in Bonneval, in which Laplance and Leclaire affirm that the origin of the unconscious must be sought in the process which introduces the subject into the symbolic universe. This position remains fundamental, and Civitarese (2014) himself recognises that in some respects Bion's theory of the unconscious is close to that of Lacan, as both support an intersubjective conception of the psyche. Civitarese naturally does not fail to point out the shortcomings of Lacanian theory, which prevent us from accounting for the articulation of the analyst's unconscious subjectivity, who always remains *maître* of the situation, even when (s)he would like to escape the role of idealised depository of the knowledge that the patient assign them. Hence also, Derrida's criticism of the primacy of the signifier, which can never precede the signified, except by questioning the very idea of the sign-of, and the philosopher's denunciation of the Lacanian claim to be able to grasp the "letter" of the unconscious and to arrive at a definitive truth of things. The hypothesis that the formation of the unconscious is an intersubjective process which presides over the formation of the subject and which introduces the subject into the symbolic, is in any case a decisive starting point. The real problem then becomes understanding the ways in which this process takes place, because these ways can be inflected in radically different ways.

Civitarese chooses to combine Freud with Bion, with the awareness of taking a difficult path and the risk of some misunderstanding, in particular regarding the function of repression, which in its original and secondary form, is maintained at the basis of the formation of the unconscious. For Civitarese, the unconscious is a product of language and the famous Lacanian formula of an unconscious structured like a language would capture its artificial nature as a symbolic system and the very functioning of the game between identities and differences. In his hypothesis, the repressed unconscious of the mother casts its shadow on the nascent repressed unconscious of the child, and even on that of the non-repressed (cognitive or structural). The repression therefore comes from the Other, the mother, who represses an affect-sensation, an image, linked to enigmatic sexual messages, which she herself sends to the child, and which he sets aside in the unconscious as a representation of things and as an original nucleus of repression that imprints its dynamism on the nascent psyche. Freud's theory of neurosis remains central and conditions the entire subsequent process, giving rise to an unconscious that retains the imprint of repression. However, entrusting the origin of the unconscious to repression is a doctrinaire legacy, which implies stringent constraints on the entire model of the mind. In other words, the risk is that the doctrine of repression cannot find anything other than what it presupposes.

In reality, Civitarese himself raises doubts about the idea that original removal could be the most suitable concept to describe psychic birth, doubts that he seems to resolve by rethinking the concept of original repression on the basis of Enrico Mangini's work. Mangini (2009) reconfigures primary repression into a lifelong process, which links excitement to the object relation, as a preliminary operation of secondary repression, thus giving primary repression a more relational interpretation than that of the hydraulic and solipsistic model by Freud. On this basis, the concept of the psychic representative of the drive (*Vorstellungsrepräsentaz*) assumes a "sensorial-pre-representative nature", as an "indefinite bodily sensation in search of meaning", and becomes ideative only "following the encounter with the object" (Civitarese, 2014, p. 165). Through the generous reading of Mangini, Civitarese consequently tries to overcome the aporias of the Freudian concept of primary repression and manages to describe the passage from the drive, to the affect-sensation, to the representation of a thing, i.e., the image invested with affection, now definitively psychic, outlining a tendency of drive representation towards the image. Despite this relational graft, Civitarese admits that the concept of original repression remains "nebulous" (ibid., p. 167). The difference between original and secondary repression is reduced to the simple fact that in the first the repressing agent is the mother's unconscious, as a complement to the infant's rudimentary consciousness, while in the second the subject's superego would intervene. Naturally, the superego is a late fruit, linked to the decline of Oedipus, which cannot play any role in the origin of the newborn's unconscious. To imagine the role of maternal repression, Civitarese thus recovers the semiotic level of the organisation of meaning, before the advent of language, referring to the distinction between semiotic and symbolic, between sense and meaning elaborated by Kristeva. At this level, the care of the child is subjected to the cultural norms, explicit and implicit, transmitted by the mother, for which the semiotic experience is affected by the mother's repression, and in this sense "even the procedural memories are under the shadow of the repressed" (ibid., p. 173). Moreover, this reduction of the original repression to a system of social laws and prohibitions, transmitted from the mother to the child, through the ways of interaction, starting from his or her conception, naturally links the formation of the unconscious to the destinies of *lack* and *inhibition*.

But what kind of lack? The lack of the Lacanian whishing subject, the "lack to be"? In Lacan, the constitutive alienation of the ego is linked to its specular identifications, the child who takes as his or her own the image that is *other*, the image of the mirror. The Lacanian subject remains caught up in an effect of language, on which the symptom, the relationship, the unconscious depend, which by condemning the subject to an infinite passage from one signifier to another, reduces the analytic work to an analysis of language. After all, Lacan (1966, p. 263) is convinced that "*Jokes and their Relation to the Unconscious* remains the most indisputable work because it is the most transparent, in which the effect of the unconscious is demonstrated to the limits of its subtlety", as "in the game of the Wit, of the joke, for example, it surprises the subject. With its flash, what its illuminates is the division of the subject from themselves" (Lacan, 1966a, p. 103). Giving the signifier priority over the subject therefore implies an original division of the subject, even before being warned of it, and alienation becomes a

logical structure, *Ichspaltung*. For Lacan, the effect of language is, as a con-
seguence, an original division, and the signifier in the unconscious chain
represents nothing except for another signifier, "one does not speak to the
subject. Ça talks about him, and it is there that he learns himself" (ibid.,
pp. 98–9), which becomes the effect of the word, the desire of the other.

This point of view has some critical aspects. Green (1966, p. 69), while
admitting that repression maintains a primordial role in the constitution of
the subject, as much as it bases it on misrecognition, maintains that for
Freud the "original fantasy" is the first organiser of the unconscious, and
that just the sensitisation to the original fantasy activates the repression and
constitutes the unconscious. Thus, the first repression organises the subsequent ones through an attraction exerted by the primary material repressed
Green tries to re-evaluate the economic factor, highlighting the role of instincts, and functioning by opposite pairs, in the conflict between positivity
and negativity, bearing in mind that drive and linguistic activities participate
in a common symbolic activity, proper to humanity, in which he places the
emergence of meaning from non-sense. Giving more weight to the second
topic, Green thus leads the unconscious back to its bodily roots, which acquires an even more impenetrable opacity and infiltrates the domain of the
ego, in the form of an unrepressed unconscious. In this path, Green shifts
the study of the unconscious from the repressed to what it represses and
he reconsiders the problem of desire, highlighting the link with the drive,
from which he draws a power of leavening and vertigo, which through the
pursuit of pleasure opens to the infinite horizon of the symbolic. For Green,
need, drive, and desire remain different but intimately connected categories, as they derive from each other, and both drive and linguistic activities
participate in the common symbolic activity proper to mankind.

Henry Lefebvre (1966, pp. 86–92), however, warns against possible er-
rors regarding the need-language-desire circuit and underlines that the need
to become desire must pass through the language test, for which it implies
a socially real subject, which speaks to onself, which speaks to others, and
which is spoken by others. In other words, the subject of desire implies a
distinction between me and not-me, and the recognition of the object of
desire, whereby desire can take its true form only when mother/infant differentiation begins, as noted Sarantis Thanopulos (2016). Laplance and
Leclaire, (1966, p. 35), on the other hand, hypothesise that language and the
unconscious are inextricably linked to the emergence of the death instinct,

and accord metonymy (displacement) the elementary function of the connection between one signifier and another: "metonymy, like the scar, thanks to its inexhaustible possibility of displacement, it marks and masks the lack where desire is born and perpetually precipitates, on the rock of the death instinct".

While putting any discussion of the concept of the death instinct in brackets, it should be noted that even before the death instinct of the newborn, it is necessary to take into consideration the death instinct of the mother, and of course that of the father and even of the generational axis. Winnicott (1949) recalls that the mother has good reasons to hate the child even before (s)he is able to feel hate, and that at the beginning of life it makes no sense to speak of envy or of the death instinct in the child. If we are to make sense of the work of the death instinct, it is then that of the mother (and other adults) that we must take into consideration in the formation of the unconscious. The original repression is consequently linked to the mother's unconscious, but more than to cultural norms, social laws and prohibitions, which often belong to the paternal or clan laws; we need to think of a split system, not necessarily repressed, of thoughts, desires, rejection, contempt and hate, that the mother can carry within herself, in the relationship with the product of her conception, on which her relational, affective and social history, including generational history, weighs. Who and what does her child represent for the mother? What is her ability to welcome the newcomer? What is the level of support and acceptance that the mother feels from the father, from the family and social group to which she belongs? Is there really a father, and what is his actual role? These questions and a thousand others weigh on the mother-child relationship, creating an irreparably split system of communication, which is affected by the relationship between the mother and her family; between this and the clan to which she belongs, between the clan and the social context, between the mother and her deepest parts, between the mother and the father, or the thousand forms in which the paternal function can be fulfilled, including those of the rapist and the sperm donor.

Can we then still speak of original repression? Haydée Faimberg (1993b, p. 89), in her works on *telescopage*, states that "If, with Freud, we postulate a primary repression as a theoretical necessity to explain the unconscious system, in this sense there would be an irreparably split subject". Faimberg thus postulates two types of splitting: the first linked to the functions of appropriation and intrusion, typical of the narcissistic regulation of the object, which causes a splitting of the ego in the child; the second linked instead to the original repression which establishes two different systems, the conscious and the unconscious, and therefore a foreign organisation that belongs to another, which causes alienation with feelings of extraneousness. The mother's repression hence creates a split in the child and not a repression, which remains a more mature defensive mechanism, which acts on representations, and which consequently presupposes a functioning alpha function.

This aspect is central to understanding the difference between the Bionian and the Freudian unconscious. With Grotstein, we have admitted a partial equivalence between Freud's repressed unconscious and Bion's dynamic unconscious, as both are formed from material previously "represented" at the level of consciousness, or in Bion's terms, from material transformed, "dreamed" by the alpha function. The hypothesis of the alpha function, however, weakens the action of repression, which loses the function of creating the unconscious, leaving the correct functioning of the two systems to the alpha barrier, which remains in balance with each other, in the possibility of a binocular vision. In other words, becoming unconscious becomes a transitory state that allows consciousness to work and maintain its tasks. The problem then moves to the level of the inaccessible unconscious, and to the split off parts of the Self. The psychotic part of the personality, the beta area, and the split off parts of the self are not permanently inaccessible, they can burst in with sudden acting out, as is evident in the borderline situation with its alternating states of the self. The problem is that these states leave little awareness, they remain split, for this reason these patients struggle to learn from experience and are unable to have binocular vision, to see through *caesura*. From this point of view, therefore, it is not repression that creates problems, but splitting, which, starting from traumatic object relations, creates split areas of the Self, and what with Bion we call the inaccessible unconscious. The origin of the unconscious then remains a mythical theme, and as René Kaës (1993) writes the origin is in any case "that which escapes us", from which we are excluded and caught up in the desire for another, or more than another, which precedes us. The subject of the unconscious consequently becomes the subject of heredity and thus the subject of the group or several groups, and the question of the formation of the unconscious comes to converge with that of psychic transmission. The problem of the origin of the unconscious thus shifts to a before and a where that continually escapes.

Bion's narration of origin

Bion is not disposed to too much speculation. The subject is "a group" and sinks into a proto-mental, which goes beyond any subject/object, individual/group, mind/body distinction. Having made the hypothesis of the proto-mental, however, Bion is not willing to make it work with too much speculation. He returns to the study of operating mechanisms, such as projective identification, the alpha function, the beta element and the alpha element, to understand how the unconscious is actually formed.

For Bion, the formation of the unconscious is a process that requires the alpha function, and as a result at birth there is no unconscious. A position congruent with Winnicott's (1958) observation when he states that at birth there is neither repression, nor the repressed unconscious. For Bion (1962, p. 35), the newborn has only a glimmer of consciousness and can only rely on the mother's unconscious, or rather on her capacity for containment and reverie to get out of the initial chaos: "the good breast and the bad breast are emotional experiences. The physical component, milk, discomfort of satiation or the opposite, can be immediately apparent to the sense and we can therefore accord a chronological priority to beta-elements over alpha-elements". It is then the mother who assumes the function of acting as the unconscious of the newborn.

> The limited consciousness defined by Freud, that I am using to define a rudimentary infant consciousness, is not associated with an unconscious. All impressions of the self are of equal value; all are conscious. The mother's capacity for reverie is the receptor organ for the infant's harvest of self-sensation gained by its conscious.
>
> (Bion, 1967, p. 116)

As a result, in the formation of the unconscious, the other is essential from the outset, and the mother-infant relationship possesses a quality, upon which the development of the child's mind rests, and upon which the actual relationship with the father insists, and even the fractal Oedipus, or rather the introjection of the oedipal relationships of various generations, and of course the ecological niche, environment, culture, society, history, i.e., a set of everything that today we tend to identify with the psychoanalytic field.

The quality of the relationship thus passes through the alpha function of the mother, of which reverie is the most important factor, but also contact: the holding and handling; the sensory dimension, the aesthetic, and the haptic dimension, which is both tactile vision and optical touch, and naturally also through the rhythm, the ability to tunein, to go in unison (at-one-ment), and the atonement; the sacrifice, the ability to reconcile and to step back in order to create and gauge that "transitional" environment that Winnicott has admirably described. The alpha function of the child develops in this relationship, as an introjection of a couple ♀♂, which stands for the parental couple, but which becomes an intrapsychic relationship between a part of him or herself that thinks another part of him or herself:

> From the point of view of meaning thinking depends on the successful introjection of the good breast that is originally responsible for the performance of α-function. On this introjection depends the ability of any part of *I* to be ♂ to the other part's ♀.
>
> (Bion, 1963, p. 32)

The α-function is then introjected as ♀♂, and this implies that the newborn's first real great challenge is to master the primal scene, or rather the father-mother relationship, which represents the origin and source of every split, which acts both interpersonally and intrapsychically, and generates in the newborn not so much a split as a Kleinian evolutionary mechanism, but a split as a compartmental dissociation of separate states of the Self. In situations of envy, Bion hypothesises the inversion of the function ♀♂, which becomes – ♀♂ and destroys the meaning rather than creating it, but we can also imagine that an antagonism between the parents, and therefore a primal scene imbued with hate, can lead to traumatic relationships and pathological splits. Moreover, this emotional climate in which the child grows up is perhaps the origin of the field, or rather the first manifestation of the field, in which the mother-father exchange takes place, and on which the effects of the transgenerational, of the ghosts and secrets that transcend generations, are exerted. In situations where splitting prevails, we witness a pathological increase in projective identification as a defensive means to evacuate situations of unthinkable pain. However, what happens in situations of lack, where the negative prevails, in situations of the unsaid, family secrets, expelled mourning, non-recognition, in which it is the denial or rejection (*verwerfung*), rather than the repression that creates perceptive voids, areas of anesthesia, areas not alive, not dead…? In these situations, according to the hypothesis of Pistiner de Cortiñas, rather than an excess of projective identification, we have a detention of projective identification, with the formation of zones which absorb energy, or which radiate negative energy. These situations flow into the inaccessible unconscious as parts of the Self or cores of experiences that never really reached consciousness, or because they were subjected to an original split, dissociation, denial, a systematic non-recognition or simply because the structures necessary for memory (hippocampus, temporal cortex and orbitofrontal) are not mature enough. In these cases, in the pre-verbal and pre-symbolic era, the "filing" would take place in the posterior temporo-parieto-occipital cortical areas of the right hemisphere, and therefore would remain outside the consciousness and linguistic signification, going to constitute the essence of implicit memory (Mancia, 2004).

This being the case, Bion bases the development of thought and the unconscious on the most primitive mechanisms of the mind, mechanisms that he studies starting from psychosis, but which have a precise confirmation in the early stages of the mother-child relationship and determine the quality of the relationship. The Freudian concept of the repressed unconscious, and even more so the non-repressed unconscious, however, disregards the relationship with the other, remaining in the fiction of a self-constructing subject.

Repetition and expansion. Fantasy and radical imagination

Chuster (2010, p. 140) points out that Bion's unconscious is characterised by a double movement of repetition and expansion, a process which on the one hand is "always creating and expanding, while, at the same time, maintaining a conservative movement of repetition of forms". The Bionian unconscious is then something much vaster than the Freudian unconscious, as Bion himself used to say, something that Chuster calls "emptiness of Being, the infinite beyond human existence" (ibid.) and that Bion also calls "O". Moreover, this unconscious is repetition of forms and at the same time expansion and creation. Psychoanalysis is a process that stimulates the growth of the field it investigates, so there is a moment in which it can be said that unconscious has been created, because what was there before has now expanded. Thus, the origin of the unconscious is a process that repeats itself continuously in the analytic process. Nonetheless, this theory would be incomplete if it did not take into consideration Bion's concept of pre-conception. For Chuster, the theory of pre-conceptions is fundamental, as it is the oldest mental element, which is already manifested in the intrauterine environment. It establishes a difference between the human and animal psyche, it is a sort of Kantian a priori form, an embryonic mind which is maintained even after birth, and which rests on the concept of radical imagination. Chuster borrows this concept from the philosopher Cornelius Castoriadis, to indicate the original element of intuition, which he differentiates from projective identification. In the Kleinian perspective, however, projective identification remains an omnipotent fantasy that already presupposes the existence of the unconscious. It is essential then to distinguish fantasy from imagination.

Unconscious fantasy would have to do with fantasy, as the ability to remember and link together various elements of memory. The radical imagination, capable of acting before the recognition of any object, as original, would instead be activated by the rhythms, acoustic and kinetic, of the maternal heart, of the child himself, by the peristaltic movements, by the voice of the mother, the father, but also by the cries of pain and joy, and the emotions, especially the violent ones expressed in the family environment during pregnancy. It is this radical imagination that, starting from the rhythms, "causes a kind of explosion that opens up spaces and creates a kind of cylinder, or an empty window, whose moldings are made of time" (ibid., p. 150). Time that begins to organise the world to come, unknown situations that will present themselves in the gaseous environment, but which somehow have already happened, so they are like a *memory of the future*. And this experience of expansion, "is always original and is connected to the domain of the imagination. It is not a question of repetition, which pertains to the realm of fantasy" (ibid.). Chuster considers these windows that are formed in intrauterine life, a preparation for future situations, and identifies them with Bionian pre-conceptions. These windows, formed in the embryonic mind, still devoid of landscape, when they come into contact with the mother who reappears shortly after birth, making the breast available, acquire the triadic dimension: the newborn, the breast and the mother. Using the differential between fantasy and imagination it is then possible to grasp and observe the existence of an area of the human mind that creates something that is not an image or a photograph of reality, but something new, which did not exist before. Chuster hypothesises that in interpretation there is a complementarity between the repetitive aspects of the patient and those parts of the unconscious that remain inaccessible, which he compares to what Freud calls "mycelium of the mushroom, the network close to chaos, prior to any meaning" (ibid., p. 159). These dissociated and scattered elements on a chaotic network, in a painful state of uncertainty, which produces anti-emotion defenses (-K, -L, -H), must go through the integration of love, hate and thirst for knowledge. Only the imagination and an interpretation that puts respect for life in general and ethical-aesthetic principles in the foreground can allow the development of these experiences that are placed before the word. In order for the interpretation to be creative, it must remain open, without a definitive conclusion, and it must rest on the creative imagination of the analyst. Only in this way can an expansion of the mind and of the analytic link be achieved.

Bion admits that it is difficult to identify how consciousness arises, and that we can speak of conscious and unconscious only after the alpha function has come into play. The infant can only evacuate sensory data and its emotions, feelings of hunger, cold and fear of dying into the mother. For this Bion (1962, p. 36) shifts the problem to the mother's reverie:

> If the feeding mother cannot allow reverie or if the reverie is allowed but is not associated with love for the child or its father this fact will be communicated to the infant even though incomprehensible to the infant. Psychical quality will be imparted to the channels of communication, the links with the child.

Thus,

> If the projection is not accepted by the mother the infant feels that its feeling that it is dying is stripped of such meaning as it has. It therefore rejntroiects, not a fear of dying made tolerable, but a nameless dread.
>
> (Bion, 1967, p. 116)

The newborn's glimmer of consciousness is in fact unable to carry out this function and what then settles in him or her is not an alpha function, but a repulsive object of projective identification, in place of a welcoming and understanding object "the infant has a wilfully misunderstanding object – with which it is identified" (ibid., p. 117). If therefore, as Civitarese admits, in Bion the unconscious coincides with the alpha function, the formation of the unconscious can only follow the vicissitudes of this function.

The alpha function is then the navel on which the processes that press on the individual and condition his or her development converge, whether they are intrapsychic, relational, generational or ecological. To remain in the family context, Bion affirms that the capacity for reverie, an essential factor of the alpha function, must be associated with love for the child and for that of the father, and it is only in the symbiotic ♀♂ relationship, in which one depends on an other for mutual benefit, that there is real development. Thought and the thinker correspond and modify each other through this correspondence, thought proliferates and the thinker develops, because (s)he can access the truth. This means that the newborn, even before birth, is involved in the father-mother relationship, in their interpersonal and intrapsychic splits, in the said and the unsaid, the transgenerational and of course the biological, hereditary and accidental. It could be said that if the unconscious is linked to the alpha function, we must assume that there are clinical situations in which it makes no sense to start from the conscious and the unconscious. In these cases, Chuster states it is necessary to start from the idea of inaccessible. These are clinical situations with various types of confusion; between sleep and wakefulness, between achievements and values, such as between error and damage, criticism and denigration, loss of youth and aging, intimacy and lack of confidentiality, voracity and efficiency and such or psychosomatic situations or somato-psychotics, autoimmune diseases, patients who cannot tolerate pain and are unable to suffer it, etc.

In these cases, Bion hypothesises that there are mental vestiges or archaic elements that can break into the surface at any moment. Bion speaks of thalamic fear, of somites, of pleasure and pain, of pressure through the amniotic fluid, of the body, of mnemonic traces like shadows that the future casts before it, he speaks of the fetus and of Es.

> It seems to me that there are certain premature and precocious developments that are too premature and too precocious to be tolerable. Therefore, the foetus, the id, does its best to sever that connection. At a later stage the individual can shut himself up.
>
> (Bion, 1976, p. 126)

The reference to the id is significant, as it refers to something undifferentiated, to the proto-mental system, or to something that can be "pre-natal, or pre-birth of a psyche or a mental life [...] Can we detect in these expressions of conscious rational communications vestiges of something coming from a part of the personality which is in fact physical?" (Bion, 1975a, p. 47).

Repression or split

Civitarese's (2014, p. 167) hypothesis that "the repressed unconscious (of the mother) projects her shadow not only on the nascent repressed unconscious of the child but also on that of the non-repressed (cognitive or structural)", could then be rethought. It seems more plausible that it is the mother's inaccessible unconscious that projects its shadow onto the nascent unconscious of the newborn, or that nevertheless influences its formation. Following Bion and his totally relational conception, we must think that it is the split behaviour, the form of the relationship and the emotional atmospheres that condition the formation, development or otherwise of the alpha function and therefore of the newborn's unconscious. In reality, ideas such as the repressed unconscious, the unrepressed unconscious and even the inaccessible unconscious maintain a substantial halo that does not help us understand the processes that originate the field. Bion (1975a, p. 49) not only affirms: "Investigated the caesura; not the analyst; not the analysand; not the unconscious; not the conscious; not sanity, not insanity. But the caesura, the link, the synapse, the (counter-transference, the transitive-intransitive mood". He also states that

> mouth is one anchor, breast is the other. Both of these terms have been treated as if they were the essential features of the analogy. It is exactly this point that marks the divergence of the path of growth from the path of the decay. The breast and the mouth are only important in so far as they serve to define the bridge between the two. When the 'anchors' usurp the importance which belongs to the qualities they should be imparting to the bridge, growth is impaired.
>
> (Bion, 1971, pp. 26–7)

The mother is consequently the unconscious of the newborn, and it is her reverie that allows him or her to contain his or her anxieties and to form his or her own alpha function, and therefore, the ability to think, dream and develop the unconscious. However, in order to retain a good reverie the mother must have a good ability in containment, and have a good relationship with her internal objects; in other words, she must have introjected a good Oedipus. Naturally, you must also have a good relationship

with the father, and so, in summary, there must be a good relationship between container and contained for the possibility of a third party to develop.
This means that the previous generations, the fractal Oedipus, press on the
mother-child relationship, or rather the echo of the generational relationships that will condition our relationships, or our ability to relate. The split
must, for this reason, be understood as a *spaltung*, a radical split, to which
the newborn is often subjected from the beginning, between mother and/or
father, but also intrapsychic, within the mother and/or father, because the
self is multiple: we are a *group*, we are not the unconscious of the wit or the
puns of the Viennese ladies.

Chapter 8

Representation (*Vorstellung*) and presentation (*Darstellung*)

Centrality of representation in Freud

What does Freud mean by representation? And how legitimate is it to bring Freudian psychoanalysis back to the centrality of representation? Representation is a general concept, which Freud takes from German philosophy. Vorstellung is the "idea", every cognitive act, in its relation to the thing, which in modern philosophy, from Descartes to Husserl, indicates the relationship of thinking with reality, the "outside of itself of thought" (Borutti, 2006, p. XIII). Representation thus stands in the place of something that is not there, evokes presence and shows an intentional statute of thought, but it must maintain with the represented object a specific iconic-mimetic valence, which philosophy has gradually declined in various ways. If representing is thinking intentionally, having an idea of something absent, under this definition we must recognise the coincidence of representation with the mental, which always refers to something else, while the physical object always and only refers to its owen self. However what does it mean that Freudian psychoanalysis is centred on the model of representation, and what are the limitations of this model?

Freud bases his model of the psychic apparatus on the rejection of the Cartesian position which equated psyche and consciousness, but maintains the centrality of representation, extending it to the unconscious. The text of the conscience is incomplete, it cannot account for slips, behaviours, symptoms or even dreams. The hypothesis of the unconscious, which philosophers, psychologists and people of letters had long taken into consideration, and therefore, imposes itself as a scientific necessity for developing a method capable of reintroducing meaning and coherence into the gaps of consciousness. The Freudian unconscious can be described with visual metaphors such as "Indian reserve", "dark and malevolent place", to highlight how it

DOI: 10.4324/9781032655239-11

is inhabited by representations incompatible with the ego, which have never had access to consciousness (primal repression), or that have been pushed back secondarily (secondary repression). Repression, which forms the unconscious, consists in fact in expelling and keeping something away from consciousness. This something, in *Studies on Hysteria*, simply is "any experience which calls up distressing affects – such as those of fright, anxiety, shame or psychical pain – may operate as a trauma of this kind" (Freud, 1892–5, p. 4), but starting from *The Interpretation of Dreams*, they can only be repressed "sexual wisheful impulses from infancy" (Freud, 1900, p. 605).

The central point is that for Freud (1915b, p. 166) repression *does not annihilate* "the idea which represents an instinct", but simply prevents it from becoming conscious. In the unconscious, therefore, a representative image of the instinct remains, separate from the affect, which can be moved to another representation. Affection also remains in the unconscious, but only as potential, which can be awakened and traced back to consciousness, and as Civitarese (2014, p. 168) observes "the mind strives to deceive affection with the kaleidoscope of representations". For Freud (1915b, p. 179), the quantitative factor of the instinct can be totally repressed, take on another quality, or be transformed into anxiety, but in the case in which the development of affect proceeds directly from the unconscious system to consciousness, it always has the character of anxiety, "for which all 'repressed' affects are exchanged". Freud is convinced that the opposition between conscious and unconscious cannot be applied to the instinct:

> An instinct can never become an object of consciousness – only the idea that represents the instinct can. Even in the unconscious, moreover, an instinct cannot be represented otherwise than by an idea. If the instinct did not attach itself to an idea or manifest itself as an affective state, we could know nothing about it.
>
> (ibid., p. 177)

Vorstellungsrepräsentanz

The Freudian unconscious is thus first of all repressed infantile sexual desire, which emerges through the camouflage work of the dream, but also in the symptom, in the parapraxis, the joke, which "present", involuntarily, what consciousness does not manages to "represent" hitself voluntarily. Freud, therefore, does not think of an unknowable unconscious, like that of the romantics, but of a knowable unconscious, "thoughts", "ideas" and above all "desires", which "with the help of a certain amount of work they can be transformed into, or replaced by, conscious mental processes" (ibid., p. 168). For that reason, in *Metapsychology*, Freud refers only to the repression of the instinct representation, *Vorstellungsrepräsentanz*, a complex concept that inherits all the ambiguities of the concept of instinct, oscillating between somatic excitation, ideational representative and affect quantum. In Civitarese's words, the concept of ideational representation recounts and theorises in a dizzying synthesis, "the history of the transformations that from sensory impressions and impulses arrive at consciousness (symbols, language)" (Civitarese, 2014, p. 159).

Accordingly, there are conscious representations and unconscious representations, but in the case of drive motions, feelings and unconscious sensations, the term *vorstellung*, representation, may not be adequate. Ricoeur (1965) observes that *repräsentanz* is not properly a representation, but a function of representation which expresses that there is something psychic which represents the drive, which reveals it, presents it purely and simply. The term *Vorstellungsrepräsentanz* has subsequently created quite a few problems for translators, because it would simultaneously indicate a cognitive mimetic representation (*Vorstellung*) or a mental image deriving from a perceptive memory trace, and connected to it in an isomorphic but more abstract way, and a representative function not isomorphic, but symbolic, which before representing something simply reveals it. Le Guen (2008), in his Freudian dictionary, writes that *Repräsentanz* or *Repräsentant* designate a capacity to represent, as opposed to *Vorstellung*, which is the effective representation of a thing, object or word. For this reason the various translations of *Vorstellungsrepräsentanz*: ideational representation, representative representation, representation given by a representation, are all compromises. Mangini (2009) maintains that the psychic representatives of the drive are not true representations, but affects-sensations, and that the representation of a thing, i.e., the image of the object which lends itself to discharging the drive tension, is formed only when the psychic representative of the drive meets a representation.

Vorstellung, representation and *Darstellung*, presentation

Ricoeur, when translating *Repräsentanz* with presentation (*présentation*), hence grasps the fundamental distinction between *Vorstellung*, representation, and *Darstellung*, presentation. This is on which Laurence Kahn (2007) insists, when recalling that with presentation consciousness comes into contact with what it cannot represent. On this distinction, which Freud (1900, p. 144) had actually already introduced in *The Interpretation of Dreams*, defining the conscience as "a sense organ which perceives data that arise elsewhere", the problem of the representability or figurability of unconscious contents unfolds, which refers to the strategies to which the psyche resorts in order to obtain the presentation of the repressed material without this being able to be recognised (displacement, condensation, overdetermination). Borutti (2006) recalls that *Darstellung,* presentation, in Kant, and above all in Wittgenstein, links representation to the imaginative function, which makes it capable of representing the thing in the figure, according to certain rules, but at the same time connecting it to an edge of unrepresentability. The *darstellung* then opposes the concept of representation, *Vorstellung*, as a mental and conceptual reproduction of the thing, and it is linked to the concept of *fiction*, as an imaginative form of experience, "a 'presentation' in a figure, and at the same time an 'exposition'" (ibid., p. 3), which opens to the relationship between representable and unrepresentable, a relationship that is always at the basis of the production of meaning, in its emergence from an opaque and formless background. *Darstellung* is hence "indirect presentation of a being that withdraws, a presentation that has internalized the prohibition to say the thing directly and exhaustively. In the semantic field of this word-concept, saying and not being able to say representatively are therefore united" (ibid., p. 4). The legitimacy of the psychoanalytic method is thus based on the assumption that the unrepresentable and ineffable (*a-phané*) unconscious can break into the territory of representation with its manifestations, (*fanìe*), which allow us to investigate it. Consciousness, however, can only come into contact with the "presentation" of what it fails to represent. This is the essential difference between "representation" and "presentation", between *Vorstellung* and *Darstellung*, and the importance of the work of presentation, *Darstellbarkeit*, which through displacement, condensation, overdetermination, allows the "psychic material", the camouflage necessary for the repressed to be presented while escaping censorship. The dream work (*Traumarbeit*) is then a work of camouflage of the unconscious desire, a distortion (*Verstellung*), which is both manifestation and distortion, which corresponds to the opposite of the analyst's work of deciphering. "The nucleus of the *Ucs*- consist of instinctual representatives which seek to discharge their cathexis; that is to say, it consists of wishful impulses" (Freud, 1915b, p. 186), writes Freud.

For this reason, it is not the instinct itself that belongs to the unconscious, but its ideational representation, or rather the representation of the thing (*sachvorstellung*), as a visual image linked to the object, the semblance of a thing, while belonging to the conscious is the representation of the thing plus the representation of word (*wortvorstellung*), which is by its very nature acoustic, made up of words. The instinct in Freud so remains centred in the realm of the visual and the representational, and can only be represented by an idea, in other words, repression rejects the translation into words of the first, authentic, object investments. These movements of desire, subject only to the pleasure principle, unalterable over time, have mobile investments, which can move from one representation to another, condense into a single one, in the absence of contradiction, but the repressed emotional state remains "only a potential beginning which is prevented from developing" (ibid., p. 178), hence the idea that affection remains the "Cinderella" of Freud's theory of the instincts.

The quantum of affection

Nevertheless, how to reconcile this position with the idea that Freud expresses in the last part of *Repression*?

> We recall the fact that the motive and purpose of repression has nothing else than the avoidance of unpleasure. It follows that the vicissitude of the quota of affect belonging to the rappresentative is far more important of the idea.
>
> (Freud, 1915a, p. 153)

Freud therefore tries to develop a method that reintegrates into the realm of meaning "thoughts", "ideas" and above all the most distant desires, which have the character of "indestructibility" and which refer not only to our childhood but also to the archaic and myth, but he does not forget the quantitative factor, the amount of affect. The dream, by virtue of its belonging to discourse, is even more suitable than the symptom for showing the mechanisms of deformation through which infantile wishes and instincts find their expression. The dream for Freud is already a vicissitude of the instinct, but which requires mnemic traces – of images taken from everyday life – which it achieves thanks to a typical regression towards the perceptive system. Freud (1900, p. 448) affirms that "dream might be described as a substitute (*Ersatz*), for an infantile scene modified by being transferred on to a recent experience". Ricoeur observes that by interpreting the infantile scene as a real memory, Freud effectively weakens the dimension of the imaginary to the advantage of real perception. Time is thus a reference to a childhood scene, but disguised and transferred to the present, so that the original sources remain hidden. In *The Ego and the Id*, Freud (1923, p. 19) specifies that

> only something has once been Cs. perception can become conscious, and that anything arising from from within (apart from feelings) that seeks to become conscious must try to transform itself into external perceptions: this becomes possible by means of memory-traces.

For Ricoeur this is linked to the preference accorded by Freud to representation, which in dream work is considered a hallucinatory revival of a primitive scene which was truly part of perception. In the function of representation, therefore, a point emerges where the problem of force and meaning coincide, because Freud realises that the removed representation must maintain its investment in order to maintain its capacity for action in the Unconscious system. Hence, Freud, after the dynamic and topical, introduces the economic point of view to complete his *Metapsychology*. Freud is, therefore, trying to reintroduce the "quantitative factor", the emotional charge of the psychic representation, and of course he rediscovers the link with the pleasure-pain principle, but also his uncertainties with respect to what a repressed emotional state means: while a repressed representation remains a real formation in the Uc system, a repressed emotional state we don't quite know what it consists of, if not in a potential that is not permitted to develop. However, Ricoeur, like Green himself, in the end hypothesises that the Freudian unconscious exhibits more the sign of energetics than that of the signifier: "The nucleus of the *Ucs*- consist of instinctual representatives which seek to discharge their cathexis; that is to say, it consists of wishful impulses" (Freud, 1915b, p. 186). Impulses that however remain waiting for a surrogate representation to which to link their purpose. Here, the path from the instinct to the expressed emotion becomes complex and appears as an extraordinary attempt to show the transition from the bodily to the mental, or rather the transformation of sensory and emotional stimuli into mental images, according to the sequence that Civitarese (2014) condenses into effective passages: drive (*Triebs*) → affect-sensation (*repräsentanz*) → image (*Vorstellung*) → representation of thing (image invested with affect); therefore, something definitively psychic, which expresses a *tending* of drive representation towards the image.

The illusions of representation

Green (2000a) observes that when Freud links *après coup* and foreclosure, especially in *The Wolf Man*, he in fact alludes to a stage in which the total refusal of castration is equivalent to its non-existence, so that more than a denial, it is about a judgment which declares that there is nothing to judge. It is the path of disavowal of the fetishist, which together with the compulsion to repeat seem to be placed on this side of the resources of representation. For Green it is also the way of reintroducing the experience of time into the psychism, which can be traced back to unrepresentable situations that sink into rhythm, into tuning, which Green approaches to the concepts of salience (rhythmic discontinuity) and pregnancy (foundation of the *continuum*), linked to the research of René Thom. Nonetheless, as we know Freud deals with splitting a bit like the fetishist with regard to the penis, "he does not deny having seen a penis, but he does not dare claim to have seen one".

The problem of the impossibility of representing certain states of the Self, which Bion defines as inaccessible states, and therefore the pain connected to them, needs to make a paradigm shift. However, psychoanalysis cannot address the thorny problem of the limits of representation, without taking into account the formidable philosophical problems and inexhaustible conflicts of ideas that are concentrated in this concept. To avoid the well-known problems of self-referentiality, psychoanalysis must deal with the meaning that science attributes to the concept of representation. An attentive author such as Enzo Funari (1991) argues that representation is the basic condition for any psychic experience to occur, and that in fact the theme of representation accompanies the attempt to found a psychological point of view, free from explanatory appeals drawn from other disciplines, such as biology, neurophysiology, linguistics and semiotics. Perhaps, however, these are no longer the times in which psychoanalysis can do it alone. Limiting the concept of representation to a psychological vision is no longer acceptable or useful today. The neurosciences themselves place the problem of representation at the centre of their biological paradigm, and that's not good news. Albeit with some variations, neurosciences conceive representation as a synthesis endowed with the qualities of globality, coherence, constancy and stability, which, although emerging from a neural configuration, is realised as an image, in some way in relation to the object it represents (Morin, 1986). The Churchlands (2007), leading exponents of so-called eliminationist materialism, write that the objection that pain contains an irreducible qualitative aspect can be overcome by a *reduction* to its neuronal and biological correlates. Through this reduction, the so-called *qualia* of pain can be traced back to *representations*, which as such are understandable within a scientific model: concepts such as belief, free will, conscience and pain can and must be explained and redefined once the research will have shed light on the nature of the underlying brain functions. The authors underline that this is a non-trivial question, "because it implies a judgment of validity regarding psychological studies and of reality about the phenomena described by psychology" (ibid., p. 2). Precisely, the Churchlands ask themselves: "What will become of psychological definitions and concepts once their functions have been traced back to the properties of specific networks of neurons or neurobiological mechanisms?" (ibid).

Paradoxically, therefore, the problem of representation is placed both at the centre of Freudian psychoanalysis and of the biological approach, emerging as a transversal core of reductionism.

Does the same apply to Bion's system? Civitarese underlines how Bion introduced the transformations precisely to overcome the model of representation. More precisely, Bion uses Kant and the concept of the *thing-in-itself* to overcome the representationalist paradigm of classical psychoanalysis, centred on the object and the idea of truth as correspondence. For this he turns to the Kantian theory of knowledge, founded on the subject of knowledge. Kant thought that *things-in-themselves* and the *noumena* they emanate were knowable only through the sensations we have of them, which we perceive as *phenomena*. Bion (1965, p. 24) accepts this position and equates phenomena to the transformations that each one produces of the *facts-in-themselves*, for which he clearly distinguishes between "the patient's experience O and the analyst's experience O", and between the processes that both carry out in transforming this experience. In Kant, however, awareness of the external world takes place through pure intuitions of space and time, which nonetheless remain *a priori* conditions of knowledge, while every intuition is always sensitive, so that thought can become knowledge only insofar as it is placed in relation with objects of the senses (experience). After following Kant's thinking, shifting attention from the object of knowledge to the subject and considering the *facts-in-themselves* as unknowable, Bion is then forced to abandon the Kantian model because his real problem is the intuition of mental reality, which does not belong to the domain of the sensible world. Not only that, Bion's problem is to grasp the invariants of a constantly changing reality, to intuit the unrepresentable, the at-one-ment, and above all to grasp the change and growth in the relationship, which pass through the construction of a intersubjective truth and a development of the analytic function of the personality. Bion's challenge is, as a result, dramatically difficult, and the question is to what extent can Bion's thought be grafted into that of Freud's, or does it need a radical paradigm shift?

Chapter 9

Intuition and reality of O

Introduction of intuition as an opening to a new epistemology

Psychoanalysis has never loved the concept of intuition and has kept it in an ambiguous position, generally assimilating it to that of insight. The word intuition comes from the Latin tueri, "look", which combined with "in" becomes "to look inside". Nonetheless, while insight implies becoming aware of the logical relationships between a problem and an answer, in intuition there is only a sensation of coherence; rapid, sudden and without any logical, rational connection. It is a premonition that is felt in the body, a flash of consciousness, which reveals the unknown and maintains the link with the invisible and the infinite. Thus intuition can precede insight, but it does not coincide with it. Freud (1932) placed intuition among illusions, together with divination, as the fulfilment of desires linked to emotional needs. A position that derives directly from his choice to keep psychoanalysis within the dominant scientific framework, which in spite of everything remained that of the positivist. Paradoxically, the desire to bring determinism into the study of the unconscious makes Freudian psychoanalysis a science with a rationalistic connotation and very far from the canons of current science, increasingly involved with probability, the irrational, the indeterminate and even the impossible. Einstein (1954) does not disdain to use intuition, which Freud expunges from his method: "There is no logical way to discover these elementary laws, the only way is intuition, which is helped by the feeling one feels for the order behind the appearance".

Unlike Freud, Bion is convinced that the psychic qualities with which psychoanalysis has to do remain ineffable and cannot be grasped by the senses, but by intuition, as equivalent to the use of the senses in medicine, and he thinks that the intuitive ability must be exercised with a permanent,

DOI: 10.4324/9781032655239-12

lasting and continuous discipline, because it is hindered by memory, desire and understanding, which remain based on the senses. To grasp the patient's reality in analysis, Bion also puts aside the consciousness that Freud indicates as the psychic counterpart of the sense organs and introduces a more general postulate, which he represents with "O", the psychoanalytic vertex, that the analyst must become to encounter the patient's ultimate reality, which can only be intuited. Phenomena are known through the senses, but to become O, the analyst must free themselves from "thinking that depends on a background of sense impression" (Bion, 1970, p. 28). The introduction of "intuition" and "O" is often referred to in Bion's "mystical" (Grotstein, 2007) or "undisciplined" (O'Shaughnessy, 2005) period, not without some misunderstanding, which slowed down the full understanding of the new paradigm that he actually built. Bion introduced the concept of intuition from the beginning, and this concept has nothing to do with the so-called "mysticism", but rather with his rejection of the positivist paradigm and the introduction of a new epistemology linked to Bergson, Poincaré, Husserl Whitehead, etc.

Since the study on groups, Bion in fact declares his intention to use intuitions developed from the psychoanalytical point of view. In *Elements of Psychoanalysis* he confirms that he wants to refine and develop intuition, and in *Transformations* he differentiates an "intuitive psychoanalysis" from an "axiomatic psychoanalysis" (Bion, 1965, p. 122).

P.C. Sandler (2005) combines Bion's intuition with the Kantian idea of apprehension of reality without the intermediation of rational thought, but current research rather indicates that Bion takes this concept from Bergson and Poincaré. In *Matter and Memory*, Henry Bergson (1896) distinguishes two ways of knowing; the *intellectual-analytical,* relative and point of view-dependent way of describing physical objects; the *intuitive way*, a global, immediate form of knowledge, more useful for grasping the continuous flow of life, an absolute knowledge that with imagination and in harmony with the object is inserted into the state of the object's mind in such a way as to resonate until it coincides with it. For the French philosopher it is, therefore, the intuitive way that can reach the "ultimate reality", the absolute and the infinite, but on the condition of great effort and a method capable of relinquishing the previous uses of thought and perception being employed.

Bion looks to Bergson, but also to Poincaré, Husserl and Carnap, which refute the positivist position that truth can only be achieved through empirical evidence. Consequently, Bion turns to contemporary epistemology in order to address the new problems proposed to him by the clinic, starting with group therapy and psychosis. For Bion, only intuition is really capable of addressing the problem of how to grasp the psychic reality that is beyond known sensory realisation. Bion then conceives of intuition as a holistic cognitive modality that belongs to the whole system and allows one to get in touch with "O", with what happens in the session and with the "ultimate reality" of the patient's mind. Hence from the outset, Bion states that he wants to develop an intuitive psychoanalysis and constructs a method for refining and using intuitive decisions. This method is incorporated in the grid, where the focus can be on the development of the patient's thinking (vertical axis) or on the patient's use of his communication (horizontal axis) (Rugi, 2019a, 2022).

The entrance of O

Intuition and O are, for this reason, closely linked and central to Bion's theory and the possibility of understanding transformations passes through the effective understanding of the nature of O. The entry of O, right from the first pages of *Transformations*, takes place with the disturbing noise of reality, rather than with the bombastic one of mystical rhetoric. Bion (1965, pp. 16–7) says that

> First I shell apply the theory to my own account of the session: something occurred during the session -the absolute facts of the session. What the absolute facts are cannot ever be known, and this I denote by the sign O.

When he chooses "O" to denote reality, Bion admits that he has in mind Kant's "unknowable thing-in-itself", but immediately appears concerned about an overly philosophical semantic aura and specifies that his choice has the advantage that "the facts are limited to that experience shared by patient and analyst" (ibid., p. 29). It is only this that the analyst can process and transform, so his or her main concern must be with "the material of which he has direct evidence, namely, the emotional experience of the analytic sessions themselves" (ibid., p. 7). Of this reality, the analyst must be interested above all in grasping the evolution in the session, when it emerges from the dark and formless with the evanescent characteristics of dreams. This "O" is the real goal of the analyst. The interpretation, to be effective, must then be able to correctly grasp O, and to express it in words.

But which O? Not an "any" O, any circumstance of the patient's life, but an O, which "in any analytic situation is available for transformation by analyst and analysand equally" (ibid., p. 48). During construction, however, O takes on many other meanings, until it becomes a complex and elusive concept, in which we feel the idea of origin, of an abstract sign, which refers to the infinite, to the divinity, to the Platonic form... and which takes on a different meaning depending on the contexts and levels, passing from reality itself, the absolute facts, to the divinity, the noumenon, the infinite, the absolute truth.

In the first instance, O is introduced to indicate the "absolute facts" that take place in the session, thus the Kantian thing-in-itself, which remains unknowable, if not through its transformations, and which everyone operates on reality subjectively. Bion uses the concept of the thing-in-itself to overcome the representationalist paradigm of classical psychoanalysis, centred on the object and the idea of truth as correspondence. After following Kant's thinking, shifting attention from the object of knowledge to the subject and considering the facts themselves as unknowable, Bion is, therefore, forced to abandon the Kantian model because his real problem is the intuition of mental reality, which does not belong to the domain of the sensible world.

Invariants and transformations

With the concept of transformation Bion tries to describe the learning process in the analytic experience. For this reason, *Transformations* represents Bion's epistemological effort to give a scientific guise to that complex set of processes that go from the patient's original experience to what happens in the session. The transformation must naturally lead to something shared, something on which patient and analyst can and should agree. In consequence, Bion from the beginning of the text introduces the concept of invariant which always accompanies that of transformation and without which the transformations would remain an infinite series of closed and incommunicable variations; a flow without memory. We know the invariants that Bion attributes to the three main types of transformations: *the transference*, in those with a rigid motion, or neurotic one; the *moral component*, in the projective or psychotic ones; *rivalry, envy, greed, thieving,* in hallucinosis. But what is the true foundation of invariants, or rather the basis, the ground of understanding each other? All of Bion's work on transformations is a gigantic attempt to "illuminate and solve the problems that lie unsolved at the heart of certain forms of mental disturbance" (Bion, 1965, p. 39) and these problems revolve around the fate of the β- element, of the emotional reality that the patient cannot metabolise. Bion places the relationship and thus the patient/analyst emotional experience at the centre of analytic work, revolutionising the very foundations of psychoanalysis as a method of treatment. Attention passes from the contained to the containers, or rather to their relationship and thus to the analytic process, which coincides with the way in which the ability to think as an intersubjective experience develops, starting from the analyst/patient relationship, which repeats that of mother/child.

Interpretation as transformation

The transformation must consequently lead to something that the patient and the analyst can agree on, and show how the relationship and the language produce change and growth. At a first level, interpretation is a transformation that serves to show the invariants of the emotional facts that occur in the session. The invariants that Bion ascribes to the three main types of transformations concern psychopathology and are useful for diagnosing pathological transformations of meaning, but the theory of transformations would not achieve its true purpose if it did not also take into account the transformations that lead to growth, which Bion calls transformations in O. For Bion, "The point at issue is how to pass from 'knowing' 'phenomena' to 'being' that which is 'real'"? (ibid., p. 148). This is the question of how interpretation works. The problem is that there is a gap between phenomena, which can be known, and reality-in-itself, which remains unknowable, i.e., reality can only become. For this reason, "the interpretation must do more than increase knowledge" (ibid.). It must succeed in passing from knowing self, to becoming self. In this sense, psychoanalysis can be understood as a process of subjectivisation through links that imply mutual recognition.

The invariant. The zero point

It is then necessary to hypothesise that there is a zero point of the invariant in normal growth development, a point from which the newborn's rudimentary consciousness begins to emerge from the chaos, thanks to the encounter with the mother. At its zero degree, the invariant could therefore correspond to the emotional unison between mother and newborn, I→EU, which in its repeated encounter experiences opens up to the creation of meaning, in a game of comparison/recognition that allows the release from the chaos

primordial[1]. In Winnicott's opinion it is in this encounter that the experience of being is created. The infant and the object are one, "the breast is
the self and the self is the breast", in which Winnicott (1971, p. 146) echoes
Freud's sibylline phrase "I am the breast" (Freud, 1938, p. 299), but lower-
ing it into a wonderful intersubjective image, in which the newborn begins
to witness his or her own psychical birth in the mother's gaze. Nonetheless,
we have to think that this first "visual" encounter was preceded by many
other encounters, that it is already the memory of a sound envelope, which
cradled the fetus with the acoustic and kinesthetic rhythms of the maternal
heart, of the peristaltic movements, of the a thousand sensory, emotional
and traumatic events that accompanied him or her in his or her gestation.
Moreover, it is from this sensory envelope that for Chuster the radical imagination originates. An original imagination, capable of acting before the
recognition of any object, activated by the physiological rhythms of pulsating life, by the caressing voice of the mother and father, but also by the cries
and violent emotions expressed in the family environment. It is this radical
imagination which, starting from the rhythms, opens spaces and creates a
sort of mental cylinder whose moldings are made of time, which begins to
organise the world to come, punctuated by unknown situations, but somehow already occurred, in that which Bion calls *memory of the future*. It is
in this keeping in time, in these repeated encounters between mother and
child, that a sort of dance of life takes place, a complex attunement, which
represents the ground for any future meaning. After birth, this movement
in time gradually takes shape in the primacy of visual perception, but carries with it a multimodal memory which it never ceases to feed on. Thus,
the premises are created for what Ed Tronik (1998) calls "dyadic expansion of consciousness", which through the shared co-creation of meaning,
reduces chaos and entropy, promoting the expansion of consciousness. And
this process for Tronik is a complex psycho-biological state, a continuous
state of signification which implies various forms of awareness and unconsciousness, such as Bollas' *unthought known*, *reverie* and *mentalisation*, capable of promoting growth and development, increasing coherence
and complexity. This continuous process of signification, therefore, implies
that the other is necessary from the very beginning for the development of
the mind, because the newborn initially has only a rudimentary consciousness, that "is not associated with an unconscious. All impressions of the
self are of equal value; all are conscious. The mother's capacity for reverie
is the receptor organ for the infant's harvest of self-sensation gained by its

conscious" (Bion, 1967, p. 116). The discoveries of implicit memory, of the unremoved unconscious, of an implicit relational knowledge and of the unthought known; therefore, oblige psychoanalysis to go beyond the theory of repression and representation.

The mother is, as a result, the unconscious of the newborn, and it is her reverie that allows the newborn to contain his or her anxieties and to form his or her own alpha function – and therefore the ability to think, dream and develop the unconscious. Placing the zero degree of the invariant in the mother/infant unison also allows us to understand that the truth factor of the transformation is located in the very quality of the intersubjective relationship, a quality that passes through the rhythm, the warmth, the involvement, the thousand nuances of the attention, acceptance, tenderness and compassion which go to achieve mutual recognition. A process that is repeated every time in the analytic relationship. But we must not forget that this first mother-child encounter is not the true origin, that it itself is already prepared by a long process of "cohabitation", not only in the uterus but also in the mind, for which it appears increasingly evident how the origin is always what eludes.

The various sides of O

In the interpretative process that leads to growth and therefore to the passage from being aware of O to becoming O, Bion postulates various passages: *intuition→at-one-ment→embodiment*. In these passages, we perceive the progression from the idea to the body, through the word, because a psychoanalytic process looks more like a cosmogenesis, a process of birth and growth, than a verifiable process. The path to O is hence complex. Bion seems to accept Bergson's idea of a contemplative-intuitive type of mental functioning, directed not towards external reality as received by the senses but towards pure self-knowledge and contact with the "ultimate reality", which he calls O. Nonetheless in this "O" sign, we feel the presence of many other meanings. For example, the idea of origin and zero, of an abstract sign, which refers to infinity, to divinity, to the Platonic form ect.

Nuno Torres and R.D. Hinshelwood (2013) observe that Bion knew the ideas of A. N. Whitehead (1911), of whom he had annotated *An introduction to mathematics*, in which the philosopher-mathematician describes the importance of the symbol 0 (zero). The concept of 0 was introduced in the eighth century by the Arabs, but was also known in India, and had an extremely abstract connotation that eschewed immediate utilitarian calculations, opening on to a metaphysical vision. Whitehead was a follower of Bergson from whom he had taken the idea of nature as a process and lowest degree of mind, whereby matter and mind are not conceived as different substances, but endowed with the same basic properties, differentiated only by the rhythm, vibration and duration. In his evolutionary vision, Whitehead was able to combine Bergson's ideas and Heraclitus's doctrine of everything flowing, with a mathematical fervour that saw in notation and formalisation the possibility of freeing the mind for higher tasks. Together with Bertrand Russel, Whitehead wrote the famous *Principia Mathematica*, which was proposed as a coherent and complete work, that is, such that every true statement of arithmetic could be derived from within it. Bion's programme of formalising the various psychoanalytic theories in order to visualise the functioning of the system and follow its transformations (conforming to the rules) in clinical reality presents many points of contact with Whitehead's ideas. In both cases, it is a question of observing the coherence of an abstract system within a real system. The set of Freudian and Kleinian theories had the same presumption of coherence and systematicity as the *Principia Mathematica*, and Bion's original project for the Grid was born out of an ecumenical intention to find a logical and dynamic system of mental functioning capable of bringing together the various psychoanalytic currents torn by the controversial discussions between Freudians and Kleinians, without questioning their content or validity. The union of these concepts – Bergson's intuition, Whitehead's ideas on the concepts of zero and notation – thus represents a suggestive epistemological background, which may have induced Bion to use the sign "O" to indicate the multiple dimensions of being and of reality. If this hypothesis has some foundation, "O" cannot be considered only a reference to a mystical and unattainable reality but also a logical sign, a notation, which refers to various dimensions of being: thing-in-itself, truth, God, divinity, ultimate reality, language, formless and infinite void, real, Platonic form, the infinite, the unconscious, the One...darkness, zero, origin... according to a multiple vertex perspective. For this reason, the meaning of O changes according to the context, but always referring to something unattainable, unrepresentable, unthinkable and at the same time constantly evolving. Civitarese (2018) identifies three main vertices in which to group the meanings of O: (a) as real, Kant's thing-in-itself; (b) as an unconscious emotional experience of the session shared in the here and now; (c) as sociality and language in the processes of subjectification and knowledge. To these vertices, I would like to add a fourth, that of *becoming real*, because basically the transformations that count in psychoanalysis are those that allow the passage from knowing reality to becoming real, T→O.

This last aspect is perhaps the one that best allows us to understand the global meaning of Bion's operation and therefore of the concept of O, which escapes any partial definition, and which finds its realisation only in the processuality of the analytic path, as a process which leads to growth, change and becoming. "O" stands, therefore, as origin, infinite, unconscious, as unattainable Reality and Truth, and divinity and absolute. Likewise, it also appears as emotional sharing, agreement between minds, as a tension towards truth, as a metaphor for the process of growth and change, as a reality in becoming, as a passage from the infinite to the finite; from the chaos of perception to thought, and therefore as an evolution of the psychoanalytic function of the personality and development of the unconscious. In other words, Bion seems to indicate with the sign O a whole series of vertices and manifestations of being – phenomenological and philosophical – which refer to the knowledge of reality, and therefore to growth as a development of the ability to think and to learn from experience, processes that can only be described through models and metaphors, such as the religious metaphor of the Incarnation. The path that leads from knowing reality to becoming reality "may be seen most clearly expressed in the doctrine of the Incarnation" (Bion, 1965, p. 139).

My hypothesis is, therefore, that the presumed mysticism of Bion is none other than a cyclopean attempt to describe the mystery of the passage from knowing the reality of the Self, to becoming the real Self, and thus the catastrophic change, or the transformation into O, of the patient. In the passage from intuition to being in unison, a difficult epistemic leap takes place, the transit from "apprehension of the object" to "becoming"; from "form" to "incarnation". The analyst follows the analysand in search of what he or she really feels, and the essential aspect is not to impede the development of the session, but to wait calmly for the emergence of O, driven by the instinct for truth, and yet, when it emerges, it bursts out "omnipotently", threatening, like a truth that we know but which frightens us and which we think we cannot tolerate. Interpretation, as a result, cannot be limited to capturing the fear and/or the pain, but must contain the patient, helping him or her to dream and to tolerate the truth that (s)he thinks (s)he is incapable of tolerating and thinking for him or herself. "The interpretation is an actual event in a evolution of O that is common to analyst and analysand" (Bion, 1970, p. 27). More than a hermeneutic of the symptom, Bion's psychoanalysis is then configured as a semiosis in process, an investigation into transformations, in which the analyst must be able to amplify the area of thought and consciousness in the direction of dreams and therefore create the conditions for thinkability, of something that has never become a symbol. Furthermore, this can only happen within a relationship. Psychoanalytic treatment as a result promotes a process of learning from experience, in which the tension towards truth is food for mind, which enriches the subject's un/conscious symbolisation apparatus and promotes a true structural change, an incarnation, an embodiment.

Note

1 I→EU, where I is the invariant, E is emotional, U, is unison, see olso Civitarese G. 2018.

Chapter 10

At-one-ment, atonement, incarnation

Becoming the patient

What does it mean to be in unison with the patient's reality? Bion uses the term reverie to indicate the analyst's constant monitoring of the analysand's emotions, but he speaks of at-one-ment, of unison, when the analyst reaches out to the patient and intuits his or her true emotional experience. Bion describes this process as "to dream the session", or "to become-at-one" with the patient, which will be followed by the evolution of O, i.e., the catastrophic change, the passage from being aware of O to becoming O (Bion, 1992, p. 118; 1965, p. 146). So, what does "the process of at-one-ment with O" consist of? (Bion, 1970, p. 33).

In this process, it is important to exercise the renunciation of desire, memory and understanding, which favours the act of faith, which does not belong to the K system (knowledge), but to the O system, to have faith in the reality of the psychoanalytic experience, which remains ineffable. The analyst must be interested in understanding the evolution of this reality, when it emerges from the dark and formless with the evanescent characteristics of dreams. This "O" is the real goal of the analyst, which the interpretation must be able to grasp correctly and express in words. In order to be apprehended, to become a thought, and to be represented by a grid element, O, it must evolve. In analytic work the analyst must wait until a pattern emerges and then (s)he intuits psychic reality, (s)he must follow the patient until (s)he finds the invariant and intuits what (s)he is really feeling, his or her true emotional experience. For Grotstein (2009, v. II, p. 31) it is a "ultimate act of empathy", in which analyst and patient enter into a symmetrical state of resonance, whereby "to dream the session" or "to become-at-one" the patient properly indicates a recall within the analyst emotions virtually identical to those of the analysand. However, I believe that this is only the

DOI: 10.4324/9781032655239-13

first part of the at-one-ment process, the moment in which in the analyst "a relevant constellation will be evoked" (Bion, 1970, p. 33), due to a sort of unconscious emergence of emotions and memories, which, however, does not exhaust the process, which can be said to be concluded only when the analyst "becomes" the patient, as foreseen by Bergson's intuitive way and as only mysticism, art and Zen have been able to describe.

In *Zen and Archery*, Eugen Herrigel (1948) writes that "bow, arrow, target and ego" must become one, and this implies the renunciation of desire, will and even ego. Modern poetry for Fernando Pessoa is a *look without opinion*, in which the perception of reality must avoid any a priori vision, any conceptualised way of seeing, it is like looking through a continuous division of forms and perspectives, which refer to the instability and multiplicity of reality (Pimenta, 1978). Moreover, this fracture is captured with precision by Dieter Roth (1973) for whom poetic consciousness takes place only in the concrete and modifying experience of each passing moment: "The bird that is an eye, the eye that is a bird". In other words, if there is a bird inside the eye, then the eye at this moment is a bird, so there is an identification with the learned object every single time, a sort of communion, an exchange of identity. The literature has also tried to describe this process. Yannick Haenel in *Tiens ferme ta couronne*, describes the hunt from the film *The deer hunter*, by Michael Cimino. Haenel (2017, p. 49) writes that in real hunting the hunter and the prey become one,

> a successful hunt implies that you have defeated the animal even before shooting, i.e., you are confronted with it throughout all the night and as a result of chasing it through the woods you be emptied of what separates you from him.

In consequences, the hunter and prey become the same thing, but if the hunter pulls the trigger it's all over. Not so in Cimino's film, where the hunter, Robert De Niro, after the tragic experience of war, returns to hunt deer, but this time he gives up shooting. And it is in this renunciation that Haenel places the origin of creativity and of literature itself.

Does something similar happen in analysis? Perhaps the analytic couple is also engaged in a process similar to hunting. The analyst follows his or her patient in a thousand paths of his associations, silences, repetitions, hitches, until (s)he finds the invariant; it is like an exhausting hunting trip in search of what the patient really feels. Thus, Bergson's intuitive way and Bion's at-one-ment imply an identification with the object, a sort of communion, an exchange of identities, as in Zen and modern poetry. Bion in fact distinguishes the at-one-ment from the process of knowledge and identification of empathy which implies an awareness of one's moods and the relationship between two separate objects which cannot be reduced to primordial communication: mother/child, analyst/patient.

So, what happens when the subject becomes the object, the analyst the patient, the container the contained? Bion uses the term "at-one-ment", which with dashes indicates union, "unison", but without dashes it means atonement for sins committed, as in Jean McEvan's masterpiece *Atonement*, but also sacrifice, reconciliation between God and man. The term "atonement" derives from the Jewish mystical tradition, frequent in the Old Testament, less so in the New, and indicates Yom Kippur, the day of atonement, the most sacred feast for the Jews, which refers to the day Moses descended from Mount Sinai and the repentance of the Jewish people being accepted. Bion (1967, p. 145) refers precisely to this meaning in the *Commentary*, when he states that the interpretation must clarify the manifestation relating to expiation, atonement, which has an essential role in a balanced development of the mind, because it is linked to the fear of megalomania, the fear of assuming a position of creativity, and putting oneself in the place of the Creator. It is therefore a complex word, which brings with it a vast halo of religious meanings and which refers to sacrifice, especially of Christ, that Bion introduces to describe the type of knowledge that takes place between analyst and patient. In his sophisticated analysis, Civitarese (2019) also points out that the decomposed word, at-one-ment, also indicates the temporal progress of a subject who is always out of his or her mind, which extends from the past to the future and vice versa.

Transformation in O

Transformations, unison and incarnation are thus processes that attempt to describe how psychoanalysis works, how words and relationships can lead to structural change. The transformation into O is compared to becoming incarnate in the sacrament of the Catholic religion, to becoming the "Godhead" within us. The analyst can broaden knowledge, but the necessary step to bridge the gap between knowing phenomena and being reality must come through a special part of the analysand, his or her internal "Godhead", which must consent to incarnate in his or her person. In the interpretative process that leads to growth, and thus to the passage from being aware of O to becoming O, we can then identify different moments: *intuition→at-one-ment→ atonement → incarnation*, in which the progression from idea to body is realised through the word.

Bion had understood that the problem was not to make the unconscious conscious, to cancel repression, to increase insight, but unlike intersubjectives, he did not fall into the trap of reducing interpretation to pure introspection, exacerbating the relationship/interpretation dichotomy. Bion places the relationship and therefore the patient/analyst emotional experience at the centre of analytic work, revolutionising the very foundations of psychoanalysis as a method of treatment. In fact, without a totally relational concept of mind, i.e., the idea that to make one mind, another is needed, without the idea of care as growth, without the idea that meaning is born in the hard work of mutual recognition, the psychoanalysis would remain an explanatory therapy that explains nothing, a therapy in words as its denigrators say.

Bion consequently tries to make us understand how relationships and words can change our way of experiencing emotions and of behaving, which presupposes a structural change of our own apparatus for thinking. This is why he places transformations, the concept of unison and incarnation, as processes that attempt to describe how psychoanalysis works, at the centre of his work, and these concepts are so advanced that Falck Leichsenring (2019) places them in the list of future research.[1]

To understand what happens in the consulting room, Bion aims his microscope at the analyst/patient, analyst/group relationship, knowing well that this relationship is an open window on the primordial chaos of the birth of thought and of the affective and social cosmos. Bion, therefore, conceives analytic work as a sort of contract for truth, in which patient and analyst undertake to strive for the truth, which, although unattainable, nonetheless remains food for mind. Interpretation as a transformation that has the purpose of showing the invariants of the facts that take place in the session, so remains the central element of the analytic work, together, of course, with silence, which gives the patient the possibility of listening to his or her own thoughts. Bion's adherence to the psychoanalytic method is so rigorous that it has become proverbial, and we should remember that he used the same setting and method also for severe or so-called psychotic patients. Hence, the stereotype of identifying Bion's strictly style with a style that is too rigid. For Bion there is no possibility of a free conversation, so much so that Grotstein (2007) recalls that he was ironic about the way Americans did analyses, who according to him conversed with their patients. Bion translates his rigor into the Grid which is an attempt to monitor the relationship moment by moment, and therefore to logically represent the complexity of the mental functioning of the analyst and the analysand in their reciprocal interaction. In analysis, for Bion the most interesting interpretations are naturally those that promote the birth of the mind and nourish its growth, indicated as transformation in O. Interpretation must therefore favour the passage from being aware of O to becoming O, from knowing reality to becoming real. The essential thing is not to inhibit the evolution of the session, to wait in a welcoming and respectful silence for the emergence of O, driven by the instinct for truth, and yet when this emerges, it bursts in omnipotent, threatening, like a truth that scares and that we think we cannot tolerate. Interpretation must for this reason provide what Grotstein (2009) calls a "security concession", which represents the ultimate meaning of containment as transference, and which helps the patient to tolerate that truth which he alone thinks he is unable to tolerate. It is in this sense that Bion's psychoanalysis is configured as a semiosis in process, an investigation into transformations, in which the analyst must be able to amplify the area of thought and consciousness in the direction of dreams, and therefore create the conditions for thinkability, of something that has never become a symbol. The interpretation cannot then come from above, neither from the theory, nor from the supposed subject of knowledge, but come from a lived and suffered experience of the analyst, who thus shows that he/she has overcome the depressive position. Accordingly, the oscillation between *patience* and *security* is taken by Bion as an indication of a good job.

However, the real point under discussion remains "how to pass from 'knowing' 'phenomena' to 'being' that which is 'real'" (Bion, 1965, p. 148), in other words how can interpretation allow the passage from knowledge of the phenomena of the real Self to becoming the real Self? This of course is olso the question of how interpretation works, because there is a gap between phenomena and the thing-in-itself; phenomena can be known, but reality has "become". For this reason, "interpretation must do more than increase knowledge" (ibid.). Bion compares the introjection process of interpretation to the "impingement on the individual of an object containing in itself the potentiality of all distinctions as yet undeveloped, a group, a conjunction and the need to bind the 'groupishness' of the group with a name, a column 1 element" (ibid., p. 150). What happens is then a sort of meshing, in which the object and the individual seek their mutual adaptation, the harmonious relationship between container and contained, until the need for a link or "complementarity" is triggered (ibid., p. 53).

The three models of growth

To describe this process Bion proposes three models – ultimate reality and phenomena, Platonic forms, incarnation – bearing in mind that all three have a similar configuration. The Kantian model of the thing-in-itself does not explain the transition to O, because if the thing-in-itself is inaccessible, we do not know what to base the objectivity of knowledge on, and the a priori forms of time and space and reliance on God are not sufficient. The problem hence arises of how to arrive at a sufficiently shared vision, because everyone transforms reality, O, in a subjective way.

Bion then introduces a second model, that of the Platonic theory of form, in which the appearance of a beautiful object serves to remind the observer of the beauty or goodness that was once known, but is now no longer. For Plato, all knowledge is *anagnorisis,* re-recognition, which, however, is based on memory, it is *anamnesis,* as a reminiscence of something that the soul had already learned and known before becoming incarnate. The object, whose phenomenon serves as a memory, is a form, and people or things can be "reminders" of the Platonic form. Bion then resorts to Plato to give a basis to his theory of innate pre-conceptions, because the innate expectation of a breast is incompatible with the Kantian system as it would reopen precisely that idealism that the philosopher wanted to overcome. In consequence, Bion's pre-conceptions do not correspond to Kant's "empty thoughts", but are closer to Platonic Forms, as Bion himself indicates when he states that Plato supports the theory of pre-conception (ibid., p. 138). Nonetheless even this model is set aside. Bion realises that to describe "becoming", it is more useful to resort to the mystical term of "incarnation", in which the "Good" or "Beauty" are not what reminds the personality of a form (pre-conception), but an "incarnation", which "enables the person to achieve union with an incarnation of the Godhead, or the thing-in-itself, (or Person-in-Himself)" (ibid., p. 139). The transformation into O has in fact to do with becoming, and becoming implies "incarnation", i.e., that the patient unites with his or her incarnated part of the Godhead, as a "spiritual substance". Bion then turns to Christian theology through Dante, who in canto XXXIII of Paradise comes to contemplate the First Cause, in which divine love brings together in "one volume" the "unwrapped", untied reality of the many things in the universe.[2] However, Bion quotes a subsequent tercet, which suggestively begins with O, where in a daring circular image, Dante declines the three moments of divine understanding, which alone understands itself, it is intellect and understand.[3] Furhemore, that insistence on "understanding" refers to the Logos, opening up to the mystery of the union of human and divine nature which took place in the "Word".

However, Dante's suggestion does not fully satisfy the needs of Bion who turns to Meister Eckhart, in whom the concept of incarnation is most clearly expressed. Bion uses the distinction between God and Godhead, which for the mystic of Erfurt, "are as distinct as the earth and the sky" (Schürmann, 1972, p. 134). For Meister Eckhart, a German Dominican theologian, it is necessary to free ourselves from God, and reach the Godhead that is in us, to become creators of ourselves. Meister Eckhart's position, censured as a heretic by the papal bull *In agro dominico*, appeals to the Aristotelian philosophy of the receptive intellect, which must be "virgin" of all images, if it wants to know all images, just as the palate must be free from all aromas if you want to perceive the taste of all aromas, but above all it refers to the philosophy of the "noble man" who moves in search of the truth (Meister Eckhart, 1999).

Bion then reformulates the theory of resistance in terms of resistance to becoming O. Resistance has the aim of keeping certain thoughts, feelings and "facts" unconscious, through an adherence to the statements of column 2, which one knows are false, but which do as a barrier to statements believed to be true. Interpretations can in fact be accepted in K, but rejected in O, because accepting an interpretation in O means not only knowing a part of oneself, but "being" or "becoming" that part of the Self. The resistance based on hate and fear of the transition TK→TO manifests itself as a preference for being aware of something over becoming something.

The interpretations that make the transition from being aware of O to becoming O must therefore have some characteristics that Bion identifies in the concept of "complementarity", understood as a development from pre-conception to conception, from row D to row E, which they involve a process of saturation of an unsaturated element, which in turn can be made available for further saturation. In practice, it is a question of contrasting the patient's statements with "an interpretation which is such that the circular argument remains circular, but has an adequate diameter" (Bion,

1965, p. 153). If this diameter is too small, it becomes a point, if it is too large, a straight line. Both situations represent primitive moods, i.e., not associated with a mature experience. The ability to use a "useful" circular argument depends on having sufficient experience to provide material through which to circulate the argument, to the point where the "complementary statements" can become fixed. The analyst can only make an interpretation starting from the elements that the analysand him or herself has snatched from his or her "formless and infinite void", but if (s)he tells the patient what (s)he already knows, then the diameter is too small, if instead the interpretation is too "abstruse", the diameter is too large (ibid., p. 167). The abstruse interpretation can be connected to the analyst's desire to appear more farsighted than the patient, which implies a challenge and belongs to the field of hyperbole. Before giving an interpretation, it is then necessary to wait for the statement to be sufficiently developed, i.e., for its dimension to be evident in column 2. The analyst must also achieve awareness of his or her own resistance to the reaction (s)he expects from the analysand.

Incarnation

In spite of this, what then does "incarnation" mean? Bion borrows this term from religion to indicate a very concrete phenomenon, that of structural change, assuming the risk of possible misunderstandings, but aware that to draw on the mysterious fund of the work of the word (Verb) the religious metaphor remains the most adequate. For Bion

> It is possible through phenomena to be reminded of the 'form'. It is possible through 'incarnation' to be united with a part, the incarnate part, of the Godhead. It is possible through hyperbole for the individual to deal with the real individual.
>
> (ibid., p. 148)

The problem is, therefore, if it is it possible through psycho-analytic interpretation to effect a transition from knowing the phenomena of the real Self to being the real Self. In other words, how to go from knowing phenomena to being what is real. Bion assimilates this gap to that between knowing about psychoanalysis and being psychoanalysed. For this the interpretation must do more than increase the knowledge. The transformation into O is thus compared to becoming incarnate in the sacrament of the Catholic religion, to becoming the

"Godhead" that is in us. In fact, phenomena can be known, but reality can only have become. In other words, the analyst can broaden knowledge, but the final step necessary to bridge the gap between knowing the phenomena and being reality must come from a special part of the analysand, "namely, his 'godhead', which must consent to incarnation in the person of the analysand" (ibid).

Hence, there are various vertices from which O can be investigated; *the religious vertex*, in which the sign O can be represented by the godhead; the *Miltonian vertex*, in which O is represented by "the void and formless infinite" from which the object that is known is won from; *Dante's vertex*, in which O is represented by canto 33 of Paradise; the *mathematical vertex*, where O is represented by the term "unfinished". As for the mathematical vertex, the results appear rather disappointing to Bion himself, who in the end seems to make a bitter self-criticism, when he declassifies his use of mathematics as a sort of "Lewis Carol" game and tries to dispel the impression to support the idea that a discipline should be considered scientific only if it is formalised (ibid., p. 170). Bion points out that the transition from sensitivity to awareness cannot occur without a mathematical development, and he gives the example of the Trinity, which shows how the progression from empty and formless infinity, or Meister Eckart's dark and formless Godhead, occurs through the association with a number, the Trinity, or a geometric figure, the triangle or the circle. Nevertheless, he admits that the religious metaphor of the incarnation is the most useful for describing the becoming of psychic reality. For this, he introduces the concept of Faith, Faith in the existence of an ultimate reality and truth, of the unknown and the unknowable. However, this Faith must be free from any element of memory and desire, which remain tied to sensitive elements. What matters to him in the analysis is the evolution of O. A thought has sensitive realisations as a background but only the act of faith has something unconscious and unknown as a background because it did not happen. The act of faith is not associated with the + K system, but with the O system. The K link can only operate on a sensory background, give knowledge about something, and must be differentiated from the O link, which is essential for transformations into O and to experience hallucinosis. In order for analysis to work, it must therefore lead the analysand to reconcile with him or herself, to feel at one with him or herself. To do this, the analyst has the only opportunity to use interpretation, which cannot be torn from the patient's emptiness and formlessness but only from what the patient has managed to extract from his or her emptiness and formlessness.

Hence, the importance of using the language of effectiveness, a language that makes action and its choice thinkable, capable of transforming pain, capable of disarticulated defensive jargons, of subverting the rigid framework of meaning, in order to achieve archaic residues, pre-natal emotions, thinkerless thoughts, wild intuitions, which remain split, until one develops the ability to cross the caesuras, and penetrate the barrier. In addition, this language often inhabits the spaces of poetic creation, and like the poetic word it must come from a lived and painful experience of the analyst. The concept of unison/at-one-ment/meeting of minds consequently creates a path that provides for continuous intersubjective verification and continuous mutual recognition, bringing together the aesthetic aspect and the cognitive aspect, the how and the what of truth. Thus the at-one-ment becomes an experience that Civitarese (2018) rightly defines as fractal, as it is found at the basis of all encounter and recognition experiences, at any level, from the mother-infant encounter, to the analyst-analysand, to the intimate one of every real relationship of love, even in our relationships with the objects we love, books, art, nature, etc. It is the mystical encounter Borges speaks of when union with the Godhead takes place, in the ecstasy that abolishes all symbolic distinction, in the image of an infinite Wheel, in which each of us is nothing but a miserable thread, which makes Tzinacàn understand the mystery of the universe, which renders any conception of identity useless. In this process, attention moves from the contained to the containers, or rather to their relationship, which coincides with the way in which the ability to think as an intersubjective experience develops, starting from the analyst/patient relationship, which repeats that of mother/child. The truth, as a result, emerges from the bottlenecks of the contents of truth, from the fallacy of autobiographical memory, to embrace an ethical-aesthetic path of agreement between minds, which by weaving shared contents, in fact opens up to the exploration of the most primitive areas of the mind, and therefore to the growth, which is nothing more than being free to become yourself.

Notes

1 Leichsenring F., The Profession of Psychotherapist, Congress, Bicocca University, Milan, 2019.
2 Dante, Paradiso, canto 33, vv. 85–87.
3 Dante, Paradiso, canto 33, vv. 124–126.

References

Abraham N. & Torok M. (1987), *L'écorce et le noyau*, Paris: Flammarion.

Alweiss L. (2002), "Heidegger and 'the concept of time'", *History of the Human Sciences*, 15(3): 117–32.

Anzieu D. (1985), *Le Moi-peau*, Paris: Bordas.

Aron L. & Harris A. (ed.), (1993), *The Legacy of Sándor Ferenczi*, Hillsdale, MI: Analytic Press.

Augustine (2017), *Confessions*, New York: Modern Library.

Baranger W. & Baranger M. (1969), *Problemas del campo psicoanalítico*, Buenos Aires: Kargieman.

Bateson G. (1979), *Mind and Nature. A Necessary Unity*, New York: E.P. Dutton.

Belting H. (2013), *Faces. Eine Geschichte des Geischts*, München: Verlag C.H. Beck oHG.

Benini A. (2017), *Neurobiologia del tempo*, Milano: Raffaello Cortina.

Bergson H. (1896), *Matière et Mémoire*, Paris: Presses Universitaire de France; *Matter and Memory*, translated by N.M. Paul and W.S. Palmer, New York: Zone Books, 1911.

Bergson H. (1907), *L'évolution créatrice*, Paris: Presses Universitaire de France, 1969.

Bergson H. (1930), *Le possible et le réel*, in Oeuvres, Paris: Édition du Centenaire, Presses Universitaire de France, 1970.

Bion Talamo P. (1987), "Perché non possiamo dirci bioniani", *Gruppo e funzione psicoanalitica*, 8: 279–84.

Bion Talamo P. (2013), in Torres N. & Hinshelwood R.D. (2013), *Bion's Sources: The Shaping of His Paradigms*, London: Routledge.

Bion W.R. (1948), "Psychiatry at a Time of Crisis", in *The Complete Works of W.R. Bion* (T.C.W.B), Mawson C. (ed.). First published 2014 by Karnac Books Ltd; First issued in paperback 2019, London and New York: Routledge, Taylor & Francis Group, v. 4.

Bion W.R. (1961), *Experiences in Groups, and Other Papers*, London and New York: Routledge.

Bion W.R. (1962), *Learning from Experience*, Lanham, MD: Rowman & Littlefield Publishers.

Bion W.R. (1963), *Elements of Psychoanalysis*, London: Karnac Books.

Bion W.R. (1965), *Trasformations*, London: Karnac Books.

Bion W.R. (1967), *Second Thoughts*, London: Karnac Books.

Bion W.R. (1967a), *Notes on Memory and Desire*, in T.C.W.B. v. 6.

Bion W.R. (1970), *Attention and Interpretation,* Lanham, MD: Rowman & Littlefield Publishers.

Bion W.R. (1971), *The Grid,* in T.C.W.B., v.10.

Bion W.R. (1975a), *Caesura*, in T.C.W.B., v. 10.

Bion W.R. (1975b), *A Memoir of the Future. Book One: The Dream*, in T.C.W.B., v. 12.

Bion W.R. (1976–9), *The Tavistock Seminars,* in T.C.W.B., v. 9.

Bion W.R. (1976a), *Four Discussions*, in T.C.W.B., v. 10.

Bion W.R. (1976b), *Evidence*, in T.C.W.B., v. 10.

Bion W.R. (1977a), *New York*, in T.C.W.B., v. 9.

Bion W.R. (1977b), *The Italian Seminars*, in T.C.W.B., v. 9.

Bion W.R. (1977c), *A Memoir of the Future, Book Two: The Past Presented*, in T.C.W.B., v. 13.

Bion W.R. (1978), "A Paris Seminar", in T.C.W.B., v. 9.

Bion W.R. (1979), *A Memoir of the Future, Book Three: The Down of Oblivion*, in T.C.W.B., v. 14.

Bion W.R. (1982), *The Long Weekend 1897–1919: Part of a Life*, in T.C.W.B., v. 1.

Bion W.R. (1985), *All My Sins Remembered: Another Part of a Life. The Other Side of Genius: Family Letter*. in T.C.W.B., v. 2.

Bion W.R. (1992), *Cogitations,* in T.C.W.B., v. 11.

Bion W.R. (1997), *Timing Wild Thoughts*, London: Karnac Books.

Blake W. (1790), *The Marriage of Heaven and Hell*, Oxford: Oxford University Press, 1975.

Blanchot M. (1955), *L'Espace littéraire*, Paris: Gallimard.

Blanchot M. (1969), *L'entretien infini*, Paris: Gallimard; Italian translation, *L'infinito intrattenimento*, Torino: Einaudi, 1977.

Boffito S. (2020), « Psicoanalisi, credo », Nel paese delle meraviglie : lettura e letteratura in Memoria del futuro, in Civitarese G. (ed.), *Bion e la psicoanalisi contemporanea, leggere Memoria del futuro,* Milano: Mimesis, pp. 47–59.

Bollas C. (1987), *The Shadow of the Object: Psychoanalysis of the Unthought Known*, London: Original Edition Free Association Books.

Bollas C. (1995), *Cracking up. The Work of Unconscious Experience*, London: Routledge; Italian translation, *Cracking up. Il lavoro dell'inconscio*, Milano: Raffaello Cortina, 1996.

Bollas C. (1999), *The Mistery of Things*, London: Routledge.

Boltanski L. (1993), *La Souffrance à distance*, Paris: Éditions Métailié.

Borges J.L. (1952), "La escritura de Dios", in Borges J.L. (ed.) *El Aleph*, Buenos Aires: Editorial Losada; Italian translation, *L'Aleph*, Milano: Feltrinelli, pp. 114–120.

Borges J.L. (1960), "Nueva refutación del tiempo", in Borges J.L. (ed.) *Otras Inquisiciones*, Buenos Aires: Emercé; Italian translation, "Nuove confutazioni del tempo", in Borges J.L. *Altre inquisizioni*, Milano: Feltrinelli, 1983, pp. 169–186.

Borgogno F. (2003), "Sopravvivere alla morte psichica: Storia analitica con una paziente schizoide deprivata", in Rinaldi L. (ed.), *Stati caotici della mente,* Milano: Raffaello Cortina, pp. 189–213.

Borgogno F. (ed.), (2004), *Ferenczi oggi*, Torino: Bollati Boringhieri.

Borutti S. (2006), *Filosofia dei sensi*, Milano: Raffaello Cortina.

Bromberg P.M. (1998/2001), *Standing in the Spaces. Essay on Clinical Process, Traumas, and Dissociation*, Hillsdale, N.J: The Analytic Press, Inc.

Bromberg P.M. (2006), *Awakening the Dreamer: Clinical Journeys*, Mahwah, N.J.: The Analytic Press, Inc., Publishers; Italian translation, *Destare il sognatore,* Milano: Raffaello Cortina, 2006.

Churchland P.S. & Churchland P.M. (2007), *Neurofilosofia*, in Enciclopedia della Scienza e della tecnica, Treccani, www.treccani.it/enciclopedia/neurofilosofia_%28Enciclopedia-della-scienza-e-della-tecnica%29.

Chuster A. (2010), "Origins of Unconscious", in Van Buren J. & Alhati S. (ed.), *Primitive Mental States. A Psychoanalytical Exploration of the Origins of Meaning*, New York: Routledge, Taylor & Francis Group; Italian translation, "Le origini dell'inconscio", in Van Buren J. & Alhanati S., (ed.), *Stati primitivi della mente. Una ricerca psicoanalitica*, Roma: Astrolabio-Ubaldini, 2013, pp. 143–162.

Civitarese G. (2012), "La Griglia e la pulsione di verità", *Rivista di Psicoanalisi*, LVIII(2): 335–60.

Civitarese G. (2014), *I sensi e l'inconscio*, Roma: Borla.

Civitarese G. (2017), *Sublimes Subjects: Aesthetic Experience and Intersubjectivity in Psychoanalysis*, London: Routledge; Italian translation, *Soggetti sublimi. Esperienza estetica e intersoggettività in psicoanalisi*, Milano: Mimesis.

Civitarese G. (2018), Tradurre l'esperienza: il concetto di trasformazione in Bion e nella teoria post-bioniana del campo analitico, 78° Congrés des Psychanalystes de Langue Français, Ginevra, 2018.

Civitarese G. (2019), "The Concept of Time in Bion's 'A Theory of Thinking'", *The International Journal of Psychoanalysis*, 100(2): 182–205.

Civitarese G. (2020), *L'ora della nascita. Psicoanalisi del sublime e arte contemporanea*, Milano: Jaca Book.

Corrao F. (1977), "Per una topologia analitica", in Corrao F. (ed.) *Orme*, vol. 1°, Milano: Raffaello Cortina, pp. 51–72.

Correale A. (1985), "Introduction", in Pines M. (ed.), *Bion and Group Psychotherapy*, London: Routledge Kegan Paul plc; Italian translation, Pines M., (ed), *Bion e la psicoterapia di gruppo*, Roma: Borla, pp. 5–27.

Cramer F. (1988), *Chaos und Ordnung, Die komplexe Struktur des Lebendigen*, Stuttgart: Deutsche Verlag-Anstalt GmbH.

Deleuze G. (1968), *Différence et répétition*, Paris: Presses Universitaires de France.

Dennet D.C. (2003), *Freedom Evolves*, New York: Viking Press.

Di Paola F. (1995), *Il tempo della mente. Saggio sul pensiero di Wilfred Bion*, Ripatransone: Edizioni Sestante.

Edelman G. & Tononi G. (2000), *A Universe of Consciousness. How Matter Becomes Immagination*, New York, NY: Basic Books; Italian translation, *Un universo di coscienza. Come la materia diventa immaginazione*, Torino: Einaudi, 2000.

Eigen M. (1985), "Towards Bion's Starting Point: Between Catastrophe and Faith", *The International Journal of Psychoanalysis*, 66(3): 321–30; Italian translation, in Neri C., Correale A. & Fadda P. (ed.), *Letture Bioniane*, Roma: Borla, 1987.

Einstein A. (1954), *Ideas and Opinions*, New York: Bonanza Book.

Eliot T. (1943), *Four Quartets*, New York: Harcourt, Brace and Company.

Etchegoyen R.H. (1986), *Los Fundamentos de la tecnica Psicoanalitica*, Buenos Aires: Amorrortu Editores.

Fabbri P. (1991), "La babele felice "babelix, babelux [...] ex babele lux", in Preta L. (ed.), *La narrazione delle origini*, Roma-Bari: Laterza, pp. 230–246.

Faimberg H. (1993a), "Le mythe d'Œdipe revisité", in Kaës R., Faimberg H., Enriquez M., & Baranes J.J. (ed.), *Trasmission de la vie psychique entre générations*, Paris: Dunod; Italian translation, in Kaës R., Faimberg H., Enriquez M., & Baranes J.J. (ed.), *Trasmissione della vita psichica tra generazioni*, Roma: Borla, 1995, pp. 175–196.

Faimberg H. (1993b), "Le 'télescopage' des générations", Italian translation, "Il 'télescopage' delle generazioni", in Kaës R., Faimberg H., Enriquez M., & Baranes J.J. (ed.), *Trasmissione della vita psichica tra generazioni*, Roma: Borla, 1995, pp. 175–196.

Fairbairn W.R.D. (1943), *Psychoanalytic Studies of the Personality*, London: Tavistock Publications.

Floridi L. (2014), *The Fourth Revolution. How the Infosphere Is Reshaping Human Reality*, Oxford: Oxford University Press.

Fornaro M. (1990), "Biopsicologia e scienza: per una nuova lettura di Wilfred R. Bion", *Gli Argonauti*, 44: 37–60.

Freud S. (1887–1904), *The Complete Letters of Sigmund Freud to Wilhelm Fliess 1887–1904*, translated and edited by J. M. Masson, Cambridge, MA, and London: The Belknap Press of Harvard University Press.

Freud S. (1891), *On Aphasia*, Authorized Translation whith an Introduction by E. Stengel, London: Imago Publishing Co., 1953.

Freud S. (1892–5), *Studies on Hysteria*, S.E. v. 2.

Freud S. (1894), *The Neuro-Psychoses of Defence*, S.E. v. 3.

Freud S. (1895), *Project for a Scientific Psychology*, S.E. v. 1.

Freud S. (1899), *Screen Memories*, S.E. v. 3.

Freud S. (1900), *The Interpretation of Dreams*, S.E. vv. 4–5.

Freud S. (1901), *The Psychopathology of Everyday Life*, S.E. v. 6.

Freud S. (1908), *Family Romances*, S.E. v. 9.

Freud S. (1911), *Formulations on the Two Priciples of Mentale Functioning*, S.E. v. 12.

Freud S. (1912), *Recommendations to Physicians Practising Psycho-Analysis*, S.E. v. 12.

Freud S. (1915a), *Repression*, S.E. v. 14.

Freud S. (1915b), *The Unconscious*, S.E. v. 14.

Freud S. (1920), *Beyond the Pleasure Principle*, S.E. v. 18.

Freud S. (1923), *The Ego and the Id*, S.E. v. 19.

Freud S. (1923a), *Neurosis and Psychosis*, S.E. v. 19.

Freud S. (1923b), *A Short Account of Psycho-Analysis*, S.E. v. 19.

Freud S. (1924), *A Note Upon the "Mystic Writing-Pad"*, S.E. v. 19.

Freud S. (1925a), *Negation*, S.E. v. 19.

Freud S. (1925b), *Inhibitions, Symptoms and Anxiety*, S.E. v. 20.

Freud S. (1929), *Civilisation and Its Discontents*, S.E. v. 21.

Freud S. (1932), *New Introductory Lectures on Psycho-Analysis*, S.E. v. 22.

Freud S. (1937a), *Analysis Terminable and Interminable*, S.E. v. 23.

Freud S. (1937b), *Costructions in Analysis,* S.E. v. 23.

Freud S. (1938a), *An Outline of Psycho-Analysis*, S.E. v. 23.

Freud S. (1938b), *Findings, Ideas, Problems*, S.E., v. 23.

Funari E. (1991), "Dimensione fenomenologica dell'attività rappresentativa", in Ammanniti M. & Stern D.N. (ed.), *Rappresentazioni e narrazioni*, Roma-Bari: Laterza, pp. 53–66.

Gaddini E. (1981), "Itinerari nella creatività di Bion", *Rivista di Psicoanalisi*, XXVII: 3–4.

Gargani A.G. (2008), *Wittgenstein. Musica, parola, gesto*, Milano: Raffaello Cortina.

Gerber I. (2022), "Bion and the Infinite Unconscious – An Intuitive Science", in Grimalt A. (ed.), *Bion, Intuition and the Expansion of Psychoanalytic Theory*, London and New York: Routledge, pp. 131–137.

Godbout C. (2004), "Reflections on Bion's Elements of Psychoanalysis", *International Journal of Psychoanalysis*, 85: 1123–36.

Graves R. (1955), *Greek Myths*, Edinburgh: Penguin Books.

Green A. (1966), in Laplanche J. & Leclaire S. (1966), *L'inconscient: une édute psychanalytique,* Paris: Desclée de Brouwer; Italian translation, *L'inconscio. Un saggio psicoanalitico*, Parma: Pratiche Editrice, 1980, pp. 63–79.

Green A. (1973), *Le discours vivante,* Paris: Presses Universitaire de France.

Green A. (2000a), *Le temps eclaté,* Paris: Les Éditions de Minuits. Italian translation, *Il tempo in frantumi*, Roma: Borla, 2001.

Green A. (2000b), *La diachronia in psychanalyse*, Paris: Les Éditions de Minuits; Italian translation, *La diacronia in psicoanalisi*, Roma: Borla, 2006.

Gregory R.L. (2009), *Seeing through Illusions*, Oxford: Oxford University Press.

Grossman V. (1980), *Vita e destino*, Milano: Adelphi, 2008.

Grotstein J.S. (2007), *A Beam of Intense Darkness. Wilfred Bion's Legacy to Psychoanalysis*. London: Karnac Books.

Grotstein J.S. (2009), "…But At The Same Time And On Another Level…", in *Psychoanalytic Theory and Technique in the Kleinian/Bionian Mode*, London: Karnac Books.

Haenel Y. (2017), *Tiens ferme ta couronne*, Paris: Editions Gallimard; Italian translation, *Tieni ferma la tua corona*, Vicenza: Neri Pozza, 2018.

Han Byung-Chul (2015), *Die Errettung des Schönen*, Frankfurt am Main: Fisher Verlag.

Han Byung-Chul (2020), *Palliativgesellschaft Schmerz heute*, Berlin: Matthes &Seitz.

Hayanal A. (2004), "La rivoluzione psichica del 'wise baby'", in Borgogno F. (ed.), *Ferenczi oggi*, Torino: Bollati Boringhieri, pp. 29–37.

Heidegger M. (1927), *Sein un Zeit*, Tubingen: Max Niemeyer Verlag; Macquarrie and Robinson Translation, *Being and Time*, Albany: State University of New York Press, 1996.

Heidegger M. (1954), *Was Heisst Denken?* Max Niemeyer Verlag; translated by F.D. Wick and J.G. Gray, 1968, New York: Harper; Italian translation, *Che cosa significa pensare?* V. 1 & 2, Milano: SugarCo, 1978.

Herrigel E. (1948), *Zen in der Kunst des Bogenschießens,* Konstanz: Weller.

Hillman J. (1996), *The Soul's Code. In Search of Character and Calling*, New York: Random House Publishing Group.

Hinshelwood R.D. (1989), A *Dictionary of Kleinian Thought*, London: Free Association Books.

Jullien F. (2009), *Le transformations silencieuses,* Paris: Éditions Grasset & Fasquelle; Italian translation, *Le trasformazioni silenziose*, Milano: Raffaello Cortina, 2010.

Kaës R. (1993), "Le sujet de l'héritage", in Kaës R., Faimberg H., Enriquez M., & Baranes J.J. (ed.), *Trasmission de la vie psychique entre générations*, Paris: Dunod; Italian translation, "Il soggetto dell'eredità", in Kaës R., Faimberg H., Enriquez M., & Baranes J.J. (ed.), *Trasmissione della vita psichica tra generazioni*, Roma: Borla, 1995, pp. 16–32.

Kahn L. (2007), "L'inconscio, un concetto limite", *Psiche*, I: 15–34.

Kant I. (1787), *Critica della regione pura*, Roma-Bari: Laterza, 1983.

Kristeva J. (1993), *Les nouvelles maladies de l'âme*, Paris: Librairie Arthème Fayard.

Lacan J. (1966), *Écrits*, v. I, Paris: Edition du Seuil; Italian translation, *Scritti*, v. I, Torino: Einaudi, 1974.

Lacan J. (1966a), in Laplanche J. & Leclaire S. (1966), *L'inconscio. Un saggio psicoanalitico*, Parma: Pratiche Editrice, 1980.

Laplanche J. & Leclaire S. (1966), *L'inconscient: une édute psychanalytique*, Paris: Desclée de Brouwer; Italian translation, *L'inconscio. Un saggio psicoanalitico*, Parma: Pratiche Editrice, 1980.

Lefebvre H. (1966), in Laplanche J. & Leclaire S. (1966), *L'inconscient: une édute psychanalytique*, Paris: Desclée de Brouwer; Italian translation, *L'inconscio. Un saggio psicoanalitico*, Parma: Pratiche Editrice, 1980, pp. 86–92.

Le Guen (2008), Dictionnaire freudien, Paris: Presses Universitaire de France.

Levinas E. (1993), *Dieu, la Mort et le Temps*, Paris: Éditions Grasset et Fasquelle.

Libet B. (2004), *Mind Time. The Temporal Factor in Consciousness*. Cambridge: Harvard University Press; Italian translation, *Mind Time*, Milano: Raffaello Cortina, 2007.

López Corvo R.E. (2002), *Diccionario de la obra de Wilfred R. Bion,* Madrid: Biblioteca Nueva.

López-Corvo R.E. (2006), "The Forgotten Self: With the Use of the Bion's Theory of the Negative Links", *Psychoanalytic Review*, 93: 363–77.

Lotto B. (2017), *Deviate: The Science of Seeing Differently*, New York, Boston, MA: Hachette Books.

Mancia M. (1989), "Sulla nascita del Sé", *Rivista di Psicoanalisi*, 34(4): 1053–73.

Mancia M. (1998), *Coscienza, sogno, memoria*, Roma: Borla.

Mancia M. (2004), *Sentire le parole. Archivi sonori della memoria implicita e musicalità del transfert*, Torino: Bollati Boringhieri.

Mangini E. (2009), "Sulla rimozione originaria", *Rivista di Psicoanalisi*, 55: 201–302.

Maturana H.R. & Varela F.J. (1980), *Autopoiesis and Cognition. The Realization of Living*, Dordrecht, Holland: D. Reidel Publishing Company.

McAllister J.W. (1996), *Beauty and Revolution in Science*. Ithaca, N.Y.: Cornell University Press.

McDougall J. (1990), *Plaidoier puor una certaine anormalité*, Paris: Editions Gallimard; Italian translation, *A favore di una certa anormalità*, Roma: Borla, 1993.

McDougall J. (2003), "L'economia psichica della dipendenza: una soluzione psicosomatica al dolore psichico", in Rinaldi L. (ed.), *Stati caotici della mente*, Milano: Raffaello Cortina, Editore, pp. 135–153.

Meares R. (2000), *Intimacy and Alienation. Memory, Trauma and Personal Being*, London: Routledge.

Meister Eckhart (1260–1328), *Dell'uomo nobile*, Milano: Adelphi, 1999.

Meltzer D. (1978), *Kleinian Development. 3. The Clinical Significance of the Work of Bion*, London: Karnac.

Meltzer D. (1986), *Studies in Extended Metapsychology*, London: The Roland Harris Education Trust.

Meltzer D. (1987), Il modello della mente secondo Bion: note su funzione alfa, inversione della funzione alfa e griglia negativa, in Neri C., Correale A., Fadda P., (ed.), *Letture bioniane*, Roma: Borla, pp. 76–83.

Meltzer D. (1992), *The Claustrum. An Investigation of Claustrophobic Phenomena*, London: The Roland Harris Education Trust.

Merleau-Ponty M. (1945), *Phénoménologie de la perception*, Paris: Libraire Gallimard; Italian translation, *Fenomenologia della percezione*, Milano: Bompiani, 2003.

Merleau-Ponty M. (1964), *Le visible et l'invisible*, Paris: Éditions Gallimard; Italian translation, *Il visibile e l'invisibile,* Milano: Bompiani, 1994.

Merleau-Ponty M. (1984), *La prosa del mondo*, Roma: Editori Riuniti, 1984.

Molinari S. (1981), "Freud di fronte al mito di Edipo", *Rivista di psicoanalisi*, 2: 275–93.

Morin E. (1977), *La méthode. I. La nature de la nature*, Paris: Éditions du Seuil.

Morin E. (1986), *La méthode. III. La connaissance de la connaissance/1*, Paris: Éditions du Seuil.

Nancy J.L. (2000), *Le regard du portait*, Paris: Galilée; Italian translation, *Il ritratto e il suo sguardo*, Milano: Raffaello Cortina, 2002.

Natoli S. (1986), *L'esperienza del dolore*, Milano: Feltrinelli.

Neri C. (1995), *Gruppo*, Roma: Borla.

Neri C., Correale A., & Fadda P. (ed.), (1987), *Letture Bioniane*, Roma: Borla.

O'Shaughnessy E. (2005), "Whose Bion?" *The International Journal of Psychoanalysis*, 86: 1523–8.

Ogden T.H. (2009), *Rediscovering Psychoanalysis. Thinking and Dreaming, Learning and Forgetting*. Hove, East Sussex: Routledge.

Ogden T.H. (2022), *Coming to Life in the Consulting Room. Toward a New Analytic Sensibility*, London and New York: Routledge.

Oliviero A. (2018), "L'inconscio e la scienza. Intervista di Felice Cimatti ad Alberto Oliviero, L'inconscio scientifico", *Rivista Italiana di Filosofia e Psicoanalisi*, 5: 21–31.

Pascal B. (1670), *Pensieri*, Torino: Einaudi, 1974.

Pimenta A. (1978), *Il silenzio dei poeti*, Milano: Feltrinelli.

Pistiner de Cortiñas L. (2005), "Scienza e finzione nel gioco psicoanalitico", *Koinos Gruppo e Funzione Analitica*, XXVI (2): 9–36.

Pistiner de Cortiñas L. (2009), *The Aesthetic Dimension of the Mind. Variations on a Theme of Bion*, London: Karnac.

Pontalis J.B. (1977), *Entre le rêve et la douleur*, Paris: Éditions Gallimard; Italian translation, *Tra il sogno e il Dolore*, Roma: Borla,1988.

Pratolini V. (1960), *Lo scialo*, Milano: Mondadori.

Preta L. (1991), (ed.), *La narrazione delle origini*, Roma-Bari: Laterza.

Prigogine I. (1996), *La fin des certitudes. Temps, chaos et le lois de la nature*, Paris: Édition Odile Jacob.

Prigogine I. & Stengers I. (1988), *Entre le temps et l'éternité*, Paris: Librairie Arthème Fayard.

Proust M. (1954), *Le temps retrouvé*, Paris: Editions Gallimard; Italian translation, *Il tempo ritrovato*, Torino: Einaudi, 1978.

Resnik S. (2003), "L'uomo congelato", in Rinaldi L. (ed.), *Stati caotici della mente*, Milano: Raffaello Cortina Editore.

Resnik S. (2006), *Biografie dell'inconscio*, Roma: Borla, 2007.

Ricoeur P. (1965), *De l'interprétation. Essai sur Freud*, Paris: Éditions du Seuil.

Rilke R.M. (1923), *Elegie Duinesi*, Torino: Einaudi, 1978.

Riolo F. (1986), "Dei soggetti del Campo: un discorso sui "limiti"", *Gruppo e Funzione Psicoanalitica*, sett. dic. VII(3): 196–204.

Riolo F. (2009), "Break-through", in Corrente G. (ed.), *Con Bion verso il futuro*, Roma: Borla, pp. 29–39.

Riolo F. (2010), "Trasformazioni in allucinosi", *Rivista di Psicoanalisi*, 3: 635–49.

Roth D. (1973), *Typische Scheisse*, Neuwied: Luchterhand.

Rovelli C. (2004), *Che cos'è il tempo? Che cos'è lo spazio?* Roma: Di Rienzo.

Rovelli C. (2017), *L'ordine del tempo*, Milano: Adelphi.

Rovelli C. (2020), *Helgoland*, Milano: Adelphi.

Rugi G. (1989), "Simbolo, Memoria e Trauma in Munch", in Cortenova G. (ed.), *Da Van Gogh a Schiele. L'Europa espressionista*, 1880-1918, Milano: Mazzotta, pp. 26–33.

Rugi G. (1996), "Anatomia del Grido", *Psiche*, IV, (1): 81–100.

Rugi G. (1997), "Laio incontra Edipo", *Psicoterapia e Scienze Umane*, XXXI, (1): 41–55.

Rugi G. (2011), "Ripensare il dolore. A partire da Freud", *Psichiatria e Psicoterapia*, Fioriti, Editore, 30(2): 131–49.

Rugi G. (2014), "Gruppo-massa e gruppo in assunto di base. Un'ipotesi sulla via somatica del dolore", *Koinos. Gruppo e funzione psicoanalitica, nuova serie*, II, (1): 125–31.

Rugi G. (2015), *Trasformazioni del dolore. Tra psicoanalisi e arte. Freud, Bion, Grotstein, Munch, Bacon, Viola*, Milano: FrancoAngeli.

Rugi G. (2019a), *Diagnosi e disturbi mentali. Percorsi e livelli della conoscenza tra modelli e singolarità*, Milano: FrancoAngeli.

Rugi G. (2019b), "Intuizione e incarnazione. Una visione bioniana del qualcosa in più dell'interpretazione", *Koinos. Gruppo e funzione psicoanalitica*, VII(2): 67–84.

Rugi G. (2022), "Intuition in Bion. Between search for invariants and creative emergence", in Grimalt A. (ed.), *Bion, Intuition and the Expansion of Psychoanalytic Theory*, London and New York: Routledge.

Sandler P.C. (2005), *The Language of Bion. A Dictionary of Concepts*. London: Karnac Books.

Schürmann R. (1972), *Maestro Eckhart o la gioia errante*, Roma-Bari: Laterza, 2008.

Serres M. (2015), *Le Gaucher boiteaux. Puissance de la pensée*, Paris: Éditions Le Pommier; Italian translation, *Il mancino zoppo. Dal metodo non nasce niente*, Torino: Bollati Boringhieri, 2016.

Sini C. (1991), *Il simbolo e l'uomo*, Milano: Egea.

Steiner J. (1993), *Psychic Retreats. Pathological Organizations in Psychotic, Neurotic and Borderline Patients*, London: Routledge.

Stengers I. (1991), "Stili di scienza, stili di narrazione", in Preta L. (ed.), *La narrazione delle origini*, Roma-Bari: Laterza, pp. 37–53.

Symington J. & Symington N. (1996), *The Clinical Thinking of Wilfred Bion*, London: Routledge; Italian translation, *Il pensiero clinico di Bion,* Milano: Raffaello Cortina, 1998.

Tabak de Bianchedi E. (1987), "In chiave di contenitore-contenuto", in Neri C., Correale A., & Fadda P. (ed.), *Letture Bioniane*, Roma: Borla, pp. 91–92.

Thanopulos S. (2016), *Il desiderio che ama il lutto*, Macerata: Quodlibet.

Tonelli F. (1984), *La caduta della Sfinge. L'enigma della tragedia di Edipo*, Ravenna: Longo Editore.

Tonelli G. (2021), *Tempo. Il sogno di uccidere Chrónos*, Milano: Feltrinelli.

Toraldo Di Francia G. (1979), "Presentazione", in Prigogine I. (ed.), *La nuova alleanza. Uomo e natura in una scienza unificata,* Milano: G. Longanesi, pp. V–XII.

Torres N. & Hinshelwood R.D. (2013), *Bion's Sources: The Shaping of His Paradigms*, London: Routeldge.

Tronik E.Z., & Boston CPSG (1998), "Dyadically Expanded States of Consciousness and the Process of Therapeutic Change", *Infant Mentale Health Journal*, 19(33): 290–9.

Valéry P. (1930), *Morceaux choisis, Prose et Poésie,* Paris: Librairie Gallimard.

Valéry P. (1946), *Monsieur Teste*, Paris: Gallimard.

Van Buren J. & Alhati S. (ed.), (2010), *Primitive Mental States. A Psychoanalitical Exploration of the Origins of Meaning*. New York: Routledge, Taylor & Francis Group; Italian translation, *Stati primitivi della mente, una ricerca psicoanalitica*, Roma: Astrolabio-Ubaldini editore, 2013.

Vanzago L. (2016), "L'esperienza del dolore. Modelli concettuali a confronto", *Philosophical Readings*, VIII(1): 46–52.

Varela F., Thompson E., & Rosch E. (1991), *The Embodied Mind*, London: The MIT Press.

Vernant J.P. (1967), "Oedipe sans complexe", *Raison présente*, 4: 3–20.

Vernant J.P. (1986), "Le tyran boiteux: d'Œdipe à Périandre", in Vernant J.P. & Vidal-Naquet P. (ed.), *Mythe et tragédie deux*, Paris: Éditions La Découverte; Italian translation, "Il tiranno zoppo: da Edipo a Periandro", in Vernant J.P. & Vidal-Naquet P. (ed), Mito e tragedia due, Torino: Einaudi, pp. 31–64.

Vila-Matas E. (2005), *Dottor Pasavento*, Barcelona: Debolls!llo.

Whitehead A.N. (1911), *An Introduction to Mathematics*, London: Williams and Northgate.

Whitehead A.N. (1929), *Process and Reality. An Essay in Cosmology*, Cambridge: Cambridge University Press; Corrected Edition, New York: Free Press, 1979.

Winnicott D.W. (1949), "Hate in the Counter-Transference", *International Journal of Psycho-Analysis*, 30: 69–74.

Winnicott D.W. (1958), "Birth Memories, Birth Trauma and Distress," in Winnicott D.W. *Through Paediatrics to Psycho-Analysis*, London: Tavistock Publications.; Italian translation, Winnicott D.W. "Ricordi della nascita, trauma della nascita ed angoscia (1949)", in *Dalla pediatria alla psicoanalisi*, Firenze: Martinelli, pp. 211–233.

Winnicott D.W. (1971), *Playing and Reality*, London: Tavistock Publications; Italian translation, *Gioco e realtà,* Roma: Armando, 1974.

Winnicott D.W. (1974), "Fear of Breakdown", *International Review of Psychoanalysis*, 1: 103–7.

Wittgenstein L. (1958), *The Blue and Brown Books*, Oxford: Basil Blackwell.

Žižek S. (2002), *Benvenuti nel deserto del reale*, Roma: Meltemi.

Index

For Product Safety Concerns and Information please contact our EU
representative GPSR@taylorandfrancis.com
Taylor & Francis Verlag GmbH, Kaufingerstraße 24, 80331 München, Germany

www.ingramcontent.com/pod-product-compliance
Lightning Source LLC
Chambersburg PA
CBHW050351270326
41926CB00016B/3687

* 9 7 8 1 0 3 2 6 5 8 3 4 6 *